EU LAW AND INTERNATIONAL ARBITRATION

This timely book addresses the main areas of tension between EU law and international arbitration, looking at both commercial and investment treaty arbitration. It opens pathways for practical solutions based on communication between the different regimes. At the same time, it offers a sound theoretical basis that allows for addressing the core problem as normative conflict between legitimate public interests and the 'privatisation of justice'.

The book is divided into five parts. It introduces key aspects of the overall tension between EU law and international arbitration, before setting out the theoretical framework, arguing that EU law, international commercial arbitration, and investment treaty arbitration are operationally closed systems. The author then addresses the core problem of finding the limits to contracting out of the EU legal order, which is linked to the question of trust-building and hence the legitimacy of the respective legal regimes. The book concludes with a short summary of each chapter and key theses.

Combining a theoretical and normative stance with a more pragmatic approach to very topical issues, this book offers invaluable insights for academics and practitioners, private and public, commercial and investment treaty lawyers alike.

EU Law and International Arbitration

Managing Distrust Through Dialogue

Konstanze von Papp

• HART •

OXFORD • LONDON • NEW YORK • NEW DELHI • SYDNEY

HART PUBLISHING
Bloomsbury Publishing Plc
Kemp House, Chawley Park, Cumnor Hill, Oxford, OX2 9PH, UK
1385 Broadway, New York, NY 10018, USA
29 Earlsfort Terrace, Dublin 2, Ireland

HART PUBLISHING, the Hart/Stag logo, BLOOMSBURY and the Diana logo are trademarks of Bloomsbury Publishing Plc

First published in Great Britain 2021

A catalogue record for this book is available from the British Library.

Library of Congress Cataloging-in-Publication data

Names: von Papp, Konstanze, author.

Title: EU law and international arbitration : managing distrust through dialogue / Konstanze von Papp.

Description: Oxford, UK ; New York, NY : Hart Publishing, an imprint of Bloomsbury Publishing, 2021. | Includes bibliographical references and index.

Identifiers: LCCN 2021000176 | ISBN 9781509931170 (hardback) | ISBN 9781509947140 (paperback) | ISBN 9781509931187 (pdf) | ISBN 9781509931194 (Epub)

Subjects: LCSH: International commercial arbitration—European Union countries. | International and municipal law—European Union countries.

Classification: LCC KJE4169 .P37 2021 | DDC 347.24/09—dc23

LC record available at https://lccn.loc.gov/2021000176

ISBN: HB: 978-1-50993-117-0
ePDF: 978-1-50993-118-7
ePub: 978-1-50993-119-4

Typeset by Compuscript Ltd, Shannon

To find out more about our authors and books visit www.hartpublishing.co.uk. Here you will find extracts, author information, details of forthcoming events and the option to sign up for our newsletters.

PREFACE

The aim of this book is to shed light on the existing tensions between EU law and international arbitration, addressing international commercial arbitration (ICA) as well as investment treaty arbitration (ITA). Both are comprised under the heading of international arbitration on the basis that they share their origin, that is, an agreement to arbitrate. In other respects, it is well acknowledged that ICA and ITA follow a completely separate logic and must be distinguished from each other.

The purpose is to trace the mostly self-referential logic of the EU legal order on the one hand, and of consensual arbitration on the other. At the same time, this book will provide a theoretical basis and explain the practical implications of the current lack of interaction between the EU and international arbitration. Accordingly, it addresses both academics and practitioners. Practitioners may want to focus less on the theoretical parts; chapter two especially is primarily of academic interest.

I will make several specific suggestions for improvement of the relationship between EU law and international arbitration. Regarding ICA, these include the reconsideration of the original proposal by the EU Commission when recasting the Brussels Regulation. This would essentially mean treating arbitration agreements in the same way as choice-of-court agreements. Regarding ITA, a more coherent approach regarding the arbitrability of EU law-related cases is needed. One should draw the line not between *intra-* and *extra*-EU scenarios, but between international arbitration where EU Member State courts remain available to assist, and international arbitration where court involvement is much more limited – in particular, arbitration under the auspices of the International Convention on the Settlement of Investment Disputes (ICSID).

Regarding both ICA and ITA the dialogue between the EU courts – that is, the Court of Justice of the European Union (CJEU), including its General Court and the EU Member State courts – and arbitration tribunals should be improved. Ideally, this could be achieved by making the preliminary reference procedure available for arbitration tribunals (at least ICSID tribunals). This would require either a change in the CJEU's case law, or a treaty amendment.

In any event, the potential for a dialogue could be enhanced by offering an expedited preliminary reference procedure for EU Member State courts if these become involved in the early stages of an arbitration. It is not only in the EU's interest to provide clarity regarding relevant EU law issues in a timely manner, but also in the interest of international arbitration. Efficiency used to be an important advantage of arbitration, although this is not the case anymore. Nevertheless, one of the main promises of international arbitration is that it leads to a binding and *enforceable* award – a concept which is undermined if awards ultimately turn out to be unenforceable in the EU.

The argument of this book is rooted in legal analysis, but offers a broader theoretical approach by using systems theory, regarding the legal system as one societal sub-system amongst others. Metaphorically speaking, in the big hall of society illustrated on the front cover, the law is just one particular staircase, with different landings along the way. Anyone choosing this particular staircase must follow its direction. But there are other staircases, leading elsewhere. The challenge for legal specialists, as well as for actors from other disciplines, is to find one platform that can be reached by all.

Konstanze von Papp
Hamburg
November 2020

ACKNOWLEDGEMENTS

The ideas developed in this book have been inspired by my experience in private practice and have taken shape in academic discussion. I am grateful, therefore, to my former colleagues in London, Oxford, and Keele who, for many years, made me feel part of an international community.

At the same time, large parts of the book were written upon my return to Germany in 2019. In this respect, I want to thank my German colleagues for welcoming me back so warmly; I am grateful to the Federal University in Brühl (HS Bund) and Hamburg University of Applied Sciences (HAW) for providing all necessary research support.

In terms of both legal and non-legal input, I am especially grateful for the discussions at the *Investment Law and Policy (ILAP)* workshop series at University College London, where I was able to present some ideas underlying this book.

I have benefitted greatly from insightful comments on draft chapters from Stefan Enchelmaier and Florian Wagner-von Papp, both of whom I want to thank very much indeed.

Last, but not least, I want to thank the copy editor, Paula Devine, and Roberta Bassi, Rosemarie Mearns and Linda Staniford at Hart Publishing for their encouragement and excellent support of this project.

I dedicate this book to Florian, Dominic and Felix.

CONTENTS

TABLE OF CASES

International

ICC

ICJ

ICSID

UNCITRAL

WTO

Netherlands

Sweden

United Kingdom

United States of America

TABLE OF LEGISLATION

European Union

International

United States of America

1

Introduction

The relationship between EU law and international arbitration is far from settled. It has moved from constituting 'separate worlds' of 'mutual indifference',[1] to involving 'challenges',[2] or 'practical problems',[3] which are by no means resolved. However, instead of moving towards solutions, the tide appears to be turning back to mutual indifference. This would be unfortunate and not in the interests of either the EU or international arbitration.

I. The EU and International Arbitration in the International Legal System

A. The EU as Supranational Entity

One of the major difficulties is the architecture of the EU itself, being somewhere between a fully-fledged federal state and a mere international organisation (ie its *supranational* character). From the perspective of an international lawyer, the EU therefore sits somewhat uncomfortably between being a 'domestic' legal system, subject to international law in much the same way as any other state and a 'regional (economic) organisation', itself generating international law. This double qualification of the EU leads to problems beyond the specific area of international arbitration. It is addressed in EU

[1] George Bermann, 'Navigating EU Law and the Law of International Arbitration' (2012) 28 *Arbitration International* 397.

[2] European Commission Communication Towards a comprehensive European international investment policy, COM(2010)343 final (7.7.2010), with regard to 'ill-adapted' ICSID structures for participation by the EU.

[3] Burkhard Hess, Thomas Pfeiffer and Peter Schlosser, Report on the Application of Regulation Brussels I in the Member States, Study JLS/C4/2005/03 (Heidelberg Report) para 115 regarding the exception of arbitration from Council Regulation (EC) No 44/2001 of 22 December 2000 on jurisdiction and the recognition and enforcement of judgments in civil and commercial matters [2001] OJ L12/1 (the 'Brussels Regulation'), now amended as Regulation (EU) No 1215/2012 of the European Parliament and of the Council of 12 December 2012 on jurisdiction and the recognition and enforcement of judgments in civil and commercial matters (recast) [2012] OJ L351/1 (Brussels Regulation (recast)).

external relations law,[4] various sub-disciplines of general international law[5] and, increasingly, in the law of state responsibility.[6]

The 'specific nature' of the EU,[7] which originates in the fact that it was set up with its own institutions, leaves a question mark over the relationship between EU law and international law. This has important practical consequences for the resolution of conflicts between the two systems. It has also implications for the role or applicability of EU law in international law and adjudication and, conversely, for the role and applicability of international law in EU law and adjudication. Solutions depend on whether one takes the perspective of EU law or international law.[8]

B. International Arbitration as Part of International Law

At first sight, international arbitration is somewhat easier to classify. It is part of international law, although it is not a substantive area of law but rather a specific form of international adjudication which is used across various areas of international law disciplines. Like general international law, international arbitration is based on bilateral or multilateral treaties between states (ie it is intergovernmental in nature).

The most important multilateral treaties that should be mentioned here are the United Nations Convention on the Recognition and Enforcement of Foreign Arbitral Awards of 10 June 1958 (the 'New York Convention', hereinafter NYC), and the International Convention on the Settlement of Investment Disputes between States and Nationals of Other States of 30 September 1966 (ICSID). To be clear, there are also mechanisms of state-to-state arbitration, for example under the Dispute Settlement Mechanism of the World Trade Organisation (WTO), but the focus here will be on international arbitration either between

[4] See, eg, Marise Cremona (ed), *Structural Principles in EU External Relations Law* (Oxford, Hart Publishing, 2018); Piet Eeckhout and Manuel López-Escudero (eds), *The European Union's External Action in Times of Crisis* (Oxford, Hart Publishing, 2016).

[5] The position depends on whether the EU itself is bound by the relevant international agreement, as is the case in WTO law, where the Dispute Settlement Body treats EU measures overall as domestic (state-like), see in particular Panel Report, *EC – Measures Prohibiting the Importation and Marketing of Seal Products*, WT/DS401/R (25 November 2013). See Christina Binder and Jane Hofbauer, 'The Perception of the EU Legal Order in International Law: An In- and Outside View' (2017) 8 *European Yearbook of International Economic Law* 139, 168 et seq. The situation is broadly similar under the Energy Charter Treaty, see Christian Tietje, 'The Applicability of the Energy Charter Treaty in ICSID Arbitration of EU Nationals vs. EU Member States' *Beiträge zum Transnationalen Wirtschaftsrecht*, 78 (2008). Available at: http://telc.jura.uni-halle.de/sites/default/files/altbestand/Heft78.pdf.

[6] And by the EU itself in Regulation (EU) No 912/2014 of the European Parliament and of the Council of 23 July 2014 establishing a framework for managing financial responsibility linked to investor-to-state dispute settlement tribunals established by international agreements to which the European Union is a party, (2014) OJ L257/121.

[7] Opinion 2/13 *Accession of the EU to the ECHR* ECLI:EU:C:2014:2454.

[8] Regarding the former, see Jan Klabbers, *Treaty Conflict and the European Union* (Cambridge, Cambridge University Press, 2009). A more recent analysis covering WTO, ECHR and the investment regime from both an EU and an international perspective see Binder and Hofbauer, 'The Perception of the EU Legal Order in International Law' (n 5).

individuals or between *individuals and states* (investor–state dispute settlement, ISDS).

Arbitration between individuals can only take place in international *commercial arbitration* (ICA), while arbitration between individual investors and states can take the form of either ICA (if based on a contract between investor and state), or investment treaty arbitration (ITA). These three scenarios need to be clearly distinguished. Nevertheless, they do have crucial procedural features in common, in particular the quasi-judicial decision-making by party-selected arbitration tribunals that are largely independent from national courts. These tribunals operate in a non-hierarchical way with no formal doctrine of precedent and no possibility of appellate review within the arbitral system – with the exception of a very narrow form of oversight within the ICSID system,[9] or under certain institutional arbitration rules like those of the International Chamber of Commerce (ICC).[10] Outside the arbitral order, national courts can play a significant role, which will be looked at below (see II B below).

II. Restrictions on International Arbitration by the EU's Judicial System

This system of adjudication based on international law does not fit easily within the EU's supranational structure. One reason is the EU's judicial system (EU judiciary) as such, the other the EU's foundational principles. Both are closely linked to each other through the Court of Justice of the European Union.

A. The Role of the Court of Justice of the EU

Starting with the first, the EU judiciary consists of the Member State courts, and the EU's Court of Justice in the broader sense. According to Article 19 TEU, this includes the Court of Justice (CJEU), the General Court (formerly called the Court of First Instance), and any specialised court(s) that after the demise of the Civil Services Tribunal may be created in the future.

The Member State courts function as 'ordinary' EU courts to the extent they are applying EU law.[11] In that role, they are hierarchically inferior to the Court of Justice, which remains the final authority on the interpretation of EU law.[12]

[9] In the form of annulment proceedings under Art 52 ICSID.

[10] ICC awards need formal approval by the ICC Court, see Art 34 of the 2012 ICC Rules (as amended 2017).

[11] Opinion 1/09 *European and Community Patents Court* ECLI:EU:C:2011:123 para 80.

[12] This follows from Arts 19 TEU, 267(3) and 344 TFEU. See Konstanze von Papp, 'The Role and Powers of the Court of Justice' in Emmanuel Guinchard and Marie-Pierre Granger (eds), *The New EU Judiciary: an Analysis of Current Judicial Reforms*, European Monographs 102 (The Netherlands, Wolters Kluwer, 2018) 101, 105.

However, the latter sits not only at the top of the judicial hierarchy, but is also understood as the EU's 'motor of integration', given that the EU is an ongoing project of economic and political integration.[13] In this role, the CJEU has been at times actively developing the EU's legal or 'Constitutional' foundations. In the early 1990s, these were summarised under just four doctrines: direct effect, primacy, implied powers, and human rights. Crucially, these were said to be topped up by judicial remedies and enforcement.[14]

The list of EU Constitutional doctrines has grown over time and, in the Court's own words, now consists of a 'structured network' of rules and principles that still has primacy, direct effect and EU fundamental rights at its core, but also includes the principles of autonomy and mutual trust (sincere cooperation).[15] To these, the Court adds the Constitutional structure of the EU, its institutional framework and the integration process itself as the EU's 'raison d'être'.[16] Recently, the Court has also added the principles of conform interpretation (of national law in light of EU law) and state liability.[17] In any event, the Court continues to repeat the importance of the judicial system.[18]

Noteworthy at this stage are, in particular, the autonomy of EU law, the principle of mutual trust, and the principle of equivalence and effectiveness. This is where the above-mentioned link between EU foundations and its judicial structure can best be seen. The reason is that the CJEU has played a crucial role in defining these unwritten principles. They can be understood as being process related,[19] and hence have important implications for the relationship between EU and international arbitration.

In a nutshell, these unwritten principles have the following effects on international arbitration. First, there is the question of arbitrability (ie the gateway for an individual dispute to reach an arbitration tribunal). EU law is exclusively interpreted by the CJEU, which relies on the Member State courts for reference of any open questions under Article 267 TFEU. For international arbitrations to which an EU Member State is a party, this means that they must not involve questions of EU law: Member States are prohibited from submitting any EU law related disputes to a forum other than the CJEU (Article 344 TFEU). This has been held to apply also to investor–state disputes.[20]

[13] Ibid.

[14] Joseph HH Weiler, 'The Transformation of Europe' (1991) 100 *Yale Law Journal* 2403, 2413–22.

[15] Opinion 2/13 *Accession of the European Union to the European Convention for the Protection of Human Rights and Fundamental Freedoms* (ECHR Accession) ECLI:EU:C:2014:2454 paras 166–70. For a detailed discussion of autonomy see ch 2 I C.

[16] Ibid, paras 165, 171–72.

[17] Case C-573/17 *Daniel Adam Popławski* ECLI:EU:C:2019:530 paras 52 et seq.

[18] Opinion 2/13 *ECHR Accession* (n 15) at para 174.

[19] For EU external relations law generally, see Cremona, 'Introduction' (n 4), stressing the duty of sincere cooperation, principle of conferral, institutional balance, mutual solidarity, subsidiarity and autonomy as process related as opposed to substantive principles that focus on the relationship between different actors.

[20] Case C-284/16 *Slovak Republic v Achmea BV* ECLI:EU:C:2018:158.

Second, there are issues regarding the enforcement of arbitration agreements. The Member State courts in their role as 'ordinary' EU courts are linked by mutual trust. This means that when they apply EU law such as the Brussels (recast) Regulation,[21] they are no longer merely courts of different nation states, bound only by international treaties and comity. Instead, to take the best-known example, the procedural powers of Member State courts in civil and commercial matters are strictly confined even in the absence of specific EU law provisions. In practice, this has translated into an EU-wide prohibition of anti-suit injunctions to enforce arbitration agreements, since that would interfere with mutual trust as basis of the Brussels Regulation.[22]

Third, general principles of EU law impact on the enforcement of arbitral awards within the EU. Even when applying their own national law, Member State courts are bound by the principles of equivalence and effectiveness. Hence, they must interpret their national public policy exemptions to the enforcement of arbitral awards in line with EU public policy.[23] It is up to the CJEU as *primus inter pares* to decide what parts of EU law constitute EU public policy.

The EU's supranational features overall mean that it is in a special position when it comes to defending its 'domestic' legal order vis-à-vis any form of potentially undue interference by international law. It must also ensure that there is enough space for further development (or alteration of direction) of the ongoing integration process. This is made difficult by the fact that there are still no clear conceptual alternatives to the nation state model.[24] This might also explain the much criticised, very reluctant approach taken by the CJEU towards accession to the European Convention of Human Rights (ECHR).[25]

Nevertheless, it falls short of a full justification. As will be discussed in more detail in chapter two, the CJEU is defending its own position as the ultimate decision-maker even if there is only a possibility that EU law may be said to be at stake in an international dispute. I will refer to this as the 'EU judicial supremacy'. This can put the EU squarely on a collision course with general international law[26] and, more specifically, with international arbitration.

[21] See ch 3, I.

[22] Case C-185/07 *Allianz Spa v West Tankers* ECLI:EU:C:2009:69.

[23] Case C-126/97 *Eco Swiss China Time Ltd v Benetton International NV* ECLI:EU:C:1999:269.

[24] Similarly, Matej Avbelj, *The European Union under Transnational Law: A Pluralist Appraisal* (Oxford, Hart Publishing, 2018).

[25] Opinion 2/13 *ECHR Accession* ECLI:EU:C:2014:2454. For an overall approving view see Daniel Halberstam 'It's the Autonomy Stupid! A Modest Defense of Opinion 2/13 on EU Accession to the ECHR, and the Way Forward' *Michigan Public Law and Legal Theory Research Paper Series* No 432 (February 2015). Available at: http://ssrn.com/abstract=2567591.

[26] Piet Eeckhout, 'Integration of Public International Law in EU Law: Analytical and Normative Dimensions' in Eeckhout and López-Escudero, *The European Union's External Action in Times of Crisis* (n 4) 189.

B. 'Party Autonomy' Challenged by EU Judicial Supremacy

International arbitration is typically understood as a self-contained legal regime (see chapter two) based on party consent, which allows for disputes to be solved mainly *outside* national courts. This independence is most obvious in ICSID arbitrations, which do not have a *seat* jurisdiction providing judicial oversight, and which result in self-executing awards.[27] Beyond the specific ICSID context, the 'autonomous' nature of international arbitration[28] needs to be qualified, since non-ICSID arbitration remains, to some extent, embedded in domestic legal systems. In particular, there is a potentially substantial role for national courts at the seat of the arbitration, but also any other court with international jurisdiction.

This can be seen most clearly when one party refuses to honour the arbitration agreement, or the final award: the party that wants to enforce the arbitration agreement will normally do so at the seat of the arbitration. The party that thinks it can litigate instead will do so at any place with international jurisdiction over the relevant subject matter. Importantly, both sides to some extent have a *choice of forum*. The same is true for the successful party who wants to enforce the award in judicial enforcement proceedings. This choice of forum entails a choice of procedural law. By the general public, this is often negatively perceived as unwanted forum shopping. For private lawyers, this is just a normal process of complying with their ethical obligation to act in the client's best interest, as long as this means remaining within the bounds of the law.[29] In any event, the choice of forum exists independently from whether one sees it in a negative or positive light.[30]

EU law causes problems for ICA since it effectively restricts that choice. It adds a uniform regulatory layer, which merges the Member State courts into the EU judiciary. This is presided over by the CJEU with the ultimate authority on the meaning of EU law. To take the above example, the CJEU has interpreted the Brussels Regulation as meaning that courts are no longer free to enforce arbitration agreements by way of anti-suit injunctions as available under English law. The formal reason is that this would reduce the powers of the court with jurisdiction under the Brussels Regulation, which we trust the court will properly exercise.[31]

These EU restrictions on Member State courts apply despite the general carve-out of arbitration in the Brussels Regulation, which has essentially remained

[27] Art 54 ICSID.

[28] Julian MD Lew, 'Achieving the Dream: Autonomous Arbitration' (2006) 22 *Arbitration International* 179.

[29] Similarly, Yuval Shany, *The Competing Jurisdictions of International Courts and Tribunals* (Oxford, Oxford University Press, 2004) 269 (forum shopping as manifestation of party autonomy).

[30] See further Freya Baetens, 'Agents of Cross-Fertilization: Abusive Forum Shopping or Legitimate Forum Choice?' in Chiara Giorgetti and Mark Pollack (eds) *Beyond Fragmentation: Competition and Collaboration Among International Courts and Tribunals* (Cambridge, Cambridge University Press, 2020).

[31] Case C-185/07 *West Tankers* (n 22). As will be explained in ch 2 below, the more recent ruling of the CJEU in *Gazprom* does not change this.

unchanged in the 2012 recast.[32] In this respect, the EU framework for private international law, as interpreted by the Court, indirectly limits party choice. The same is true for the role attributed to public policy as a ceiling to the international enforcement of arbitral awards: since *Eco Swiss*,[33] it is clear that EU Member State courts have to take EU law into account when determining public policy.

The CJEU's interpretation of EU law has, therefore, become the ultimate benchmark for the enforcement of arbitration agreements and arbitral awards in the EU. This is obviously disturbing for a dispute resolution system such as international arbitration, which praises itself for being detached from domestic legal orders or to have at least as much flexibility based on party autonomy. To put this differently, as far as commercial arbitration goes, this is an example of what has been aptly labelled 'the regulation of contractual autonomy in the EU internal market'.[34]

There are also more direct limits to party choice by EU law. These kick in when it comes to ISDS. Challenges for the interaction between EU, investment law and arbitration came to light most prominently when the EU itself appeared as an actor in the field of foreign direct investment with the Treaty of Lisbon. However, there were important issues even before that. These go to the heart of judicial powers in the EU, independent of the question of who – the EU or its Member States – will conclude future investment treaties.

The biggest problem is that ITA as such may be a form of dispute settlement that is illegal under EU law. It interferes not only with the CJEU's judicial supremacy, but has also been held to breach Article 344 TFEU, which – again, widely interpreted by the CJEU in *Achmea*[35] – forbids Member States to use any other form of dispute resolution than those provided for in the EU treaties. Member States as parties in ITA are, therefore, directly regulated by EU law. Moreover, the standard of investment protection under international law can differ from that available under EU law, which raises the issue of different treatment of EU investors. These problems are obvious in disputes between EU investors and EU Member States (*intra*-EU), but they could still extend to scenarios beyond that (*extra*-EU), at least as long as EU law might have a bearing on the case.

III. The Public/Private Divide

However, the problem is not just created by the EU. International arbitration itself suffers from conceptual dilemmas. The main tension is that it cannot be squarely attributed to either a public or a private law theory of dispute settlement.

[32] For a critical discussion see, eg, Neil Dowes and Zeng Sophia Tang, 'Arbitration in EU Jurisdiction Regime: Brussels I Recast and a New Proposal' (2015) 3 *Groningen Journal of International Law* 125. See also Louise Hauberg Wilhelmsen, 'The Recast Brussels I Regulation and Arbitration: Revisited or Revised?' (2014) 30 *Arbitration International* 169.

[33] Case C-126/97 *Eco Swiss* (n 23).

[34] Stephen Weatherill, *Contract Law of the Internal Market* (Cambridge, Intersentia, 2016).

[35] Case C-284/16 *Achmea* (n 20). This will be discussed in more detail below (ch 3).

A. Distinguishing Treaty-Based from Commercial Arbitration

This is partly acknowledged by the distinction between investment treaty and commercial arbitration, which can be seen from the following main features: first, the jurisdictional basis of investment arbitration ultimately lies in an international treaty and not in an individually agreed arbitration agreement. Second, the applicable law to investment disputes is international law and not a domestic law chosen by the parties. Third, investment arbitration – though modelled closely along commercial arbitration proceedings[36] – in substance is more akin to judicial review of administrative (ie public law) acts of states.[37] ICA, however, is based on the assumption that commercial parties on an equal footing can solve their private law-type disputes outside the courts since they normally do not raise public concern.

But the categorisation of arbitration as either ICA or ITA does not fully solve the public/private divide. As mentioned above, there are also contract-based (commercial) arbitrations against states. Here, the state is not acting in its regulatory capacity (*de jure imperii*), but more like a 'normal' commercial entity (*de jure gestionis*). It is well recognised in many jurisdictions that states can act in a sovereign and in a private or commercial capacity. International law makes the same distinction when it comes to defining sovereign immunity.

Nevertheless, this should not be understood as meaning that whenever a state enters into a commercial contract this would automatically constitute a 'private' activity. Instead, it is necessary to look at the subject matter of the relevant contract. If, for example, it involves the outsourcing of essential public services, there is à priori no reason why this should be dealt with under the heading of commercial law and arbitration.[38]

From the EU's point of view, the Member States are always subject to their obligations under EU law (ie including when they contract based on private law). A good example here are Member State obligations under EU state aid law, which often come up in ITA against an EU Member State (chapters 3 and 4) More generally, states are not necessarily on an equal footing with their commercial partners even in subject matters that are normally attributed to private law. In other words, the 'subordination'[39] that is present in investment treaty cases, accounting for

[36] See the detailed account of the drafting process of ICSID in Antonio R Parra, *The History of ICSID*, 2nd edn (Oxford, Oxford University Press, 2017).

[37] Gus van Harten, 'Investment Treaty Arbitration as a Species of Global Administrative Law' (2006) 17 *European Journal of International Law* 121. See also *International Thunderbird Gaming Corporation v Mexico* UNCITRAL/NAFTA Award (26 January 2006), Separate Opinion Wälde para 129.

[38] Stavros Brekoulakis and Margaret Devaney, 'Public–Private Arbitration and the Public Interest Under English Law' (2017) 80 *Modern Law Review* 22.

[39] Stephan Schill, 'International Investment Law and Comparative Public Law – An Introduction' in Stephan Schill (ed), *International Investment Law and Comparative Public Law* (Oxford, Oxford University Press, 2010) 15.

their public law nature, may very well extend to the 'commercial' relationship between investor and state.

This means that the dividing line between a public and a private paradigm of arbitration has to be drawn somewhere else, and not simply by assuming the former for ITA and the latter for ICA. It also implies that there needs to be clarity about the limits of party autonomy as a cornerstone of international arbitration. Public concerns about the 'secrecy' of investment treaty arbitration – especially in connection with the draft Transatlantic Trade and Investment Partnership (TTIP) – may have to be taken on board for ICA as well. This is true, at least to the extent that the dispute involves a state party. In other words, the need for more transparency[40] of ITA – especially if *not* conducted under the auspices of ICSID – might well extend to claims based on a contract as opposed to an investment treaty (ie a typical case of commercial arbitration).

B. Contractual and Jurisdictional Theories of Arbitration

The conceptual dilemma remains even if one concentrates on commercial arbitration without state parties. In ICA generally, there is a clash of theories regarding the general nature of arbitration.[41] In effect, this means that there are different views as to the reach of party autonomy and hence the role of an arbitrator. The contractual model understands arbitration as a mere creature of the arbitration agreement. This is a contract between the parties, which the arbitrator – who derives his mandate from the parties – must honour.[42] Some would even go as far as understanding arbitration as 'autonomous' in the sense that no national legal system should be able to impose its constraints on the parties.[43]

On the other side, following a so-called jurisdictional model, one can attach importance to the fact that arbitration involves adjudicatory procedures, and results in a final and binding decision that is equivalent to a court judgment. Under the latter model, there would be no reason to defer to party autonomy any more than one does when applying the relevant laws in state court proceedings. In trying to bridge those opposite views, one could use the jurisdictional

[40] Regarding ICSID, UNCITRAL and NAFTA see Nicolas Hachez and Jan Wouters, 'International Investment Dispute Settlement in the Twenty-first Century: Does the Preservation of the Public Interest Require an Alternative to the Arbitral Model?' in Freya Baetens (ed), *Investment Law within International Law: Integrationist Perspectives* (Cambridge, Cambridge University Press, 2015) 417, 435 et seq.

[41] See Emmanuel Gaillard, *Legal Theory of International Arbitration* (The Netherlands, Brill Nijhoff, 2010).

[42] See, in particular, French jurisprudence, eg, the Judgment of 27 July 1937, 1938 Dalloz 25 (Cour de cassation civil). But see Georgios Petrochilos, *Procedural Law in International Arbitration* (Oxford, Oxford University Press, 2004) 25.

[43] But the autonomy of ICA is not a precise notion since it can refer to arbitration without a seat, the determination of the applicable law without recourse to national conflict of law rules, or the application of transnational law.

theory as a limit to the purely contractual model. It would then be necessary to differentiate between the contractual basis as catalyst for the arbitration, and the arbitration itself as a process more akin to judicial procedures: this would be a 'mixed' or 'hybrid' theory.[44]

There is otherwise not much room for compromise between these theories, which led commentators to conclude that the divide cannot be expected to be resolved soon.[45] The New York Convention does not help in solving this puzzle. Article V puts excess of mandate as ground for challenge of an award in enforcement proceedings in one line with breaches of the law of the seat. This leaves to individual decision-makers the problem of finding the right balance between vindicating party autonomy and respect for the law. Without clear legal guidance, judges and arbitrators will essentially have to follow their own ideologies. The extent of private choice and flexibility will, therefore, depend on whether the relevant decision-maker comes from a private law background with a focus on contractual freedom and non-interference by the state; or from a public law background more concerned with the regulatory powers of states.

Making such differing starting points more transparent will be one central aim of this book. It is based on the underlying premise that the difficult relationship between EU law and international arbitration is merely symptomatic of a more abstract problem, namely the underlying tension between contractual freedom and legality of state action. In international arbitration, this translates into the dichotomy between party autonomy and public policy. The EU has its own problems in addressing the tension between private and public interests, which also underlies the criticism of international investment law and arbitration.[46] Put simply, one key consequence is that we need to be clearer about the limits of contractual freedom: Is party autonomy a value in itself, or does it have to serve the public interest in the longer run?

IV. Privatisation of Justice within the EU?

The core issue then becomes which disputes can be left safely for resolution *inter partes* and which raise concerns that are clearly of wider public interest, or which may create law with binding effect *erga omnes*.[47] It is well arguable that the latter

[44] Gary B Born, *International Commercial Arbitration* Vol 1, 2nd edn (The Netherlands, Wolters Kluwer, 2014) 217.

[45] Alec Stone Sweet and Florian Grisel, *The Evolution of International Arbitration: Judicialization, Governance, Legitimacy* (Oxford, Oxford University Press, 2017).

[46] See ch. 4.

[47] Stavros Brekoulakis, 'The Relevance of the Interests of Third Parties in Arbitration: Taking a Closer Look at the Elephant in the Room' (2009) 113 *Penn State Law Review* 1165, 1178 aptly addresses this as commercial arbitration's failure to 'break its bilateral restraints', which the doctrine of non-arbitrability is supposed to resolve. See text accompanying n 58 et seq.

have to be carved out from a dispute resolution system that relies on non-tenured arbitrators, and without sufficient legal certainty through a doctrine of precedent and appellate review. In the absence of such a carve-out, the question is how to develop a model for arbitration that can promote party autonomy whilst safeguarding the public interest, in particular the legality of state action. This is where EU law could and should make a valuable contribution since it incorporates the public/private divide.

A. EU Law as Transnational Law

The EU can well be regarded as a 'laboratory'[48] for transnational law-making in multiple ways. First, in the classical inter-state sense, the EU is set up as a 'transnational body of legal action'.[49] But through its market focus by 1963, the EU had already started to reach out to individuals,[50] which led to an ever-increasing impact of EU law on private law relationships.[51] This means that EU law can be seen as setting a framework for managing the public/private divide.[52] In sociological terms, EU law provides a forum where either private or public law scholars[53] can interact, each bringing their own perspective.[54] One example of such a mix of perspectives, which has then impacted on substantive law, is the EU's more regulatory take on contract law.[55] This is most obvious by the influence of EU law on consumer and employment law, but EU experience goes far beyond these areas.[56]

[48] Francis Snyder and Lu Yi, 'Transnational Law and the EU: Reflections from WISH in China' (2013) 19 *European Law Journal* 705, 708.

[49] Carrie Menkel-Meadow, 'Why and How to Study "Transnational Law"' (2011) 1 *University of California (Irvine) Law Review* 97. Electronic copy available at: http://ssrn.com/abstract=1851634. Carrie Menkel-Meadow, 'Why and How to Study "Transnational Law"' (2011) 1 *University of California (Irvine) Law Review* 97, 101. Electronic copy available at: http://ssrn.com/abstract=1851634.

[50] See Bruno de Witte, 'The Continuous Significance of Van Gend en Loos' in Miguel P Maduro and Loïc Azoulai (eds), *The Past and Future of EU Law: The Classics of EU Law Revisited on the 50th Anniversary of the Rome Treaty* (Oxford, Hart Publishing, 2010).

[51] Daniela Caruso, 'The Missing View of the Cathedral: The Private Law Paradigm of European Legal Integration' (1997) 3 *European Law Journal* 3, 9–12.

[52] Hans-Wolfgang Micklitz, 'Rethinking the Public/Private Divide' in Miguel P Maduro, Kaarlo Tuori and Suvi Sankari (eds), *Transnational Law: Rethinking European Law and Legal Thinking* (Cambridge, Cambridge University Press, 2014) 271.

[53] Caruso, 'The Missing View of the Cathedral' (n 51) at 12–14 explains this by the traditional classification by civil law jurisdictions into either private or public law (calling for more engagement with EU law by private law scholars).

[54] Similarly, Rob van Gestel, HW Micklitz and M Maduro, 'Methodology in a New Legal World' EUI Working Papers Law 2012/13, 15. Available at: http://ssrn.com/abstract=2069872.

[55] Hugh Collins, 'The Hybrid Quality of European Private Law' in Robert Brownsword, HW Micklitz, Leone Niglia and Stephen Weatherill (eds), *The Foundations of European Private Law* (Oxford, Hart Publishing, 2011) 453 refers to 'regulatory contracts'.

[56] Weatherill, *Contract Law of the Internal Market* (n 34) 21, 129 et seq.

It is suggested to take this one step further to the level of adjudication: finding limits to contractual freedom not only at the deal-making stage but also at the stage of dispute resolution by way of arbitration. EU law has started to engage with this in consumer arbitration cases,[57] without providing more generally for consumer protection against involuntary arbitration. This will be discussed in more detail in chapter three. Nevertheless, instead of an incremental approach at the enforcement stage, consumer arbitration in the EU must be based on a clear conceptual footing. One way of doing this would be to revive the doctrine of non-arbitrability (see immediately below) to ensure and clarify the involvement of public courts.

Taking such a perspective of managing the public/private divide by focusing on the relationship between arbitral tribunals and courts would set a fresh impulse for enhancing the legitimacy of international arbitration. This will then help to channel the clashes between EU law and international arbitration in light of the pursuit of justice or fairness, which is an overall theme that these regimes have in common.

B. The Doctrine of Non-Arbitrability in International Commercial Arbitration

In ICA, the doctrine of *non-arbitrability* is used to address the carve-out of cases that raise concerns beyond the parties' relationship or where that relationship is not based on an equal footing. This doctrine acknowledges that there are cases of a certain public importance or in need of formal court adjudication[58] that should not be resolved by arbitration.

Nevertheless, the scope of this doctrine has been considerably weakened over time, which can be seen by the existence of arbitration in such matters as antitrust law or consumer and employment law.[59] The latter have come under public scrutiny, for example in the US, as a negative illustration of the 'privatisation of justice'[60] which only serves the interests of the financially strong repeat players (businesses). The central point of critique here is that employees or consumers are neither aware of, nor have any other choice than to accept, arbitration clauses in the relevant contract. This could also be addressed by reviving the doctrine of non-arbitrability.[61]

[57] Case C-168/05 *Mostaza Claro v Centro Móvil Milenium SL* ECLI:EU:C:2006:675.

[58] Gary B Born, *International Arbitration: Cases and Materials* (The Netherlands, Wolters Kluwer, 2011) 422.

[59] Especially noteworthy in the US, see *Mitsubishi Motors Corp v Soler Chrysler-Plymouth Inc*, 473 US 614 (1985).

[60] See New York Times, 'In Arbitration, A "Privatization of the Justice System"' (1 Nov 2015). Available at: www.nytimes.com/2015/11/02/business/dealbook/in-arbitration-a-privatization-of-the-justice-system.html.

[61] In the US, this is being done by the suggested 'Arbitration Fairness Act' (a bill to amend title 9 of the United States Code with respect to arbitration, 115th Congress 2nd session s 2591, in the Senate of the US (22 March 2018). Available at: www.gpo.gov/fdsys/pkg/BILLS-115s2591is/pdf/BILLS-115s2591is.pdf. This proposal carves out antitrust, consumer, employment and civil rights disputes as 'public law' claims from arbitration. See also chs 3 and 4.

C. The Legitimacy Debate in Investment Treaty Arbitration

Investment treaty cases are different from the outset since they do not involve private law contracts but claims under investment treaties (ie public international law). Such claims *per definitionem* are of public interest. Even though the immediate legal effect may be *inter partes*, they will typically have broader repercussions for the general public.[62] Allowing for private enforcement of international treaties has been the exceptional achievement – for better or for worse – of international investment law, which in this respect can be compared to international human rights law.

The alternative, which is brought up in recent reform discussions, would be to leave the enforcement of investment law to the states as treaty parties. This would resemble the WTO dispute resolution model. Seen in this light, the current backlash against investment arbitration is essentially the same as the discussion about allowing public or statutory law matters to be resolved by commercial arbitration: private law-making in the sense of private enforcement of public law issues outside public courts. One could try to address this by distinguishing categories of investment disputes.[63]

In any event, the argument underlying this book is that, ultimately, the reform proposals of investment treaty arbitration need to deal with the social legitimacy of international arbitration.[64]

D. Developing an EU Arbitral Model through Dialogue

The EU's judicial system is based upon public courts – including the Member State courts (see II A above). These take guidance from the CJEU regarding EU law matters. The question of whether justice within the EU can be said to be 'privatised' hence concerns the interaction – or the lack thereof – between these courts and international arbitration.

Regarding ITA, EU law as interpreted by the CJEU clearly distinguishes investment arbitration between EU investors and EU Member States (*intra*-EU) and arbitration based on a treaty between an EU Member State and a third state (*extra*-EU). The former is being phased out[65] so, over time, the question will not be one

[62] This is often discussed under the heading of a potential *chilling effect* or 'regulatory chill' of investment arbitration, see Jonathan Bonnitcha, Lauge Poulsen and Michael Waibel, *The Political Economy of the Investment Treaty Regime* (Oxford, Oxford University Press, 2017) 238.

[63] See, eg, Christian Tietje and Freya Baetens, 'The Impact of Investor-State-Dispute Settlement (ISDS) in the Transatlantic Trade and Investment Partnership' *Study prepared for the Minister for Foreign Trade and Development Cooperation, Ministry of Foreign Affairs, The Netherlands* (24 June 2014). Available at: www.rijksoverheid.nl (singling out challenges to national *legislation*).

[64] See ch. 4.

[65] Prompted by the EU Commission's strict position as approved by the Court in Case C-205/06 *Commission v Republic of Austria* ECLI:EU:C:2009:118, Case C-249/06 *Commission v Kingdom of Sweden*

of interaction between courts and arbitration tribunals, but that of cooperation between courts in investment arbitration matters.

Extra-EU, ITA is being replaced by new dispute settlement procedures in investment agreements concluded by both the EU and its Member States (EU investment agreements).[66] These new EU investment agreements envisage a turn from *ad hoc* arbitration to an investment court system (ICS) with a standing appellate tribunal and, in the longer run, a multilateral investment court.[67] Here the question will arise how that case-law-to-be will tally with the Court's exclusive jurisdiction over EU law.

Regarding ICA, the CJEU's case law based on the Brussels Regulation (recast) has been drawing a line between the functioning of the EU judiciary and 'private justice'.[68] To some extent, the latter remains unregulated in civil and commercial matters, where the EU is formally constrained by the principle of conferred powers: it does not have full competencies in civil and commercial law. The Brussels Regulation (recast) hence works on the traditional public international law model of recognition and enforcement of foreign judicial acts, while abolishing the need for an *exequator*.

It is only at the national level that we find comprehensive codes of civil procedure or arbitration laws regulating the relationship between courts and arbitration tribunals. These are often very similar to the UNCITRAL Model law, and are broadly in line with the Member States' international obligations under the NYC. By contrast, the EU itself is not a signatory to the NYC. Nor does it have a statutory regime dealing with the interface between adjudication in public courts and arbitration. This is where more structure is needed, for which there will be suggestions in chapter four.

The purpose of the following chapters is to map the issues from different perspectives, and to provide practical suggestions for an improved interaction between the EU judiciary and international arbitration. Chapter two will start by setting out the theoretical framework underlying the argument, which will draw on systems theory. This framework will then be applied separately to EU law and international arbitration (ICA and ITA), with specific regard to the enforcement of arbitration agreements. A transnational perspective will help in identifying the link between practical problems and certain underlying assumptions, which are either grounded in contractual thinking, or in a public interest perspective.

ECLI:EU:C:2009:119 and Case C-118/07 *Commission v Republic of Finland* ECLI:EU:C:2009:715. The EU Member States have meanwhile followed suit and, in March 2020, announced the termination of their *intra*-EU investment treaties. See Nikos Lavranos, 'Comment: When 23 Member States Terminate their Intra EU BITS' (6 May 2020). Available at: https://borderlex.eu/2020/05/06/comment-when-23-eu-member-states-terminate-their-intra-eu-bits/.

[66] According to the broad reading of the new EU competencies following the Lisbon Treaty by the EU Commission, above n 2. See, eg, Catherine Titi, 'International Investment Law and the European Union: Towards a New Generation of International Investment Agreements' (2015) 26 *European Journal of International Law* 639.

[67] For the example of the Canada–EU Trade Agreement (CETA) see ch 3, II B.

[68] Above n 3. This is discussed in ch 3.

Chapter 3 will analyse EU law limits to both ICA and ITA. Regarding the former, the focus will be on the arbitration exception of the Brussels Regulation (recast)[69] on the one hand, and the role of EU public policy on the other. Regarding the latter, it will be shown that EU law approaches state contracting very differently (ie strictly regulating agreements to arbitrate by EU Member States).[70] At the same time, the CJEU treats investment tribunals the same as commercial arbitration tribunals, namely as 'private' tribunals with no access to the preliminary reference procedure.[71] Nevertheless, the Court draws a sharp distinction between *intra*-EU cases and bilateral investment treaties by the Member States, and *extra*-EU cases under EU agreements. It will be argued that this kind of line-drawing is unlikely to work.

Chapter 4 will set out the problem of legitimacy in theory and practical application to the EU and ITA, arguing that the legitimacy question has an increasing impact on ICA. It will be shown that the legitimacy debate is best understood as the pursuit of justice in the sense of societal fairness. There is a risk for international law and the legal system generally if this debate is not taken up by national and international courts.

Mutual indifference between EU law and international arbitration cements the *status quo* (ie the attempt to draw a line between 'private justice' and public courts in the EU). But such line-drawing means that the actors in international arbitration ignore issues of EU law, while the CJEU risks ignoring public law implications in private adjudication. It cannot deal with remaining distrust in the longer run. Clashes between commercial and public interests, and between arbitration and EU law will continue to arise. This will reinforce the negative perception of unregulated 'private justice' unless judges and arbitrators within the EU can and do engage with each other.

This is why EU law should enable a dialogue between the EU judiciary and international arbitration. In terms of existing structures, this is only possible by involving the court of an EU Member State. It will be suggested that incentives should be created for international arbitration to consider relevant EU law questions at the outset of an arbitration, with a view to getting any necessary clarification by the CJEU via preliminary references of EU Member State courts. *De lege ferenda*, this could also be achieved by making the preliminary reference procedure available for arbitration tribunals, at least in ICSID cases. In terms of substance, a dialogue between EU law and international arbitration should, where possible, be structured around concepts of general international law and ideally concepts that are also shared by the outside (non-legal) world.

[69] Above n 3.

[70] This is the Court's interpretation of Article 344 TFEU, which it understands as complete prohibition to arbitrate matters of EU law outside the EU's judicial system. See Case C-284/16 *Achmea* (n 20), which is discussed in ch. 3.

[71] As confirmed by the CJEU in Case C-284/16 *Achmea* (n 20).

2

The Nature of EU Law and International Arbitration

Introduction

In this chapter, the issues identified in the introduction will be placed in a systems theoretical framework. It will be seen that the circularity of EU landmark cases and the contractual understanding of arbitration impede mutual engagement of both systems. Moreover, the public/private divide also means that within EU law and arbitration respectively, there are different underlying perspectives or implicit assumptions. The analysis will hence take a transnational perspective with a focus on making these as transparent as possible.[1] Chapter one identified the key problem as freedom versus legality of state action; and it framed the question as being where the public interest puts a limit to contractual freedom. This is employing a functional transnational approach: it is using two traditionally opposed legal perspectives, namely public versus private law, in pursuit of a model for international arbitration (commercial (ICA) and investment (ITA)) in the EU.

In a first step, it will be shown that the lack of interaction between EU law and international arbitration is best explained by understanding EU law, ICA and ITA as highly specialised regimes, and as sub-systems of international law. Under systems theory, some coordination between sub-systems can only be addressed by using links that these systems share in the form of common concepts (see I B (iii) below, so-called 'structural coupling'). One such link is mandatory law, understood as rules that parties cannot contract out of, and which courts or tribunals must apply of their own accord. In a second step, the analysis will focus on tracing such mandatory rules within the concept of 'arbitrability'.

[1] Peer Zumbansen, 'Where the Wild Things Are: Journeys to Transnational Legal Orders, and Back', *King's College London Dickson Poon School of Law Legal Studies Research Paper Series*, Paper No 2016-11 (available at: http://ssrn.com/abstract=2723990), calls for such critical reflection of one's own perspective from a private or public law 'universe'. It can be left open here whether this constitutes methodology in a technical sense. See Rob van Gestel, Hans-Wolfgang Micklitz and Miguel P Maduro, Methodology in 'A New Legal World', EUI Working Papers Law 2012/13. Available at: http://ssrn.com/abstract=2069872.

I. Theoretical Framework

A. The Contribution of Regime Theory

The lack of interaction between EU law on the one hand, and ICA or ITA on the other, can be explained by understanding each as a separate 'regime'. This term originates in international relations theory and was the result of a mediation between its idealist and realist schools: regimes 'intervene' between powers, interests, and values at one end, and outcomes and behaviour at the other.[2]

Regime is defined as a 'set of implicit or explicit principles, norms, rules and decision-making procedures around which actors' expectations converge in a given area of international relations'.[3] This applies to EU law as based on its specific treaties and foundational or Constitutional principles as set out in chapter one (I A and II A). It was also seen there that EU institutions, especially the Court of Justice, play a crucial role. The latter not only ensures the judicial enforcement of EU law, but also adds a dynamic element for further EU integration.

ICA and ITA also constitute regimes in the above sense, in that they provide for decision-making procedures based on agreements to arbitrate that find their binding legal force in specific treaties (such as the New York or ICSID Convention, as well as bilateral or multilateral investment treaties). Both ICA and ITA also rely on more general principles such as party autonomy or due process and are at least partly institutionalised (eg ICSID-based arbitration; ICC or LCIA arbitration, or arbitration under the UNCTAD rules for ICA). Especially regarding ITA there is even a *de facto* precedential effect of arbitral case law,[4] involving repeat players with more or less homogenous backgrounds.[5] In summary, EU law as well as ICA and ITA are captured by the notion of regime around which their respective actors' expectations converge.

For international lawyers, the focus is less on the actors and more on the applicability of legal rules. The debate here started from the question of whether specialised international law regimes are *self-contained* in the narrow sense that they preclude recourse to the general rules on state responsibility (eg diplomatic law).[6] This was taken up by Martti Koskenniemi in his fragmentation report

[2] Stephan Haggard and Beth A Simmons, 'Theories of International Regimes' (1987) 41 *International Organization* 491.

[3] Stephen D Krasner, *International Regimes* (Ithaca, Cornell University Press, 1983).

[4] Stephan Schill, 'The Multilateralization of International Investment Law: The Emergence of a Multilateral System of Investment Protection on the Basis of Bilateral Treaties' (2008) *Society of International Economic Law Online Proceedings Working Paper* 18/08. Available at: https://ssrn.com/abstract=1151817.

[5] See the landmark empirical study by Yves Dezalay and Bryant G Garth, *Dealing in Virtue: International Commercial Arbitration and the Construction of Transnational Legal Order* (Chicago, University of Chicago Press, 1996). See further below n 15. The legitimacy of international arbitration more generally is discussed in ch 4.

[6] Bruno Simma, 'Self-contained Regimes' (1985) *Netherlands Yearbook of International Law* 111.

for the International Law Commission (ILC),[7] where he distinguished between further approaches to defining a regime as self-contained: first, there is the narrow understanding above, which focuses on secondary rules (ie those setting out specific remedies as possible reactions to breaches of primary rules). The latter are the rules laying down particular rights, duties and powers in the first place.[8] Second, there is a broader understanding, which includes special regimes that do not just regulate remedies, but also the substance of a particular subject matter – that is, primary rules – differently from general international law.[9] Third, in its broadest category, a self-contained regime also includes fields where special rules and techniques of interpretation and administration are used. Explicit reference to EU law is made here;[10] other examples are given as international human rights, international trade, or environmental law.[11]

What all these categories have in common is that they seek precedence with regard to general international law by way of reference to their respective special rules. Regarding the third category, the special character includes not just rules, but also interpretative – often teleological – principles such as 'polluter pays' or 'sustainable development' or even a more normative than purely contractual interpretation of international treaties as is especially the case in human rights law.[12] It is acknowledged that no conscious act of regime creation is necessary.[13] Instead, the regime may emerge through informal channels such as professional networks.[14] This part of the definition is of particular interest for international arbitration, where social network analysis of arbitrators and their typical backgrounds has found a 'dense network that reinforces prevailing norms and behaviours'.[15] In this informal way, both ICA and ITA can be regarded as specialised regimes of international law.

In conclusion, Koskenniemi found that self-contained regimes do not exist as closed sub-systems of international law (in the sense of a complete detachment of general international law). Instead, they should simply be understood as

[7] Report by Martti Koskenniemi, Chairman of the Study Group of the ILC, 'Fragmentation of International Law: Difficulties Arising From the Diversification and Expansion of International Law', ILC 56th Session (1 May–9 June and 3 July–11 August 2006), A/CN.4/L.682 – referred to as 'Koskenniemi'.

[8] Ibid at paras 123–25.

[9] Ibid at paras 126–28.

[10] Ibid at paras 129–33 and 148.

[11] Ibid at paras 133–37.

[12] Ibid at paras 130–31 with reference to the ECHR and the case law of the Inter-American Court of Human Rights and the Human Rights Committee.

[13] Ibid at para 158.

[14] For network theory and its application to EU Foreign Policy see Stephan Keukelaire and Arnout Justaert, 'Policy Networks and the Analysis of EU Foreign Policy' GARNET Conference, The European Union in International Affairs (Brussels 24–26 April 2008). Available at: www.ies.be/files/repo/conference2008/EUinIA_VIII_4_KeukeleireJustaert.pdf.

[15] Sergio Puig, 'Network Analysis and the Sociology of International Law' (2018) *Arizona Legal Studies Discussion Paper* No. 18–06, 12 with further references. Available at: https://ssrn.com/abstract=3130256.

a particular form of *lex specialis*, with customary international law in particular acting as a gap-filling tool.[16] This effectively combined regime theory with the unity of international law, which makes sense from the perspective of general international law.

However, it is questionable from a specialist's perspective. For example, EU law has been developed using a teleological approach, including EU-specific foundational principles and rules of interpretation. This makes the EU a self-contained regime in Koskenniemi's third category. It has led to the EU seeing itself as a new legal order that has meanwhile become independent from its origins in traditional public international law (see C below). One might counter this by saying that the EU remains firmly rooted in international law, and that the self-understanding of the regime does not matter. Nevertheless, by acknowledging that there is something like a self-understanding of the respective sub-system, one accepts the very basis for what system theorists would call *autopoiesis* (see immediately below): the system keeps reproducing itself, using itself as point of reference, and existing independently from its environment.

Regime theory in public international law is, therefore, the best point of departure for (specialist) lawyers, but it does not reach far enough. It cannot satisfactorily answer the question of hierarchies between different regimes in the case of 'regime collision', that is, a situation when one regime claims precedence in dealing with a legal issue, and another regime does not accept this. The problem is that not even the benchmark is clear. The benchmark could be the unity of international law, which would be a legal centralist perspective.[17] Alternatively, it could be some form of legal pluralism.[18]

Even if one were to accept a centralist view, using general international law as the benchmark, this would be inconclusive: traditional instruments such as the Vienna Convention on the Law of Treaties are not sufficiently well-equipped to deal with regime collisions. Rules such as *lex posterior*[19] or *lex specialis* apply only

[16] Koskenniemi (n 7) paras 152, 172–85.

[17] Eg Piet Eeckhout, 'Integration of Public International Law in EU Law: Analytical and Normative Questions' in Piet Eeckhout and Manuel López-Escudero (eds), *The European Union's External Action in Times of Crisis* (Oxford, Hart Publishing, 2016) 189. See also Gareth Davies, 'Constitutional Disagreement in Europe and the Search for Pluralism' in Matej Avbelj and Jan Komárek (eds), *Constitutional Pluralism in the European Union and Beyond* (Oxford, Hart Publishing, 2012) 269.

[18] John Griffiths, 'What is Legal Pluralism' (1986) 24 *Journal of Legal Pluralism and Unofficial Law* 1. See Andreas Fischer-Lescano and Gunther Teubner, 'Regime Collisions: The Vain Search for Legal Unity in the Fragmentation of Global Law' (2004) 25 *Michigan Journal of International Law* 999, 1017. See also Gunther Teubner and Peter Korth, 'Two Kinds of Legal Pluralism: Collision of Laws in the Double Fragmentation of World Society' in Margaret A Young (ed) *Regime Interaction in International Law: Theoretical and Practical Challenges* (Cambridge, Cambridge University Press, 2012) 23.

[19] Jan Klabbers, *Treaty Conflict and the European Union* (Cambridge, Cambridge University Press, 2009) 70 et seq refers to Lauterpacht's work to illustrate the ambivalence underlying the *lex posterior* rule as a balancing act between the special interests of the contracting states, and the general interest in the development of international law. Similarly, Koskenniemi (n 7) paras 61–62 describes the need for some flexibility, neither allowing for unlimited contracting out of the general law by some states, but at the same time recognising the need to respect the will of individual states when agreeing on a more specific rule.

to those state parties that are bound by both treaties, that is, the old and the newer one, or the general and the more specific one. Also, depending on the date of accession, one treaty may be the newer one for one state party, but not for another.

This is where a broader focus than the one on *legal* regimes is helpful. This can be achieved by using a sociological lens.[20] Systems theory moves the question of how to define the relationship between different regimes beyond the search for hierarchical structures. Instead, it acknowledges the operational closure of each system, while allowing for some interaction to the extent the systems are structurally coupled with each other as will be explained in more detail now.

B. Core Insights from Systems Theory

The necessary outlook beyond the law is offered by systems theory in the specific form that Luhmann has adopted for sociology.[21] In essence, systems theory is about distinctions. The basic distinction is that between a system and its environment. This system can be any one living thing, in particular, a human being (biological system). Given its consciousness, the human being is not only a biological, but also a psychic system. Society is a social system and, on a global level, world society would be *the* social system. The social system is divided into sub-systems, which serve specific functions.[22]

The legal system is such a sub-system of society.[23] The same is true of the economic or political systems. These further distinctions make, for example, the political system the environment of the legal system, and vice versa. Also, society, as the overall system, becomes the environment of each sub-system (and vice versa). Put differently, the legal system differentiates itself from political or economic systems, as well as from the social system as a whole.[24]

(i) The Legal System as a Functional Sub-System of the Social System

By embedding law in society, the first core insight is that the legal system is just one societal sub-system among many. Asking which *legal* rule has the highest

[20] Compare J Griffiths, 'What is Legal Pluralism' (n 18), criticising legal centralism and suggesting that pluralism be viewed as – de facto – existing legal orders covering the same social fields.

[21] Niklas Luhmann, *Introduction to Systems Theory* (Cambridge, Polity Press, 2013).

[22] Luhmann, ibid at 32 with further reference to Jay A Sigler, 'A Cybernetic Model of the Judicial System' (1968) 41 *Temple Law Quarterly* 398–428.

[23] Niklas Luhmann, *Das Recht der Gesellschaft* (Frankfurt, Suhrkamp, 1995) 34 with reference to Adam Podgorecki, Christopher J Whelan and Dinesh Khosla (eds), *Legal Systems and Social Systems* (London, Croom Helm, 1985). See also Hans-Joachim Mertens, 'Lex Mercatoria: A Self-applying System Beyond National Law?' in Gunther Teubner (ed), *Global Law without a State* (Dartmouth, Aldershot, 1997) 31.

[24] Luhmann, *Recht der Gesellschaft* (n 23) 23; 55–56. Luhmann nevertheless stresses that any operation of the legal system is, at the same time, a societal operation in the form of a communication. Ibid at 34–35.

authority to govern any factual situation means already employing the legal benchmark ('code'), distinguishing 'legal' from 'illegal'. The relevant code may be a completely different one from the perspective of another system. For example, the economic system distinguishes utility/no utility;[25] and the political system power/no power.

This higher order perspective allows for consideration not of hierarchies (top/down), but of different circles (in/out or, respectively, centre/periphery). Law becomes just one fact among others.[26] From a sociological perspective, the point of a legal norm is to create a safe haven in case present expectations turn out to be frustrated in the future: people know that legally, they will be covered – for example, by having a remedy, or by being exempted from liability – if things turn out differently.[27] And the legal system as functional sub-system of the social system can be further differentiated into sub-systems of the legal system (see below (iv)).

(ii) The Autonomous Self-Reproduction of the Legal System

The second core insight is that systems are 'autopoietic', a term which originates in biology and essentially means 'self-reproduction of life'.[28] In the literature, the autopoietic nature of the legal system has been summarised as meaning autonomous, reflexive, and self-[re]productive.[29] The underlying assumption is that the system is not 'closed'[30] but 'open' in the sense that it aims for continued existence. A system continues to exist only as long as it keeps differentiating itself from its environment or, in other words, keeps reproducing the difference between system and environment.[31] A human being (a biological system) differentiates itself by living.

[25] The code of an economic system is defined variously in the literature ('price/no price'), including by Luhmann himself ('payment/no payment'). The one used here ('utility/no utility') is taken from Luhmann, *Recht der Gesellschaft* (n 23) 26 and is arguably the most precise.

[26] Ibid at 31–33, 322. The perspective of centre/periphery instead of hierarchies has also been picked up by US legal realists and critical legal studies. See, eg, David Kennedy, 'The Political Economy of Centers and Peripheries' (2013) 26 *Leiden Journal of International Law* 7. Available at: http://blogs.sciences-po.fr/pilagg/files/2012/05/David-Kennedy-Paper-PILAGG-FM.pdf.

[27] Luhmann (n 23) at 61. This must not be confused with an *internal* perspective of the relevant legal (sub-) system, where there is, of course, a clear distinction between facts and the law, see Luhmann, ibid at 84–85. See also Niklas Luhmann, *Gibt es in unserer Gesellschaft noch unverzichtbare Normen?* Heidelberger Universitätsreden 4 (Heidelberg, CF Müller Verlag, 1993) 5.

[28] Luhmann, *Introduction to Systems Theory* (n 21) 43 (with reference to Humberto Maturana).

[29] Richard Nobles and David Schiff, *Observing Law through Systems Theory* (Oxford, Hart Publishing, 2013) 89.

[30] The law of physics assumes such closure since it aims at producing entropy by dissolving all distinctions, thus bringing about a state of no more (usable) energy, see Luhmann, *Introduction to Systems Theory* (n 21) 28. Closed systems are solely based on causality ('causally closed'). Technical systems such as computers ('trivial machines') are normally a useful example: lack of electricity (cause) will shut them down (event).

[31] Luhmann (n 21) 38–39.

Living would be the operation[32] bases on which this self-reproduction takes place. Such an operation must be recursive, self-referential, and circular – conditions that build on the older theory of closed systems.[33] Under the modern assumption of open systems, these remain 'operationally closed'. This means that it is the system itself that draws the necessary distinctions from the environment in order to ensure its own survival:[34] to take the above example, the human being achieves this by living.

How does a social system achieve this? In a nutshell, through communication.[35] Focusing on autopoiesis (ie the continuous self-reproduction of a system) Luhmann relies on operations that are self-referential, thus staying within the system. Otherwise, the system would not remain operationally closed. For Luhmann, communication is the one and only form of operation in the social system. At a basic level, an operation is self-referential if it distinguishes between the system's own operations and other things.[36] So a social system that keeps reproducing itself by way of communication also decides which events count as communication.

At a higher level, self-reference means that the social system describes itself (ie its characteristics and overall function).[37] For the legal system, it follows that legal communication is the basic operator. The most obvious examples are the passing of a statute, the filing of a claim (and any legal submission), a court judgment, a contract or a legal settlement. For less obvious examples in daily life that may give rise to legal issues, a further criterion of self-reference is needed. Luhmann describes this as the ability of an operation (communication) to connect, thereby creating structures. In a social system, learning a language can be used an as example.[38]

More specifically for the legal system, this means that only communication which applies the legal code (legal/illegal), such as 'I do/don't have the right to do x', counts as legal communication.[39] Based on communication, a social system keeps creating its own structures, defined as the system's expectations in relation to the connectivity of communications. Such structures of the legal system are rules, norms, or texts.[40]

[32] Operation is also referred to as interaction between the whole system and its parts, Nobles and Schiff, *Observing Law through Systems Theory* (n 29) 24. In Luhmann's terminology, the system does not consist of elements, but rather structure. The difference from the environment is the sole operator, Luhmann, *Introduction to Systems Theory* (n 21) xvi (editorial foreword by Dirk Baecker).

[33] Luhmann, ibid at 38. See also above n 30.

[34] Luhmann, ibid at 63.

[35] Ibid at 53–54, distinguishing Parsons' theory of action. For Luhmann, action does not always have social resonance. By contrast, communication always means that someone hears you.

[36] Luhmann, *Recht der Gesellschaft* (n 23) 53.

[37] Ibid.

[38] Luhmann, *Introduction to Systems Theory* (n 21) 70.

[39] Luhmann, *Recht der Gesellschaft* (n 23) 67. In this sense, the legal system can include daily situations, not just the actions of lawmakers or lawyers.

[40] Ibid at 41.

The abstract idea of recursive self-reproduction is better equipped to deal with different legal regimes: as functional sub-systems of the legal system they are operationally closed, each evolving around their specific concepts and rules. This allows for a higher-order perspective that is less normative. It simply describes the way in which any legal sub-system operates. This can be applied to the relationship between a 'self-contained' specialised regime of international law and general international law. The latter would be the overall legal system on a global level; the former would be one of its sub-systems. Under a systems theoretical approach, the two are system and environment, respectively. There would be no question of hierarchies. It would therefore be of no interest whether the specialised regime claims precedence. Such a perspective – external to the legal system – understands striving for self-reproduction as part of the regime's definition, and is less of a problem per se.

This external perspective has the consequence of reducing law to a fact. Norms are seen as dealing with factual expectations.[41] Their point, as the function of law generally, is to stabilise normative expectations.[42] The legal system is therefore programmed in a way that allows for structural compensation if these expectations are subsequently frustrated. For a systems theorist, the legal system does not start with a quest for principles, but simply with a distinction: Which expectations are recognised by the legal code so that they warrant – in a non-technical sense – compensation?

The legal system fills this distinction with life, based on the core distinction between legal and illegal. This is the legal code and, as such, is invariable. It must be contrasted against variable programmes (eg norms),[43] which constitute selection criteria and hence build structure (eg further norms).[44] Each legal (sub-) system uses the same code (legal/illegal) but this is programmed differently. Herein lies the source of the problem, namely, if something appears to be legal and illegal at the same time. Luhmann refers to this as the *paradox* of the legal system: for the law to work, we must assume that the distinction between legal and illegal itself is legal – so ultimately, the law is the law because the law says so.[45]

Within a system, proper programming can normally avoid that this basic *paradox* becomes visible. However it cannot always be avoided, even within the same legal system.[46] It is unsurprising, then, that it comes up in situations covered by different legal regimes: increasingly, lawyers are faced with circumstances where, under the programming of one legal regime, the act in question

[41] See above text accompanying n 26.

[42] Luhmann, *Recht der Gesellschaft* (n 23) 199, 221.

[43] Ibid at 189–94.

[44] Ibid at 242. See also above the text accompanying n 40. Special treatment is required for the notion of justice: This is not a selection criterion nor a (regular) norm, but a so-called 'contingency formula'. Ibid at 221–26.

[45] Ibid at 168.

[46] Luhmann, *Gibt es in unserer Gesellschaft noch unverzichtbare Normen?* (n 27) 2–3, 25 refers to such hard cases as those involving 'tragic choices' (eg torture is the only means by which human lives can be saved). Here, the assumption that the distinction legal/illegal is itself legal, no longer works.

would be legal, whereas the same act would be illegal under the programming of another.[47]

(iii) Structural Coupling between the (Legal) System and its Environment

The third insight derives from the association between the system and its environment. System in this respect can be a sub-system (such as international trade law). The environment is system specific and can be anyone or anything else from which the respective system (or sub-system) differentiates itself (ie another human being, a functionally different part of society or the overall legal system). In the example given, the environment from which international trade law distinguishes itself would be general international law.

Under modern systems theory there is no *causal* interaction between the system and its environment. The only way in which reactions take place in specific situations is through common concepts (ie *via* 'structural coupling' (see below)). This notion originates from biology, where it refers in particular to the eyes and the ears, which structurally couple the human brain to its environment (ie anything outside the human body).[48] It is then made fruitful for social systems: for nations, it is the concept of the constitutionally bound state that structurally couples the legal and political system.[49]

The rule of law as a constitutional principle plays an outstanding role in this respect.[50] The legal and economic systems are structurally coupled through concepts such as 'contract' or 'property'.[51] The point of structural coupling is to enable and, at the same time limit, environmental influences on the system. To take the above example: eyes and ears enable a human being to see and hear within their respective reach.[52] Structural development of the system then depends on structural coupling insofar as the system cannot produce structures other than those that are compatible with the environment. For example, birds will develop only if there is an atmosphere.[53]

Specific situations in which the environment can influence the system are called 'irritations', which the system then has to process. For example, a dispute in daily societal life – the environment of the legal system – is being framed as

[47] The *Micula* case discussed below at n 154 and in ch 4 is an illustration of this, at least, if the Court ultimately upheld the Commission's finding that the arbitral award in favour of the claimants constitutes state aid that is illegal under EU law (see ch 4, IA (iv), IIA (i) and (ii)).

[48] Luhmann, *Introduction to Systems Theory* (n 21) 86.

[49] Luhmann, *Recht der Gesellschaft* (n 23) 470. For an EU-specific context see Mathias Albert, 'Governance and Democracy in European Systems: On Systems Theory and European Integration' (2002) 28 *Review of International Studies* 293, 299.

[50] Luhmann, *Recht der Gesellschaft* (n 23) 407–26.

[51] Ibid at 450, 455, 459.

[52] Ibid at 441.

[53] Luhmann, *Introduction to Systems Theory* (n 21) 197 (with reference to Maturana).

who is legally right: the legal system can pick up and process this legal question under its own code (legal/illegal), relying on its own programmes,[54] thus further building on its own structures.[55] The same factual scenario will be processed independently in another sub-system. For example, payment of a debt is processed differently in the economic (payment as basic operation) and the legal system (payment settles a claim).

(iv) Reducing Social Complexity through Trust

The fourth insight from systems theory is the existential role of communication. Due to operational closure, communication works only *within* the system, following its own specific logic of connectivity.[56] The example given above was 'I do/don't have the right to do x'.[57] The same logic applies to the relationship between legal sub-systems and the international legal system: if we functionally divide the international legal system into specialised sub-systems,[58] *specialist legal* communication within each regime is constitutive for the respective sub-system such as international human rights or trade law. By contrast, *outward* communication is not constitutive for a system or sub-system. External relations, that is, those between a (sub-) system and its environment, hinge entirely on structural coupling. Nevertheless, specialist legal communication within, say, international trade law, still belongs to or 'implements' the international legal system and, ultimately, society.

The point of communication – as operation – is to reduce complexity.[59] So communication in the social system serves the reduction of social complexities. Such complexities arise from the fact that the future is unknown and holds many more possibilities of what could happen compared to what actually happens. In Luhmann's words, the future is overly complex. People live in the present, so they must constantly reduce future complexities in accordance with what has, in fact, materialised.[60]

One important way of reducing complexity is trust. Without trust, we would have to constantly guard ourselves against everyone and everything. This would make life too complex and ultimately prevent us from doing things. We only have certainty about the past. Looking at history means dealing with the known (ie with complexity that has already been reduced).[61] By contrast, trust is about dealing

[54] For the difference between code and programming see the text accompanying nn 40 and 44.
[55] Luhmann, *Recht der Gesellschaft* (n 23) 443.
[56] Luhmann, *Introduction to Systems Theory* (n 21) 63–64.
[57] See the text accompanying n 39.
[58] This sociological perspective alleviates the controversy between legal centralism and pluralism as to the correct benchmark for the international legal order (unity versus diversity): there can be unity without strict hierarchies; and there can be diversity without complete detachment.
[59] Luhmann, *Introduction to Systems Theory* (n 21) 121 with further references.
[60] N Luhmann, *Vertrauen: Ein Mechanismus der Reduktion sozialer Komplexität*, 2nd edn (Stuttgart, Ferdinand Enke Verlag, 1973) 12.
[61] Ibid at 20.

with the unknown: the future. We limit risks[62] by deciding whom (or what) to trust. Regarding individual persons, trust-building factors derive from the way in which the relevant person presents itself in society: the question is whether we feel certain enough that – within space for personal development – this person will act within a calculable range of possibilities.

Trust beyond trust in individuals – trust in a social system itself – is much more difficult to achieve or assess. Systems theory uses generalised mechanisms in a social system, such as truth, commitment, power or money as trust-building factors.[63] For example, money – the freedom to spend at a later date according to personal preference – reduces the complexity associated with barter. Trust in the economic system is thus channelled through trust in money, at least as long as money itself is trusted. Money is just one particular medium of communication. The same is true for truth, the function of which is also to transfer complexity that has already been reduced.

Seen in this light, systems theory enriches regime theory by shifting the focus towards communication and concepts that structurally couple general (legal) communication with the more specialist one. This can then replace the pursuit of unity or hierarchies within the international legal order. The problematic relationship between EU law and international arbitration is best explained by understanding EU law, ICA and ITA as operationally closed sub-systems of international law, which need to remain structurally coupled to the latter so as to alleviate conflict. The interface between EU law and international arbitration can then be formulated as problem of structural coupling. At the same time, this needs to be done with a view to achieving public trust by reducing complexity.

C. The Primacy and Autonomy of EU Law Revisited

EU law is best understood as a sub-system of the international legal system (above B (i)), which has been evolving over time and is still a work in progress. A system (sub-system) that keeps differentiating itself from its environment (the overall system), operates in a self-referential way: it is operationally closed with the effect that its operations (legal communications) stay within the system. The only interaction with the environment takes place via structural coupling (see B (iii) above). The problem with EU law is that its foundational principles, as interpreted authoritatively by the Court of Justice of the EU (CJEU), have, to date, been focused on operational closure rather than on potential trigger points for structural coupling with the overall international system.

[62] Luhmann, *Recht der Gesellschaft* (n 23) 34, noting that a complete elimination of risk in the future is not possible.

[63] Luhmann, *Vertrauen* (n 60) 51 with reference to Talcott Parsons.

(i) Self-Referential Nature of the EU

Costa and *van Gend* set out the basis for the EU's self-understanding as a 'new legal order', that is, an operationally closed sub-system based on the primacy[64] and direct effect[65] of EU law. The argument went as follows: the EU's (then the EC's) legal system is autonomous and must hence prevail over and have direct effect in national legal systems.[66] Since the EU created its own legal system, which is supreme and has direct effect, it is effectively autonomous vis-à-vis its Member States' legal systems. The circularity of this reasoning is well understood.[67] Obviously, its sole point of reference is the EU. These landmark cases constitute conscious regime building (see A I above). Since then, the principles of primacy and direct effect have been at the heart of EU law.[68] Since they originate in and continue to be developed by case law, the Court is ultimately building the EU legal (sub-)system.[69]

The modern principle of autonomy, which has increasingly attracted the attention of legal commentators,[70] best illustrates this. Its textual origin lies in *Costa* itself, in particular, the understanding of EU law as an autonomous source.[71] This effectively enables the Court to determine when there is a collision between the EU and any other legal system. In *Costa*, this was the national legal system. The same was true in *Simmenthal*,[72] where the Court held that national authorities

[64] Case 6/64 *Costa v ENEL* ECLI:EU:C:1964:66.

[65] Case 26/62 *Van Gend en Loos* ECLI:EU:C:1963:1. This means that if EU law provides a sufficiently clear rule to govern a specific situation, individuals in the Member States can rely on the relevant EU rule in the domestic courts, national law notwithstanding.

[66] The Court later confirmed that the primacy of EU law also applies to national Constitutions, Case 11/70 *Internationale Handelsgesellschaft* ECLI:EU:C:1970:114.

[67] See, eg, Bruno de Witte, 'Direct Effect, Primacy, and the Nature of the Legal Order' in Paul Craig and Gráinne de Búrca, *The Evolution of EU Law*, 2nd edn (Oxford, Oxford University Press, 2011) 324, 361.

[68] More recently, the CJEU has clarified that direct effect is indeed a pre-condition for EU primacy, which only bites in the case of a conflict. This, in turn, presupposes that two (different) rules – a directly applicable EU and a national one – apply. Case C-573/17 *Criminal Proceedings against Daniel Adam Poplawski* ECLI:EU:C:2019:530 paras 60–64.

[69] Known as EU legal integration, see the edited volumes by Mauro Cappelletti, Monica Seccombe and Joseph HH Weiler (eds), *Integration through Law: Europe and the American Federal Experience* Vols 1–3 (New York, de Gruyter, 1986–1987). See also ch 1, II B (judicial supremacy).

[70] For general conceptualization, see Marcus Klamert, 'The Autonomy of the EU (and of EU Law): Through the Kaleidoscope' (2017) 42 *European Law Review* 815 (distinguishing three inter-related features: the special nature of the EU legal order, the integrity of the EU's essential characteristics, and implications from the EU's constitutionalisation). See also Dimitri Kochenov, 'EU Law without the Rule of Law: Is the Veneration of Autonomy Worth It?' (2015) 34 *Yearbook of European Law* 1. For categorisation of its external dimension, see Cristina Contartese, 'The Autonomy of the EU Legal Order in the ECJ's External Relations Case Law: From the "Essential" to "Specific Characteristics" of the Union and Back Again' (2017) 54 *Common Market Law Review* 1627; and Jed Odermatt, 'The Principle of Autonomy: An Adolescent Disease?' in M Cremona (ed), *Structural Principles in EU External Relations Law* (Oxford, Hart Publishing, 2018).

[71] Case 6/64 *Costa v ENEL* (n 64) ('*source autonome*' in French; the English version refers to the 'independent' source of EU law). See Willem van Rossem, 'The Autonomy of EU Law: More is Less?' in Ramses A Wessel and Steven Blockmans (eds), *Between Autonomy and Dependence: The EU Legal Order under the Influence of International Organisations* (The Hague, TMC Asser Press, 2013).

[72] Case 106/77 *Amministrazione delle Finanze v Simmenthal* (II) ECLI:EU:C:1978:49 para 24.

must not await the Italian Constitutional Court's setting aside of a law that the CJEU had previously held to be in breach of EU law. To hold otherwise would 'imperil the very foundations of the Community', since it would deny the effectiveness of Member States' obligations under EU law.[73] The same circularity can be detected here, since it is the Court that must first define what these obligations are in any given case.

The EU's autonomy hence allows the Court to ensure that EU Constitutional law *as interpreted by the Court* cannot be ignored. Its underlying rationale is ultimately the primacy of EU law via-à-vis its Member States' legal systems.

Autonomy also enables the Court to deal with collisions between the EU and the overall international legal system. EU autonomy has been playing a crucial role in EU external relations law, starting with Opinion 1/91 on the envisaged agreement setting up the European Economic Area (EEA) in the early 1990s,[74] and culminating in Opinion 2/13 regarding ECHR accession.[75] It is also the basis of the *Achmea* judgment.[76]

To be clear, the primacy of the EU legal system characterises the EU's *internal* structure, so it cannot be relied on as such in relation to international law. In relation to third countries, the Court hence focused on the 'allocation of responsibilities defined in the Treaties',[77] notably its own competence under (now) Article 19 TEU to interpret EU law and hence ensure EU autonomy.[78] Allowing the envisaged EEA Court to interpret rules that correspond to EU rules would conflict with this responsibility of the CJEU, adding it to the 'very foundations of the Community'.[79] This line of cases represents the EU's external autonomy, that is, the EU's perspective on the relationship between agreements under general international law and EU law: these cannot stand if they conflict with the 'very foundations of the Community', including the Court's own powers. So international law agreements of the EU and its Member States may not interfere with the EU's exclusive jurisdiction, which gives rise to and, at the same time, follows on from, the EU's autonomy.[80]

[73] Ibid at para 18. See also Case C-103/88 *Fratelli Costanzo SpA v Comune di Milano* ECLI:EU:C:1989:256, and the application in recent case C-349/17 *Eesti Pagar AS v Ettevõtluse Arendamise Sihtasutus and Majandus- ja Kommunikatsiooniministeerium* ECLI:EU:C:2019:172.

[74] Opinion 1/91 *EEA Agreement* ECLI:EU:C:1991:490 para 30 (para 21).

[75] Opinion 2/13 *Accession of the European Union to the European Convention for the Protection of Human Rights and Fundamental Freedoms* (ECHR Accession) ECLI:EU:C:2014:2454. See (ii) below.

[76] Case C-284/16 *Slowakische Republik (Slovak Republic) v Achmea BV* ECLI:EU:C:2018:158. For further discussion see ch 3.

[77] Opinion 1/91 (n 74) para 35.

[78] Ibid. The Court's terminology clouds the fact that there is a difference between the internal division of powers or competences between the EU and its Member States and the responsibility of the EU, its Member States (or both) under international law. See ch 4, II B.

[79] Ibid at para 46. The reference to the 'very foundations of the Community' completes the circle back to *Simmenthal* (nn 72–73 and accompanying text), but is less convincing in EU external relations than it is in an intra-EU context.

[80] The reasoning follows the same logical circle as was found above (see text accompanying nn 66–67).

This self-referential reasoning has been strengthened in subsequent cases, where the Court has added EU-specific elements to those that constitute EU (external) autonomy. In the *Kadi* case, it ruled that judicial review on the basis of EU fundamental rights was part of the 'very foundations' of EU law.[81] Such judicial review is a 'constitutional guarantee stemming from the EC Treaty as an autonomous legal system'.[82] Hence, no international agreement can prejudice an EU fundamental rights review of a Community measure. This even applied to a decision by the UN Sanctions Committee based on a Resolution by the Security Council for which Article 25 of the UN Charter claims paramount authority.[83]

Kadi was extremely controversial.[84] It has been partially defended by reference to the importance of rights protection within the EU, given that no international forum equivalent to the CJEU was readily available.[85] But *Kadi* contained an even wider definition of the 'very foundations' of EU law: according to the Court, these include judicial review more generally, based on the principles of liberty, democracy, and respect for human rights and fundamental freedoms enshrined in (then-) Article 6(1) of the EU Treaty.[86]

Kadi hence effectively makes the 'very foundations of EU law' a benchmark for *any* obligations by the Member States *whatever their legal source* (ie whether they are arising under national or international law): if there is a conflict, EU law prevails. This is true at least as a matter of EU law since primacy is an EU *internal* feature in that it represents the EU's own view: the self-referential circle is closed.

For present purposes, this operational closure in the CJEU's *Kadi* decision is the most relevant issue.[87] It means that EU law detaches itself from general international law by using the EU foundations as a benchmark for judicial review in external relations.

The alternative would have been to consider ways to engage with general international law. Put differently, the Court could have looked for a concept that is common to both the EU and general international law in order to communicate

[81] Joined Cases C-402/05P & C-415/05P *Kadi and Al Barakaat v Council* ECLI:EU:C:2008:461 paras 281, 284–85, 290 (*Kadi*).

[82] Ibid paras 281–85, 316.

[83] For details regarding the interpretation of Security Council resolutions and an argument from the French version of Article 103 of the UN Charter to the effect that the primacy of the Charter includes UN law generally, see Peter Hilpold, 'EU Law and UN Law in Conflict: The Kadi Case' (2009) 13 *Max Planck Yearbook of United Nations Law* 141, 159, 161.

[84] Compare the reference to internal and external autonomy and the critique of *Kadi* by Gráinne de Búrca, 'The European Court of Justice and the International Legal Order after Kadi' (2010) 51 *Harvard International Law Journal* 1.

[85] See Katja Ziegler, 'The Relationship between EU Law and International Law' (2015) *University of Leicester School of Law Research Paper* No 15–04. Available at: https://ssrn.com/abstract=2554069.

[86] *Kadi* (n 81) para 303. The reference to Art 6 ties with the approach favoured by Advocate General Maduro, AG Opinion in Case C-402/05P *Kadi* ECLI:EU:C:2008:11, para 31.

[87] For a comprehensive critique, see, eg, Peter Hilpold, 'EU Law and UN Law in Conflict: The *Kadi* Case' (n 83).

in the same language. The – overruled – benchmark used by the General Court in *Kadi* would have paved the way for such an approach. The General Court had relied on *jus cogens* as the only basis on which the EU could indirectly review measures by the UN Security Council.[88] This would not just have limited the EU's judicial review power in this and similar cases. More importantly, it would have provided a concept originating in general international law. *Jus cogens* as relied on in international practice and interpreted by the International Court of Justice (ICJ) would have been used as an EU law concept. As a shared concept it could then have provided the platform for a dialogue between the EU judiciary and (other) international courts and tribunals.[89]

In short, the use of general legal concepts such as *jus cogens*, would form the basis for an interaction between the EU legal system and its environment (ie, general international law and other specialised regimes). The mechanism available for this is called *structural coupling*.

(ii) Structural Coupling between EU and General International Law?

To recall, in national societies it is the constitution and, in particular, the constitutionally acknowledged rule of law that couples the national legal and political systems. In the international legal order this constitutional function can only partly be served by international legal treaties.[90] But treaties couple the specialist regime (legal sub-system) to the overall legal system. International treaties that structurally couple the EU and the international legal system are first and foremost the EU's founding treaties in the current form of the Treaty on the European Union (TEU) and the Treaty on the Functioning of the European Union (TFEU).

The EU founding treaties come closest to what could be called an EU Constitution. This means that the validity, under EU law, of any other international law agreements by the EU, its Member States, or both, will be judged against

[88] Case T-315/01 *Kadi v Council and Commission* ECLI:EU:T:2005:332 paras 226–31 (*jus cogens* as basis for review) and paras 232–91 (application).

[89] See further below ch 4, II B.

[90] There is no equivalent at the global level to a national constitution. Models of societal constitutionalism (Gunther Teubner, *Constitutional Fragments: Societal Constitutionalism and Globalization* (Oxford, Oxford University Press, 2012)) and, more recently, G Teubner, '*Quod Omnes Tangit*: Transnational Constitutions Without Democracy?' (2018) *Journal of Law and Society* (available at: https://ssrn.com/abstract=3177062) or concepts such as demoicracy (Robert Schütze, 'Models of Demoicracy: Some Preliminary Thoughts' (2020) EUI Department of Law Research Paper No 2020/08 (available at: https://ssrn.com/abstract=3658493) can only partially fill this gap. The same is true for understanding treaties such as the NYC or ICSID as fulfilling constitutional functions, since this would be reduced to an emerging economic constitution, referred to as 'embryonic at best' by Alec Stone Sweet and Florian Grisel in *The Evolution of International Arbitration: Judicialization, Governance, Legitimacy* (Oxford, Oxford University Press, 2017) 31. A systems theoretical approach is helpful in that it alleviates the need for *the* (one) global authority: sub-dividing the international legal order alongside functional lines is *not* making any normative claims. See also Eric C Ip, 'Reconceptualizing the International Legal Regime: Law, Politics and Institutions' (2009) 2 *Northwestern Interdisciplinary Law Review* 57.

these. The actor responsible for this is the CJEU, Article 218(11) TFEU. This is where most case law in EU external action originates, in particular the CJEU's Opinion on the *EEA Agreement* and on *ECHR accession* referred to at (i) above. It is, therefore, the CJEU's case law that guides the degree to which EU law is, at any given point, actually coupled to the international legal order. Any change of events in this respect – other than changes in the case law – remain possible by way of amendments to the EU founding treaties by the Member States.

The advantage of structural coupling as a concept dealing with the association between system and environment is that it takes an *external* perspective, asking how the system (EU law) and its environment (the overall international legal system) are connected.[91] So it does not matter what either EU or general international law conclude in terms of the correct approach to a case such as *Kadi*. It was said above (see B (iii)) that the structural development of a system depends on structural coupling. For the EU, this means that the evolution of EU law in the longer run depends on what is compatible with general international law. Conversely, the development of EU law stops when EU external action is understood as a breach of EU law.

This can be illustrated by Opinion 2/13, where the Court held that accession by the EU to the ECHR must preserve the 'specific characteristics' of the EU.[92] These were said to include 'the very nature of EU law' (ie, its independent source, primacy and direct effect) as well as a 'structured network of principles, rules and mutually interdependent legal relations linking the EU and its Member States, and its Member States with each other (…), based on (…) mutual trust'.[93] The latter is linked to the principle of cooperation (Article 4(3) TFEU), according to which the Member States must ensure the application of and respect for EU law, including a duty to take appropriate action.[94] By moving on directly to the importance of the EU's judicial system and the preliminary ruling procedure, the Court signals that it understands the latter as a crucial platform for this cooperation.[95]

Opinion 2/13 focuses on the special features of the EU and EU law,[96] which makes it difficult to see the bridge for further evolution in line with general international law.[97] It remains ambiguous regarding the concept of EU autonomy,

[91] Luhmann, *Introduction to Systems Theory* (n 21) 197.

[92] Opinion 2/13 *ECHR Accession* (n 75).

[93] Ibid at paras 166–68. For more detail see Konstanze von Papp, 'Role and Powers of the Court of Justice of the EU' in Emmanuelle Guinchard and Marie-Pierre Granger (eds), *The New EU Judiciary: An Analysis of Current Judicial Reforms*, European Monographs Series Set 102 (The Netherlands, Wolters Kluwer, 2018) 101, 116.

[94] Opinion 2/13 *ECHR Accession* (n 75) paras 172–73.

[95] Ibid at paras 174–76. Judicial protection is here specifically addressed with regard to individual rights, but this can, of course, be generalised.

[96] Using categories such as the EU's 'constitutional structure' as per the principle of conferred powers; its institutional framework (Articles 13– 19 TEU); and 'the very nature of EU law'.

[97] But see Daniel Halberstam 'It's the Autonomy Stupid! A Modest Defense of Opinion 2/13 on EU Accession to the ECHR, and the Way Forward' *Michigan Public Law and Legal Theory Research Paper Series* No 432 (February 2015). Available at: http://ssrn.com/abstract=2567591.

using the new and independent nature of the EU legal system as part of its characteristics and at the same time 'autonomy' as a seemingly free-flying concept.[98] The case law references here suggest that the Court is using the argument for an EU fundamental rights review of Member State acts for an EU fundamental rights review of EU acts implementing international law.[99] In this sense, EU autonomy is less a starting point (a new, independent legal order) than the effect or conclusion of this, which again exemplifies the self-referential nature and circularity of EU law.

Seen through the prism of systems theory, autonomy comprises those elements that formally shield the EU legal system against 'irritations' (see B (iii) above) from its environment, including Member State legal systems and the international legal system. In other words, autonomy is part of the structure that underlies the EU and that its law keeps producing. EU autonomy originates in and reinforces the CJEU's exclusive jurisdiction over the interpretation and applicability of EU law, which can be paraphrased as 'judicial monopoly'[100] or 'disguised claim to sovereignty'.[101] In the terminology of systems theory, this illustrates operational closure. The Court has minimised the role that international law plays within the EU legal system (eg by disregarding the international law debate on state responsibility and its meaning for international organisations).[102] So the CJEU focused on EU-specific language without using concepts that could be picked up by general international law and would thus have structurally coupled EU law with international law.

D. Arbitration Agreements as Self-Validating Contracts?

(i) *The Self-Referential Nature of ICA and ITA*

As discussed above, ICA and ITA are both specialised regimes. They are here further understood as sub-systems of the international legal system, although there are some ambiguities.

As to ICA, its character has been discussed in the literature mostly under the notion of *lex mercatoria*.[103] One of the main controversies here is its *legal* nature

[98] Opinion 2/13 (n 75) paras 157, 166, 170 and 174.

[99] Para 170 refers to *Internationale Handelsgesellschaft* and *Kadi*.

[100] Steffen Hindelang, 'Conceptualisation an Application of the Principle of Autonomy of EU Law: The CJEU's Judgment in *Achmea* Put in Perspective' (2019) 44 *European Law Review* 383, 384.

[101] van Rossem, 'The Autonomy of EU Law' (n 71).

[102] Critically Piet Eeckhout, 'Opinion 2/13 on EU Accession to the ECHR and Judicial Dialogue – Autonomy or Autarky?' *Jean Monnet Working Paper 01/15*. Available at: http://jeanmonnetprogram.org/paper/opinion-213-on-eu-accession-to-the-echr-and-judicial-dialogue-autonomy-or-autarky/. See also n 78.

[103] Gunther Teubner, 'Breaking Frames: Economic Globalisation and the Emergence of *lex mercatoria*' (2002) 5 *European Journal of Social Theory* 199. For a comprehensive analysis of both ICA and ITA under this heading see Jan H Dalhuisen, *The Transnationalisation of Commercial and Financial Law*,

as such, and its relationship with state law and national courts.[104] In systems theoretical terms, this has led to a debate as to whether ICA really follows the legal code, or whether it should not better be seen as following the economic code. This would translate into a different view on its legitimacy, which under the economic code is not interested in what is legal, but in what is efficient.[105] The law, and even the legal system as such, becomes something that can be bargained for. Under such a view, ICA would not belong to the legal, but to the economic system (see B above).

A lawyer's response to this must be that ICA still belongs firmly to the legal system, which can be seen from the fact that we expect legally enforceable outcomes. Nevertheless, ICA can be understood as a legal sub-system that is particularly prone to irritation (see B (iii)) from the economic system, which it needs to process and deal with. As to ITA, the debate has focused on whether the abundance of bilateral treaties, interpreted by different *ad hoc* tribunals can be understood as a regime with an ordering function at all.[106] So the question of precedents and overarching *principles* has been controversial here.[107] This, under systems theory, is therefore more about the question of operational closure (ie whether ITA really constitutes its own system). An ITA specialist's response to this would be that investment law has left its bilateral origin behind to the extent that investment protection standards are interpreted along similar lines across treaties, and arbitration tribunals take note of each other's decisions.[108] In fact, where the same factual scenario is decided differently on the basis of different treaties, this is being heavily criticised.[109] Hence, there is also an expectation of consistent (self-referential) case law. Similar to the debate regarding ICA, there is also a controversy as to whether ITA really belongs to the legal sub-system. Historically, ITA has evolved from diplomatic protection and could therefore be placed within the political sub-system.[110] Under this view, law is made and

and of Commercial, Financial, and Investment Dispute Resolution: The New Lex Mercatoria and its Sources, 7th edn (Oxford, Hart Publishing, 2019).

[104] Gralf-Peter Calliess, 'Lex Mercatoria' in Jürgen Basedow et al (eds), *Encyclopedia of Private International Law* (Cheltenham, Edward Elgar, 2017) 1119.

[105] Eg Albert, 'Governance and Democracy in European Systems' (n 49) 293, 304. See also Kennedy, 'The Political Economy of Centers and Peripheries' (n 26), asking how economic interests alone could then limit political power.

[106] See Stephan Schill, 'W(h)ither Fragmentation: On the Literature and Sociology of International Investment Law' (2011) 22 *European Journal of International Law* 875, 890.

[107] See, eg, Tarcisio Gazzinni, 'General Principles of Law in the Field of Foreign Investment' (2009) 10 *Journal of World Investment and Trade* 103; compare the subsequent call for caution by Martti Koskenniemi, 'It's Not the Cases, It's the System' (2017) 18 *Journal of World Investment and Trade* 343.

[108] Schill, 'The Multilateralization of International Investment Law' (n 4).

[109] See, eg, Susan D Franck, 'The Nature and Enforcement of Investor Rights Under Investment Treaties: Do Investment Treaties Have a Bright Future?' (2005) 12 *UC Davis Journal of International Law and Policy* 47.

[110] Cedric G Dupont, Thomas Schultz and Jason W Yackee, 'Investment Arbitration and Political Systems Theory' in Thomas Schultz and Federico Ortino (eds), *Oxford Handbook of International Arbitration* (Oxford, Oxford University Press, 2019). Available at: https://ssrn.com/abstract=3351343.

changed by those in power. Nevertheless, ITA has long been based on international law treaties enabling private enforcement. The better view is, therefore, to place ITA firmly within the international legal system, while acknowledging that it is particularly prone to and must deal with irritations from the political system (see B (iii)).

In any event, ICA and ITA are consensual. Both originate from an agreement between the parties to remove their dispute from the jurisdiction of national courts. They are hence discussed under the heading of international contracts.[111] A contract can be seen as a self-referential system in itself.[112] Even if one were to disagree with this as a general matter, it could be applied to arbitration agreements (as part of commercial contracts often referred to as arbitration clauses): they are, at the same time, the basis on which the arbitration operates, and the arbitration's main point of reference for construing its process – how to choose arbitrators, where to place the arbitration in terms of seat and hence applicable arbitration laws, procedural rules etc.

An arbitration is therefore an operationally closed legal (sub-)system,[113] removed from national legal systems, which is why international arbitration is sometimes perceived as 'private'. Understanding arbitration as a legal (sub-)system works for the ideal arbitration (ie where the parties remain in agreement as to the process resulting in a binding award); in other words, as long as this indeed remains outside the national courts. Such a theoretical view squares, in principle, with a contractual understanding of arbitration (see ch 1 III B). In the language of systems theory, this expresses trust in the consensus between the parties.

Nevertheless, this understanding needs to be backed up by a more realistic perspective, considering that the dispute often reaches the level of the arbitration agreement itself. It may turn out that the trust in the arbitration agreement was misplaced (ie the parties may disagree about its existence, validity, or reach). Once the dispute comes before an arbitration tribunal, a well-known paradox arises: if the parties disagree about whether their dispute shall be arbitrated, doesn't this erase the basis of the arbitration and hence the jurisdiction of the tribunal? Conversely, where an action is initiated in the state courts, does the (potentially valid) agreement to arbitrate remove the jurisdiction of the court? A purely contractual understanding finds its limits here and what counts is the requirements for legal enforcement of the arbitration agreement.

[111] Teubner, 'Breaking Frames' (n 103). There remains, of course, a difference between an international treaty between states, and the individual contract between either the state and the investor (ITA), or between companies or individuals (ICA).

[112] See Hugh Collins, *Regulating Contracts* (Oxford, Oxford University Press, 1999), Ana Lourenco, 'Autopoietic Social Systems Theory: Co-Evolution of Law and the Economy' *Centre for Business Research, University of Cambridge Research Paper* No. 409 (2010). Available at: www.austlii.edu.au/au/journals/AUJlLegPhil/2010/4.pdf.

[113] For arbitration as a system see also Thomas Schultz, *Transnational Legality: Stateless Law and International Arbitration* (Oxford, Oxford University Press, 2014).

(ii) Enforcing the Agreement to Arbitrate: Article II of the New York Convention

In ICA, this problem is partly tackled by separating the agreement to arbitrate from other contractual agreements between the parties or, respectively, from the contract containing the arbitration clause ('container contract'). This is known as the doctrine of separability. This does not resolve the issue, however, if it is the arbitration clause itself that is at stake.

The New York Convention on the Recognition and Enforcement of Foreign Arbitral Awards of 10 June 1958 (New York Convention, NYC)[114] obliges contracting states to recognise an arbitration agreement in writing (Article II(1)), unless the agreement is 'null and void, inoperative or incapable of being performed' (Article II(3)). Accordingly, there is an international law benchmark, but it does not resolve the paradox described above: Whose job is it to review the arbitration agreement?

In European jurisdictions, the doctrine of competence–competence states that it is generally up to the arbitration tribunal to hear challenges to the arbitration agreement. This decision can normally be fully reviewed by national courts.[115] By contrast, in the US legal system, review of the arbitration agreement is normally a matter for the national courts. Only exceptionally can this be left to the arbitrators.[116] If such an exception bites, the arbitral decision regarding its own competence is reviewable by national courts, but on a very limited scale, leaving much deference to the arbitrators.[117]

Nevertheless, under both the European and the US approaches, one must consider the intentions of the parties, using certain default rules. It is generally accepted that commercial parties can agree to have their disputes solved by arbitration, thus waiving their right to have the case heard by a court. The NYC's whole point is to provide the framework in order to ensure this. There is, therefore, a sound argument that an agreement to arbitrate stands under an *international* presumption of validity, following the NYC's pro-arbitration objective (sometimes also referred to as pro-arbitration or pro-enforcement bias).[118] From a systems theoretical perspective, this captures trust in the arbitration system: the

[114] 330 United Nations Treaty Series (UNTS) 3.

[115] French law is noteworthy in this respect since the doctrine of competence–competence is particularly strong here. For more details see Konstanze von Papp, 'Biting the Bullet or Redefining Consent in Investor-State Arbitration? Pre-Arbitration Requirements after BG Group v Argentina' (2015) 16 *Journal of World Investment and Trade* 695.

[116] See the more detailed discussion below at II. Note that the jurisdictional hurdle in the US is often referred to as 'arbitrability'. I will use this term here accordingly, but at the same time add a broader perspective, see below II A and B.

[117] See von Papp, 'Biting the Bullet or Redefining Consent in Investor-State Arbitration?' (n 115).

[118] Gary B Born, *International Commercial Arbitration Volume I*, 2nd edn (The Netherlands, Wolters Kluwer 2014), § 4.04 [A][1][b][i]. Note that this does not change the fact that, in the US, its application is seen as a task for the courts. See also below (II B (i)).

New York Convention reduces complexity by trusting that the relevant actors in arbitration achieve fair results. As long as the parties arbitrate their actual dispute consensually, this trust is justified: the agreement to arbitrate indeed constitutes a self-validating contract.

But this trust may be misplaced in a given case, and even a self-critical commercial actor would acknowledge this possibility. The general presumption of validity of the arbitration agreement could therefore lead to wrong results in individual cases. Therefore, some fine-tuning is required, especially to ensure the protection of the weaker party. For example, English and German courts have held arbitration agreements invalid that would have foreclosed the application of EU rules protecting the commercial agent by choosing a different *lex causae*.[119]

Regarding the reach of arbitration agreements, the situation is slightly different. The NYC does not prescribe any rules of interpretation when it comes to assessing which disputes precisely the parties agreed to submit to arbitration.[120] This interpretative question has particular relevance for non-contractual claims: for example, does a valid arbitration clause in a contract referring to 'all claims arising under this contract' also cover claims in tort? It is less clear whether the pro-arbitration objective of the New York Convention also covers the interpretation of the exact reach of arbitration agreements. National courts have taken different approaches.[121]

In summary, ICA is based on general trust in the arbitration system, which leads to a pro-arbitration approach to an arbitration agreement. However, this stops short of leaving all questions regarding its validity or reach to arbitrators. In these cases, it is up to the courts whether the parties are sent to arbitration.

(iii) Enforcing the Agreement to Arbitrate in Investment Treaty Arbitration (ITA)

The intentions of the parties are also used as a starting point in ITA, but the framework is very different from ICA. First, there is no generally acknowledged

[119] *Accentuate Ltd v Asigra Inc*, 2009 EWHC 2655 (QB); Oberlandesgericht (OLG) München *Wertpapier-Mitteilungen Zeitschrift für Wirtschafts- und Bankrecht* (WM) 2006, 1556. These cases implement the CJEU's *Ingmar* decision, see below II B (ii).

[120] Born (n 118), § 9.02 [A]. Born goes on to argue in favour of an *international* pro-arbitration rule of construction as a matter of international law.

[121] *Fiona Trust v Privalov* [2007] 4 All ER 951 (HL) is the paradigmatic case for a pro-arbitration approach (rational businessmen would want *any* dispute regarding their relationship decided by one and the same tribunal). In the US, *Mitsubishi Motors Corp v Soler Chrysler-Plymouth*, 473 US 614, 624–628 (1985) used a pro-arbitration approach to include statutory (antitrust) claims, see below II. But contrast more restrictive US case law excluding tort claims from similarly worded clauses, *Cape Flattery Ltd v Titan Maritime LLC* 647 F 3d 914 (US Ct of Appeal, 9th Cir, 2011) 921–23. See also the more cautious approach by the Supreme Court under the specific factual circumstances of *Granite Rock Co v Int'l Brotherhood of Teamsters et al* 561 US 287 (2010). Other national courts have taken a less arbitration-friendly approach, most importantly in France, see Born, *International Commercial Arbitration* (n 118) § 9.02 [D][2].

doctrine of separability.[122] This is related to the second and more important point: in ITA, state and investor normally do not specifically agree to arbitrate future disputes.[123] Instead, the consent to arbitrate typically derives from an investment treaty, in which the home state of the investor and the host state – in the territory of which the investment is made – offer to subject themselves to arbitration. This can be initiated by investors with the respective other state's nationality. By starting the arbitration, an investor is typically said to accept that unilateral offer by the host state.[124] Doctrinally, it is just this offer that is open to construction. This means that the search for what the parties might have intended becomes an interpretation of the dispute settlement provisions of the investment treaty.

Which default rules should guide this interpretation of a state's offer to arbitrate? A purely commercial approach would still work with a default rule that is pro-arbitration, followed by presumptions that depend on the relevant national legal system. For example, the US Supreme Court extrapolated the US presumptions regarding ICA to the question of whether non-compliance with a procedural pre-condition – *in casu* the requirement to litigate for six months prior to arbitration – precluded the arbitrability of the dispute.[125] The majority of the Supreme Court concluded that it did not.[126] By contrast, a public international law approach would draw the line between *admissibility* and *jurisdiction*.[127]

[122] On the contrary, the tribunal in *SGS Société Générale de Surveillance SA v Republic of the Philippines*, ICSID Case No ARB/02/6, Decision on Jurisdiction (29 January 2004) at para 154 stressed that: '[t]he question is whether a party should be allowed to rely on a contract as the basis of its claim when the contract itself refers that claim exclusively to another forum. In the Tribunal's view the answer is that it should not be allowed to do so, unless there are good reasons …' This was based on the 'principle that a party to a contract cannot claim on that contract without itself complying with it …' This suggests a different approach in principle: he who claims on a contract has to stick with the judicial forum therein agreed. The tribunal in *SGS* backed this up by case law reference at paras 150–53, while acknowledging that this is not uncontroversial.

[123] The *SGS v Philippines* award (ibid) concerned contractual claims based on an umbrella clause in the treaty. The relevant contract contained an exclusive jurisdiction clause. But the reasoning would also work for an arbitration agreement in a contract between host state and investor.

[124] For a more detailed discussion see *K v Papp* (n 115).

[125] *BG Group v Republic of Argentina*, 572 US 25, 134 S Ct 1198 (2014).

[126] This was a highly controversial decision (with Chief Justice Roberts and Justice Kennedy dissenting), which turned on whether the six-month litigation requirement was a mere 'procedural pre-condition' or a substantive condition on consent to arbitrate. For critical commentaries from a public international perspective, see, eg, Anthea Roberts and Christina Trahanas, 'Judicial Review of Investment Treaty Awards: BG Group v Argentina' (2014) 108 *American Journal of International Law*. Available at: https://ssrn.com/abstract=2767889. Nicolas Klein, *Das Investitionsschutzrecht als völkerrechtliches Individualschutzrecht im Mehrebenensystem, Studies in International Investment Law* 27 (Baden-Baden, Nomos, 2018) 299–305; Jarod Wong, 'BG Group v Argentina: A Supreme Misunderstanding' (2016) 43 *Pepperdine Law Review* 541.

[127] Yuval Shany, 'Jurisdiction and Admissibility' in Cesare PR Romano, Karen J Alter and Yuval Shany (eds), *The Oxford Handbook of International Adjudication*, 781 (Oxford, Oxford University Press, 2014). See also Friedrich Rosenfeld, 'Arbitral Praeliminaria: Reflections on the Distinction between Admissibility and Jurisdiction after BG v Argentina' (2016) 29 *Leiden Journal of International Law* 137.

The purpose of this distinction is to avoid submitting a state to international adjudication too readily.[128] The default rule would not be party autonomy with a pro-arbitration mind-set, but state sovereignty with a prominent role for national courts.[129]

ITA concerns the resolution of international law disputes by *ad hoc* arbitration panels, modelled alongside those for commercial law disputes. This is why ITA is often considered as a hybrid, with the arbitral decisions to a varying degree depending on whether the tribunal was staffed with commercially minded arbitrators. It is hence unsurprising that investment tribunals have been drawing different conclusions on whether non-compliance with waiting periods – including domestic litigation requirements – prior to an investment arbitration affect their jurisdiction or are merely procedural in nature. In *SGS v Philippines*, which concerned an exclusive jurisdiction clause, the tribunal assumed the latter, because '… the principle that a party to a contract cannot claim on that contract without itself complying with it is more naturally considered as a matter of admissibility than jurisdiction'. This was quoted with approval for forum selection clauses more generally in a more recent award,[130] which drew an analogy with the exhaustion of local remedies rule.[131]

In practice, the effect of a merely procedural hurdle is often that the tribunal continues to decide the claim, since it would be inefficient and even futile to send the parties back to negotiation and/or domestic litigation.[132] By way of comparison, other tribunals have criticised exactly this, saying that there appears to be no consequence for the defaulting party if non-compliance with waiting periods is seen as an admissibility criterion only.[133] The distinction between admissibility and jurisdiction often clouds the underlying issue, which is what purpose is served by waiting periods or domestic litigation requirements. The idea that prior negotiations could avoid the arbitration or that domestic litigation could narrow down the dispute often appears unrealistic. Accordingly, it is more the practical usefulness of waiting periods rather than the concepts of admissibility and jurisdiction as such that are 'elusive'.[134]

[128] See the restrictive interpretation of the state's offer to arbitrate by the majority view of the International Court of Justice, *Georgia v Russian Federation*, Preliminary Objections, Judgment of 1 April 2011, ICJ Reports 2011, 70, 131 (with reference to the *Armed Activities* case).

[129] Leading to a restrictive reading of the requirements under which a state has consented to the jurisdiction of an international court or tribunal. The ICJ (ibid) phrases this as follows: 'any conditions to which such consent is subject must be regarded as constituting the limits thereon'.

[130] *Supervisión y Control, SA v Republic of Costa Rica*, ICSID Case No ARB/12/4, Award (18 January 2017) para 298.

[131] Ibid at para 299.

[132] See, eg, *Société Générale de Surveillance SA v Islamic Republic of* Pakistan, ICSID Case No ARB/01/13, Decision on Jurisdiction (6 August 2003) para 184.

[133] *Murphy Exploration and Production Company International v Republic of Ecuador*, ICSID Case No ARB/08/4, Award on Jurisdiction (15 December 2010) paras 147–48.

[134] Compare August Reinisch, 'Jurisdiction and Admissibility in International Investment Law' in Andrea Gattini, Attila Tanzi andd Filippo Fontanelli (eds) *General Principles of Law and International Investment Arbitration* (The Netherlands, Brill Nijhoff, 2018) 130, 150.

In short, ITA presents a picture that is different from ICA in that there is no general trust in the arbitration system or pro-arbitration approach. Careful line-drawing shows that the principle of state sovereignty is not easily abandoned.

For both ICA and ITA this means that arbitration agreements are only self-validating contracts as long as both parties remain in consensus. If one party refuses to arbitrate, this changes. The ideal of arbitration as a self-referential process without intervention by the courts must give way to some form of interaction between arbitration tribunals and courts. As far as commercial actors are concerned, the default rule to be maintained here must be party autonomy. If one of the parties is a state, especially in ITA, the default rule of state sovereignty must also be discussed. The private law approach and the public international law approach need to be reconciled with each other. This can only be done by using a transnational law approach, which will be addressed in Part II.

II. Arbitrability from a Transnational Law Perspective

The key characteristic of transnational law from a practical point of view is that it helps to solve factual scenarios with cross-border implications. In this sense, transnational law captures both state and private action and hence includes public and private international law.[135] Typically, any specialised regime of international law will fall under this definition (eg global environmental protection or international sports law).

Technically, transnational law refers to any legal regime that transcends the nation state. This can imply that the regime in question is mostly engaging non-state actors.[136] ICA is an example of this, at least as long as one excludes commercial arbitration against states. This could lead to a narrow definition: transnational law is distinct from classic international law in terms of its legal sources, which would include international usages or soft law. Examples are the UN recommendations relating to multinational enterprises, the *lex mercatoria* or the law of the internet.[137] Here, transnational law is furthest removed from any state as lawmaker.

In a broader sense, legal regime beyond the nation state simply means that the nation state is no longer the sole point of reference for law making. This would

[135] Carrie Menkel-Meadow, 'Why and How to Study "Transnational Law"' (2011) 1 *University of California (Irvine) Law Review* 97, 101. Electronic copy available at: http://ssrn.com/abstract=1851634. For detailed coverage of several subject matters as transnational law see Dalhuisen, *The Transnationalisation of Commercial and Financial Law, and of Commercial, Financial, and Investment Dispute Resolution* (n 103).

[136] Andreas Fischer-Lescano and Gunther Teubner, 'Regime Collisions: The Vain Search for Legal Unity in the Fragmentation of Global Law' (2004) 25 *Michigan Journal of International Law* 999, 1009–1012.

[137] Ibid at 1011 with further references. One can also include soft law created by the EU. See, from an English perspective, John Cartwright, 'Interpretation of English Law in Light of the Common Frame of Reference' in Henk J Snijders and Stefan Vogenauer (eds), *Content and Meaning of National Law in the Context of Transnational Law* (Munich, Sellier, 2009) 197.

move the focus from non-state law and also include, for example, the law of the EU as a supranational entity.

The concept of transnational law is further used more specifically for categorising hybrid areas of law, comprising private and public law elements.[138] In this sense, it is an apt categorisation of ITA, which is based on public international law treaties but adjudicated in individual cases following a commercial model (see chapter one).

By way of contrast, the transnational law approach here employed will be functional, following the theoretical framework on transnational legal ordering by Halliday and Shaffer.[139] 'Ordering' implies that one accepts a continuing role[140] for the (nation-)state, which ultimately enforces private contracts, arbitration agreements, and awards. 'Functional' means that transnational law is not understood as covering specific substantive fields of law or classifying them as public, private, hybrid,[141] or soft law. Rather, transnational law is seen as a process in which different perspectives (national/international or private/public) are tried to solve a legal problem that arises in a cross-border scenario.

The question of arbitrability, broadly understood, is such a problem: Within which limits can parties in cross-border scenarios agree to have their dispute removed from public courts? At the same time, arbitrability is here understood as more than a transnational concept. It is a concept that is common to international arbitration and national arbitration laws. It was seen above that the notion of arbitrability refers in particular to the jurisdictional question of whether an arbitration tribunal (or the national court) is competent to hear the case (see I D).[142] This means that arbitrability is structurally coupling arbitration as a contractual system[143] with the overall legal system. In *international* arbitration, it is also structurally coupling the international and the national legal systems. This raises the question within which limits parties in cross-border scenarios can agree to resolve their dispute without the involvement of national courts.

A. Contracting Out of the Law: Normative Considerations

So far, the question of arbitrability has been approached by determining whether the parties have actually agreed to arbitration. This was illustrated above by case

[138] Hans-Wolfgang Micklitz, 'Rethinking the Public/Private Divide' in Miguel Maduro, Kaarlo Tuori and Suvi Sankari (eds), *Transnational Law: Rethinking European Law and Legal Thinking* (Cambridge, Cambridge University Press, 2014) 271.

[139] Terence C Halliday and Gregory Shaffer, 'Transnational Legal Orders' in Terence C Halliday and Gregory Shaffer (eds), *Transnational Legal Orders* (Cambridge, Cambridge University Press, 2014).

[140] Albert, 'Governance and Democracy' (n 105) 295–96 refers to the 'staying power of the state', and correctly observes that governance studies have too quickly led away from the state as *the* democratically legitimised actor. See also ch 4.

[141] See the detailed categorisation by Hans-Wolfgang Micklitz, 'Rethinking the Public/Private Divide' (n 138) 279.

[142] See, in particular, n 116.

[143] See above text at nn 112–13.

law that scrutinised the consent to arbitrate, bearing in mind that Article II(3) of the New York Convention carves out arbitration agreements that are invalid, inoperative, or incapable of being performed (see I D). In this sense, arbitrability is a contractual issue: *have* the parties *agreed* to arbitrate.

We are now moving on to include a broader understanding of arbitrability: whether the parties *can* agree to arbitrate this case – assuming there is definitely an agreement to arbitrate, the question becomes whether we *allow* the issue to be resolved by arbitration. Framed this way, the issue becomes a regulatory one. It starts from the assumption that disputes linked to a particular state are normally solved by the courts of this state: international jurisdiction raises issues of sovereignty and international comity. Under many legal systems there is a right to be heard in court. Can parties contract out of this right?

The starting point of private law programming (above I B) is contractual freedom. This includes the ability to choose whether to enter into a contract in the first place, with whom to contract, and to freely negotiate the terms of the contract. This is based on the assumption that the contractual parties are on an equal footing. If this is not the case, contract law itself provides instruments that are designed to protect the structurally weaker party against the economic power of the stronger party (i). But the regulatory aspects of contract law[144] can also be approached from the outside, by protecting a specific public good (ii).[145]

(i) A Contractual Perspective: Protecting the Weaker Party through Non-Derogable Rules

Within the contractual system (see I D (i) above), one would start with party autonomy as the default rule, provided that the relevant law allows for its own setting aside. Contract law is typically based on the assumption that this is indeed the case; and it would specify which rules *cannot* be contracted out of. Underlying this framework is the presumption that private parties normally have equal bargaining power. Contractual agreements are, therefore, binding and enforceable *unless* this assumption is wrong. This is typically the case in circumstances where there is some form of subordination between the parties.

Accordingly, certain disputes or claims follow more rigid rules, with jurisdiction sometimes vested in special courts or tribunals (eg employment disputes

[144] For classification see, eg, Lourenco, 'Autopoietic Social Systems Theory' (n 112). Regarding the impact of EU law on private law relationships see Arthur S Hartkamp, *EU Law and National Private Law: Effect of EU Law and European Human Rights Law on Legal Relationships between Individuals*, 2nd edn (Cambridge, Intersentia, 2016) 167.

[145] From an EU law perspective, this category can also be referred to more broadly as contractual dealings that have repercussions for third parties or the general public in the EU, see Christiane Wendehorst, 'Internationales Privatrecht' in Katja Langenbucher (ed), *Europarechtliche Bezüge des Privatrechts*, 2nd edn (Baden-Baden, Nomos, 2008) 376, 408 (with EU insolvency laws as an example). For the distinction between unequal bargaining power and protection of public goods see also Jürgen Basedow, *The Law of Open Societies: Private Ordering and Public Regulation in the Conflict of Laws*, Hague Academy of International Law Monographs, 9 (The Netherlands, Brill Nijhoff, 2015).

since employer and employee are usually in a relationship of subordination). The same accounts, in principle, for franchise (franchisor and franchisee), consumer (business and individual consumer), or rental disputes (landlord and tenant). Behind this categorisation lies a generalised finding of unequal bargaining power between the parties. There is no need to show one party's relative weakness or commercial inexperience in a specific case. Instead, it is assumed as structurally inherent in certain relationships. Regarding consumer cases, the Court of Justice of the European Union has succinctly expressed this as follows:

> '[t]he consumer is in a weak position vis-à-vis the seller or supplier, as regards both his bargaining power and his level of knowledge. This leads to the consumer agreeing to terms drawn up in advance by the seller or supplier without being able to influence the content of those terms … Such an imbalance between the consumer and the seller or supplier may only be corrected by positive action unconnected with the actual parties to the contract.[146]

The same idea is underlying the proposed Fairness in Arbitration Act in the US (see chapter one, IV C). This contractual perspective means staying, in principle, within the national legal system chosen as applicable by the parties. The non-derogable rules provided by the domestic law (*lex causae*) that the parties meant to apply to their dealings constitutes mandatory law. They are sometimes referred to as *internal* or *domestic* mandatory rules.[147] The EU, as a sub-system of the international legal system, has such 'internal' mandatory rules, as the example of EU consumer law shows.

The above focused on the question of *who* the parties are. The situation in which certain rules protecting the weaker party must remain in place should be distinguished from one in which certain public goods are at stake:[148] this is a perspective that is external to the contract, since it works independently, focusing on the subject matter: *what* is it that the parties want to agree upon? It is the typical perspective of a regulator and will be addressed below as a public interest perspective.

(ii) A Public Interest Perspective: Protecting a Specific Public Good

One good example of a specific public good that parties need to respect in their dealings is undistorted competition. At least with regard to business-to-business

[146] Case C-168/05 *Mostaza Claro v Centro Móbil Milenium SL* ECLI:EU:C:2006:675 paras 25–26 with further references.

[147] See Adeline Chong, 'The Public Policy and Mandatory Rules of Third Countries in International Contracts' (2006) 2 *Journal of Private International Law* 27 with further references.

[148] But see Laura Maria van Bochove, 'Overriding Mandatory Rules as a Vehicle for Weaker Party Protection in European Private International Law' (2014) 3 *Erasmus Law Review* 147 (available at: https://ssrn.com/abstract=2536316), arguing that there is also a public interest in protecting the weaker party. This is true; the clear separation here is meant to illustrate the difference in perspective rather than indicate a difference in substance. See also below n 188.

claims, and especially for horizontal agreements, there is not necessarily a relationship of subordination. Accordingly, we are less concerned about unequal bargaining power. Rather, it is the subject matter as such that requires some form of elevation above the contractual system: parties are free to contract, but they cannot use this freedom with the object or effect of restricting competition.

It is the public interest in undistorted competition that serves as the benchmark for limits to private contracting. In systems theoretical terms, the market – understood as properly functioning based on undistorted competition – becomes the concept that is structurally coupling the economic and the legal system.[149]

This can be illustrated by the *Eco Swiss* case.[150] Eco Swiss had obtained a damages award against Benetton in the Dutch courts. Benetton tried to annul and stay the enforcement of this award, arguing that it was based on a contractual agreement that breached the Treaty's competition rules. More precisely, the contract was said to be a market-sharing agreement and hence void under what is now Article 101 TFEU. The CJEU held that (now-)Article 101 TFEU constituted a 'fundamental provision' of the Treaty. This meant that where an application for annulment of an award must be granted on grounds of public policy under Member State law, the same was true for failure to comply with (now-)Article 101 TFEU.[151] The Court here relied on the principle of equivalence, which – in the absence of harmonisation – allows the EU Member State courts to enforce EU rights on the basis of national rules, provided that these are no 'less favourable than those governing the same right of action on an internal matter'.[152] Subsequent case law has extended this reasoning to the EU prohibition on abuse of a dominant position (now Article 102 TFEU)[153] and the same is arguably true for EU state aid law.[154] In practice, this means that arbitration

[149] For the principle of free competition as structurally coupling the legal and the economic system see Luhmann, *Recht der Gesellschaft* (n 23) 464–65.

[150] Case C-126/97 *Eco Swiss China Time Ltd v Benetton International NV* ECLI:EU:C:1999:269.

[151] Ibid at para 37.

[152] Case C-45/76 *Comet BV v Produktschap voor Siergewassen* ECLI:EU:C:1976:191 para 13. By contrast, the principle of effectiveness adds a further layer, requiring Member State courts not to make it impossible in practice to exercise the relevant EU right, ibid at para 16. The Court formally only relies on the argument that a Member State needs to read national public policy as including EU public policy (and hence EU competition law). This and the cases below are hence illustrations that the Court is reluctant to openly refer to the principle of effectiveness in relation to ICA.

[153] Joined Cases C-295 to 98/04 *Manfredi v Lloyd Adriatico Assicurazioni SpA* ECLI:EU:C:2006:461 para 31 (without giving specific reasons).

[154] In the *Micula* case, the EU Commission's view was that an arbitration award that orders compensation for withdrawal of tax incentives in breach of EU state aid law itself constitutes (new) state aid, see Commission Decision (EU) 2015/1470 of 30 March 2015 on State aid SA.38517 (2014/C) (ex 2014/NN) implemented by Romania – Arbitral award *Micula v Romania* of 11 December 2013 (notified under document C(2015) 2112) [2015] OJ L232/43. The General Court left this question open for the time following Romania's accession to the EU, but the Commission had, in any event, overstepped its competencies by retroactively applying EU state aid rules, Cases T-624/15, T-694/15 and T-704/15 *European Food SA et al v European Commission* ECLI:EU:T:2019:423 para 91.

tribunals who want to ensure the enforceability of their award within the EU have to make the factual findings regarding potential breaches of EU competition law.[155] It should be added that, in any event, there is still the possibility of enforcement of international arbitration awards *outside* the EU.[156] The public interest in ensuring undistorted competition is similarly acknowledged in other countries. In particular, the US Supreme Court has constantly been proceeding on the basis that there is a legitimate public interest in the enforcement of US antitrust laws. This remains true in principle, despite some profound shifts in the case law (see B (i) below).

To summarise, arbitrability as a gateway into arbitration is a concept that is shared by private law (Can we construe an agreement to arbitrate or not?) and public law (Do we enforce this agreement?). In practice, the contractual approach is playing the dominant role (see B (i)), but with a similar effect to the public interest approach. The latter is then taken up under the heading of public policy at the end of an arbitration, when it comes to the enforcement of an arbitral award (see B (ii)).

B. Limits to Arbitrability: Contracting Out of a Legal Regime?

The example of competition law provides a context in which the parties do not just place their dealings within certain rules by contracting out of those they deem unfit. Rather, by choosing a seat for their arbitration and the law applicable to their dealings, the parties try to contract out of national legal systems as such, including their antitrust laws.[157] This was the situation in *Mitsubishi Motors*, where a contract for distribution and sales of Mitsubishi automobiles through Chrysler dealers outside the continental United States provided for arbitration by the Japan Commercial Arbitration Association.[158] Here the question of whether the parties have successfully contracted out becomes a gateway issue: gateway into arbitration here stands for the exit from an otherwise competent legal regime.

[155] So, the EU Commission in an opinion provided in the ICC case of *Neckarpri GMBH v EDF International SAS (v Baden-Württemberg as Additional Party)*, see Opinion of 19 September 2014 (available at: https://ec.europa.eu/competition/court/neckarpri_en.pdf) para 33. See also ch 4 below.

[156] Using the *Micula* case (n 154) as an example again, the controversies over the award were followed by successful enforcement proceedings in the US (*Ioan Micula et al v Government of Romania* US Court of Appeals for the District of Columbia No 19-7127). Enforcement proceedings were even successful in the UK during the Brexit transition period, which signals that the UK is likely to become an enforcement jurisdiction for *intra*-EU awards that may face enforcement problems under EU law (*Micula and others v Romania* [2020] UKSC 5).

[157] For the importance of the choice of the legal seat of an arbitration, which includes the arbitration laws of the country so chosen, see, e.g., the English Commercial Court in *Union of India v McDonnell Douglas Corporation*, 2 Lloyd's Rep 48 (Queen's Bench Div, Comm Ct (1992)). See also ch 3.

[158] *Mitsubishi Motors Corp v Soler Chrysler-Plymouth*, 473 US 614 (1985).

(i) The Doctrine of Non-Arbitrability and its Decline: Mitsubishi Motors *and* CDC Hydrogen Peroxide

The notion of arbitrability as a gateway into arbitration derives from Article II NYC. As mentioned above (see I D), this Article binds signatory states to recognise valid arbitration agreements. However, this obligation arises only if the dispute ('difference') between the parties concerns a 'subject matter capable of settlement by arbitration' (Article II(1) NYC). This is commonly referred to as the *doctrine of non-arbitrability*: despite an otherwise valid arbitration clause which, on its face, covers the relevant dispute; this dispute falls into a category that cannot be decided by arbitrators. This is not about interpreting an arbitration clause and hence the agreement between the parties, it is about inherently public interests (eg protecting undistorted competition – see II A (ii) above).

In theory, then, the doctrine of non-arbitrability formally carves out non-arbitrable subject matters from the duty of a state which is party to the New York Convention to refer disputes to arbitration. This can enhance the legitimacy of an arbitration at different stages (see below chapter 4). First, it allows a court that is seised during the preliminary stages of an arbitration to consider whether the dispute concerns a subject matter that is not arbitrable and should hence not be decided by the arbitrators. This can be any court with international jurisdiction, but there is a good argument for a particularly strong role for the court at the seat of the arbitration (see chapter 3). Article II(1) NYC would then, generally speaking, dispense this court from the duty to refer the dispute to arbitration.

Second, the doctrine of non-arbitrability again becomes relevant at the final stage of an arbitration, concerning the question of enforceability of an international arbitral award by the competent national authorities (ie the courts). Article V(2)(a) NYC provides that these can refuse recognition and enforcement of an award if the subject matter is not 'capable of settlement by arbitration' (ie not arbitrable) under the laws of the relevant state. Article V(2)(a) is the mirror image of Article II(1) for a later point in time. One important difference to Article II(1) exists in terms of actors: intervention is now open to any court with international jurisdiction concerning the enforcement of the award (enforcement court), which depends upon the location of the losing party's assets. Consequently, Article V(2)(a) specifies that the issue is whether the subject matter is arbitrable according to the laws of *that* country.[159]

[159] This raises the question of whether non-arbitrability can here be understood as a local standard. In practice, more relevant is the related question of whether the enforcement court could apply any limits to arbitrability imposed by another legal system, in particular the law of the seat of the arbitration. The better view is to read Article V(2)(a) literally (making room just for the law of the enforcement court) and to generally acknowledge that there are always international law limits to domestic standards. See Born, *International Commercial Arbitration* (n 118), §4.05 [A]–[C].

In practice, the legitimising role for national courts based on the non-arbitrability doctrine has been low. Starting in the 1970s, the NYC's pro-arbitration objective (see I D (ii)) has increasingly served as an argument that the formal carve-out of disputes not capable of settlement by arbitration must be construed narrowly.[160] This can be illustrated by the development of US case law on the arbitrability of antitrust claims. In the landmark case of *Mitsubishi Motors*,[161] the US Supreme Court had to decide whether a US and a Japanese party were allowed to contract out of US law – including antitrust law – and hence arbitrate their dispute. Under the prevailing case law at the time (the *American Safety*-doctrine), which had been developed for the domestic context, antitrust claims were non-arbitrable for various reasons.

Two of them are of particular interest here, since they illuminate the public interest in antitrust enforcement: first, the 'pivotal role' of private parties in aiding governmental enforcement of antitrust laws, which can be seen from the availability of treble damages in litigation. I will refer to this as the private enforcement angle. Second, a distrust in arbitrators from the business community to appreciate the importance of antitrust regulation. For the US Court of Appeals, this was particularly true in an international context, where arbitrators may be chosen from a foreign community with no experience or exposure to US law or values. This second argument thus includes a twofold assumption: *business* cannot be trusted to uphold the public interest underlying the Sherman Act, and *foreign* business even less.

The Supreme Court had little trouble in disposing of the second argument. Basically, it switched distrust with trust in arbitrators by arguing that the business community could be relied on to consider public interests. It took more effort to establish counter arguments to the private enforcement angle: 'We are left then with the core of the American Safety doctrine – the fundamental importance to American democratic capitalism of the regime of the antitrust laws.'[162] In this respect, the Court first stressed the *remedial* function of private antitrust claims over their deterrent function.[163] It then argued that, even acknowledging the deterrent function of treble damages, this could as well be served by an arbitration tribunal.[164] It went on to state the now famous 'second look' doctrine, saying that national (US) courts would, in any event, have an opportunity at the enforcement stage to ensure that the 'legitimate interest in the enforcement of antitrust laws has been addressed' by the tribunal.[165] The Court finally held that in line with

[160] Looking ahead, this is seen favourably by Born ibid at § 6.06. Critically at the time, William W Park, 'Private Adjudicators and the Public Interest: The Expanding Scope of International Arbitration' (1986) 12 *Brooklyn Journal of International Law* 629.

[161] *Mitsubishi Motors Corp v Soler Chrysler-Plymouth* 473 US 614 (1985).

[162] Ibid at 634.

[163] Ibid at 635–36.

[164] Ibid at 637.

[165] Ibid at 638.

international comity, the importance of international trade warranted a different solution for the international than for the domestic arbitration context.

Mitsubishi Motors is representative of a broader international trend to interpret the NYC as arbitration friendly. This makes sense from a commercial point of view as it reinforces the operation closure of the arbitration system (see I D). But it leads to an international law obligation of the NYC's signatory states to make an effort to support international commerce by enabling private dispute resolution. From the wider perspective of general international law, this is problematic since it puts ICA on a collision course with specialised regimes protecting public goods (eg international environmental law).

In any event, the practical impact of the non-arbitrability doctrine has declined due to this pro-arbitration approach. Competition law claims, to return to the above example, are internationally seen as arbitrable.

In the EU, this is said to follow from the CJEU's decision in *Eco Swiss.*[166] Nevertheless, it should be noted that the situation is different from the US in that arbitration is explicitly carved out from the EU's competences in regulating disputes in civil and commercial matters (see chapter 3). It is not up to the CJEU to opine on the arbitrability of private law claims. This remains for the Member States to decide – within their international law obligations.

An example of this division of power between the EU and its Member States can be seen in the *CDC Hydrogen Peroxide* case.[167] The issue here was whether jurisdiction and/or arbitration clauses in supply contracts could be interpreted as covering cartel damages claims. While the Advocate General dealt – in the same way – with both jurisdiction and arbitration clauses, the Court of Justice restricted its ruling to jurisdiction clauses.[168] The lack of EU competence regarding commercial arbitration means that national courts are free, in principle, to deal with arbitration agreements. Member State courts have reacted differently to *CDC Hydrogen Peroxide*, with Dutch courts extrapolating the CJEU's reasoning to arbitration clauses and English courts drawing the line precisely between jurisdiction and arbitration clauses.[169] Under EU law, both are possible;[170] this is simply the consequence of the remaining powers of the Member States in this area.

[166] Case C-126/97 above (n 150). See Assimakis P Komninos, 'Arbitration and EU Competition Law' (19 April 2009), at note 32 with further references. Available at: http://ssrn.com/abstract=1520105.

[167] Case C-352/13 *Cartel Damage Claims (CDC) Hydrogen Peroxide SA v Akzo Nobel NV* ECLI: EU:C:2015:335.

[168] The Court explained this, however, not with lack of competence, but with incomplete information available, ibid at para 58.

[169] Contrast *Kemira Chemicals Oy v CDC Project 13 SA* ECLI: NL:GHAMS:2015:3006 (21 July 2015, Gerechtshof Amsterdam) with *Microsoft Mobile Oy (Ltd) v Sony Europe Ltd* [2017] EWHC 374 (Ch).

[170] For a different view see Renato Nazzini, 'Global Solution Arbitrability of Cartel Damages Claims in the European Union: CDC, KEMIRA, and Microsoft Mobile' *King's College London Dickson Poon School of Law Legal Studies Research Paper Series* Paper No 2019-12. Available at: https://ssrn.com/abstract=3249051.

The *CDC Hydrogen Peroxide* case is also noteworthy for another reason. It illustrates that the doctrine of non-arbitrability is similar, in effect, to construing the reach of an arbitration agreement. The Advocate General distinguished between general arguments speaking against the inclusion of competition law claims based on the principle of effectiveness of EU (competition) law; and the possibility of a narrow construction of such clauses in the individual case.[171] The Court of Justice relied solely on the latter, holding that unless provided for by the relevant clause,[172] competition damages claims would not fall under a standard jurisdiction agreement.[173]

This has been understood as being driven mostly by 'practical' considerations in the AG's Opinion.[174] Nevertheless, it is more than this. It is squaring a purely commercial approach, which in the name of party autonomy would have called for a broad reading of jurisdiction clauses, with a public interest approach, which may have suggested the exclusion of antitrust claims. In any event, the Court chose *not* to rely on the principle of effectiveness of EU law.[175] Instead, it set out a narrow default rule of construction for jurisdiction agreements. In other words, it chose a contractual over a public interest approach. The effect of this rule of construction in the *CDC Hydrogen Peroxide* case was to restrict the forum choice by the parties. In theory, the same rationale would arguably have applied if the Court had dealt with arbitration as opposed to jurisdiction clauses. Then we would have the exact result that the doctrine of non-arbitrability achieves: the gateway into arbitration would have been closed.

This is not overlooking the fact that in the actual case, the CJEU did not opine on arbitration clauses. Nor is it intended to suggest that jurisdiction and arbitration agreements under *CDC Hydrogen Peroxide* should, or should not, be treated the same. The point is simply that non-arbitrability has the same effect as a narrow construction of an arbitration clause: it forecloses the gateway into arbitration.

In any event, construing the reach of an arbitration agreement narrowly still assumes that the dispute could well be arbitrable, but the parties have simply not agreed to this. The construction of an arbitration agreement is different from the

[171] Opinion of Advocate General Jääskinen in Case C-352/13 *CDC Hydrogen Peroxide* ECLI: EU:C:2014:2443 para 124 (principle of effectiveness regarding arbitration clauses and jurisdiction agreements conferring jurisdiction on a non-EU court), and paras 129–30 (narrow construction needed also for jurisdiction agreements within the EU).

[172] It is open to discussion whether an explicit reference to potential infringements of competition law is needed (this view was taken by the Advocate General at para 126 of his Opinion), or whether an implicit suggestion that the parties were aware of this possibility would suffice. Arguing for the latter, with explicit reference to commercial logic, Wolfgang Wurmnest, 'International Jurisdiction in Competition Damages Cases under the Brussels I Regulation: CDC Hydrogen Peroxide' (2016) 53 *Common Market Law Review* 225, 246.

[173] Case C-352/13 *CDC Hydrogen Peroxide* (n 167) paras 68–70.

[174] Damien Geradin and Emilio Villano, 'Arbitrability of EU Competition Law-Based Claims: Where Do We Stand after the CDC Hydrogen Peroxide Case?' *TILEC Discussion Paper* 2016 22. Available at: ssrn.com/abstract=2851112.

[175] See above n 152 and the accompanying text.

non-arbitrability doctrine, which categorically excludes certain types of disputes from being arbitrated. This can be illustrated by the *Mitsubishi* case above, where the US Supreme Court assessed the reach of the arbitration agreement separately from the doctrine of non-arbitrability. By contrast, the Court of Justice in *CDC Hydrogen Peroxide* refrained from any suggestion that the principle of effectiveness of EU law might require the non-arbitrability of EU competition law claims. This caution squares with the lack of EU competence in this respect.[176] Effectively, this remains a contractual approach, leaving the litigation of antitrust claims to (explicit) agreement by the parties.[177]

Overall, the doctrine of non-arbitrability has not had much practical effect. In the EU, the focus might be shifting towards a narrow construction of arbitration agreements, if – as has been the case in the Dutch *Kemira* case[178] – the Court of Justice's restrictive approach regarding jurisdiction agreements is extrapolated to arbitration clauses. Globally, it has to date been the NYC's public policy exception that has served as a tool for national courts to legitimise arbitration.

(ii) Protecting the Public Policy of the Forum

Article V(2)(b) NYC provides that the court can also refuse recognition and enforcement of an award if this would be 'contrary to the public policy of … [the relevant] country'. In light of the NYC's pro-arbitration objective (see I D (ii) above), the public policy exception is usually understood in a narrow sense. This is also corroborated by the drafting history.[179] And the promise of finality of international arbitration[180] can hold only if national courts refrain from reviewing the substance of an award in an appeal-style manner.[181] In principle, this is accepted by national legal systems as well as by EU law.

Nevertheless, there are considerable discrepancies between domestic laws regarding what constitutes public policy. One reason for this is that Article V(2)(b) explicitly refers to the public policy of the country in which enforcement is being

[176] Above text at nn 166–70. See also Geradin and Villano, 'Arbitrability of EU Competition Law-Based Claims' (n 174) 24 (stressing that the Court did not opine on the principle of effectiveness).

[177] See also ch 4 for the suggestion to be more explicit about EU law being in favour of party autonomy in principle, while clarifying limits of arbitration in the EU public interest.

[178] *Kemira Chemicals Oy v CDC Project 13 SA* (n 169).

[179] Gary B Born, *International Commercial Arbitration*, Volume III, 2nd edn (The Netherlands, Kluwer 2014), § 26.05 [C] [9].

[180] This is traditionally one of arbitration's main selling points. See Nigel Blackaby and Constantine Partasides, *Redfern and Hunter on International Arbitration*, 6th edn (Oxford, Oxford University Press, 2015), 1.101.

[181] The external view on international arbitration is quite different. There have been increasing voices in favour of the possibility of appeal in arbitration, see, eg, Noam Zamir and Peretz Segal, 'Appeal in International Arbitration: An Efficient and Affordable Arbitral Appeal Mechanism' (2019) 35 *Arbitration International* 79. In ITA, the lack of an appellate mechanism has long been at the forefront of the legitimacy debate (ch 4). These suggestions have been picked by the EU regarding investment arbitration under its new investment agreements with third countries, see chs 3 and 4.

sought. This is a local standard to begin with, which is then put into an international context (international public policy, see below). Doctrinally, one can distinguish procedural from substantive grounds of public policy. The former includes, in particular, fair trial principles. Examples of the latter are awards that would foster any serious illegality, including breach of trade sanctions or export controls.[182]

In contrast to internal or domestic mandatory rules that the parties cannot derogate from within the *lex causae* chosen as the applicable law (see A (i) above), public policy takes the perspective of the enforcement court: which rules of the *lex fori* are so fundamental that they warrant an exception from the obligation to recognise and enforce an international award? These are sometimes referred to as *external* or *international* mandatory rules.[183] They are correctly understood as overlapping with the internal or domestic mandatory rules, constituting a narrower sub-set of these.[184]

At the same time, however, the role of international mandatory rules is different in that they take a public interest perspective. Generally speaking, the CJEU has defined them as 'national provisions compliance with which has been deemed to be so crucial for the protection of the political, social or economic order in the Member State concerned as to require compliance therewith by all persons present on the national territory of that Member State and all legal relationships within that State.'[185]

There are also EU mandatory rules, which can be understood as being (EU) internal or international mandatory rules or both. An example is the Court's interpretation of the Commercial Agents Directive.[186]

In *Ingmar*, the Court held that the provision for payment of compensation upon termination of an agency contract was part of the Directive's mandatory regime in that it protected the EU-based commercial agent.[187] The parties could not, therefore, contract out of this special protection. Consequently, the UK court seised with the dispute had to apply the relevant provisions of the Commercial Agents Directive as implemented by the UK. This was true, although the *lex causae* chosen by the parties was the law of California, where the principal was based. Put differently, the protection of the weaker (EU) party was, as a matter of EU public interest, paramount to party autonomy.[188]

[182] Further examples by Born (n 179), § 26.05 [C] [9] [h]–[i].

[183] Chong, 'The Public Policy and Mandatory Rules of Third Countries in International Contracts' (n 147) with further references.

[184] Ibid.

[185] Case C-369/96 *Arblade* ECLI:EU:C:1999:575. This case concerns EU fundamental freedoms law. Its definition of so-called *lois de police* is now underlying Art 9(1) of the Regulation (EC) No 593/2008 of the European Parliament and of the Council of 17 June on the law applicable to contractual obligations (Rome I) OJ 2008 L177/6 (only slightly reworded).

[186] Council Directive of 86/653/EEC 18 December 1986 on the coordination of the laws of the Member States relating to self-employed commercial agents [1986] OJ L382/17.

[187] Case C-381/98 *Ingmar GB Ltd v Eaton Leonard Technologies Inc* ECLI:EU:C:2000:605 paras 21–22.

[188] Critically, in this respect, Wulf-Henning Roth, *Case C-381/98, Ingmar GB Ltd v Eaton Leonard Technologies Inc.* (2002) 39 *Common Market Law Review* 369, 377–81 (note). Advocate General Léger put significant emphasis on the purpose of the directive, which was to harmonise the

The exact classification of the *Ingmar* decision at the time proved difficult since the Rome Convention – now the Rome I Regulation (Rome I)[189] – was not applicable *ratione temporis*. Article 3(4) Rome I would now settle the issue by providing for non-derogable EU law provisions in case a non-Member State law is chosen. However, this Article applies only to cases where all relevant factual elements are located in one or more Member States (*intra*-EU cases). The broader proposal by the Commission did not find its way into Article 3(4), so one could conclude that *Ingmar* is implicitly overruled.[190]

Nevertheless, case law continues to build on *Ingmar*.[191] The Court suggested that *Ingmar* must be understood as relying on the 'overriding mandatory provisions' of what is now Article 9(1) and (2) Rome I.[192] Overriding mandatory provisions must be distinguished from non-derogable rules of the chosen law in that they effectively constitute a break for the regular conflicts-of-law rules: although the parties have chosen law A, overriding mandatory rules of law B – or, respectively, the EU – must be enforced. They originate in either the law of the *forum* or the law of the country in which the contract is being performed, and they supersede the applicable law.[193] At the other end, they must also be distinguished from international mandatory rules (public policy) of the *forum* (Article 21 of the Rome I Regulation) in that they serve a different function. Still, they often amount to the same fundamental provisions.[194]

The same is true for the relationship between non-arbitrable subject matters and public policy restraints in Article V(2)(a) and (b) of the NYC: a systematic reading of Article V(2) suggests a doctrinal difference between non-arbitrable subject matters (a) and limits imposed by public policy (b), but in practice they can hardly be separated.[195] Nevertheless, a line can be drawn according to their

conditions of competition between economic operators (ie the parties to a commercial agents contract). See Opinion of the Advocate General in Case C-381/98 *Ingmar* ECLI:EU:C:2000:230 para 33. This comes close to relying on the extraterritorial application of EU competition law, see also Horatia Muir Watt, 'Integration and Diversity: The Conflict of Laws as a Regulatory Tool' in Fabrizio Cafaggi (ed), *The Institutional Framework of European Private Law* (Oxford, Oxford University Press, 2006), 107, 143 (contrasting this with the Court's focus on protecting social standards in harmonised EU law). Here one can see the link between a contractual and a regulatory perspective, see above n 148.

189 Case C-369/96 *Arblade* (n 185).

190 See the references by van Bochove, 'Overriding Mandatory Rules as a Vehicle for Weaker Party Protection in European Private International Law' (n 148) 154.

191 See also Xandra E Kramer, 'The Interaction between Rome I and Mandatory EU Private Rules – EPIL and EPL: Communicating Vessels?' in Peter Stone and Youseph Farah (eds), *Research Handbook on EU Private International Law* (Cheltenham, Edward Elgar, 2015) 248.

192 Case C-184/12 *United Antwerp Maritime Agencies (Unamar) NV v Navigation Maritime Bulgare* ECLI:EU:C:2013:663 paras 40–48.

193 See Xandra E Kramer, 'EU Overriding Mandatory Law and the Applicable Law on the Substance in International Commercial Arbitration' in Franco Ferrari (ed), *The Impact of EU Law on International Commercial Arbitration* (New York, Juris, 2017) 285, who further distinguishes between overriding mandatory rules and internal market law as *sui generis* break to conflicts-of-law rules.

194 Ibid at 300.

195 Critically, in this respect, Stavros Brekoulakis, 'On Arbitrability: Persisting Misconceptions and New Areas of Concern' *Queen Mary University of London School of Law Legal Studies Research Paper* No. 20/2009. Available at: https://ssrn.com/abstract=1410285.

respective functions: non-arbitrability concerns the application of fundamental legal provisions to the arbitration agreement (of any national law with a sufficient connection to the contract, or of the *lex fori*). This may impact the enforceability of the arbitration agreement, or of the award. Public policy serves as a last resort, concerning fundamental legal provisions of the *forum* only, and only regarding the enforcement of an award.

Traditionally, public policy has been the main trigger for consideration of the public interest in ICA. For the EU, this remains true, since the principle of conferral restricts the CJEU's competence to opine on arbitrability.[196] The example of competition law has shown that the CJEU has instead addressed fundamental EU law under the heading of public policy (see A (ii) above). As seen, this translates into a strong role for the *lex fori*. The enforcement court does not necessarily have any substantive ties with the dispute at hand. It does not have to be identical with the court at the chosen seat of the arbitration; it has nothing to do with the law chosen by the parties. The *lex fori* may, accordingly, be difficult to anticipate, and it can still put limits on party choice in the same way as mandatory rules of the chosen law.[197]

The *Genentech* case illustrates how a contractual paradigm can still survive.[198] The Court took a more cautious approach than in *Eco Swiss* by avoiding finding a breach of Article 101 TFEU. *In casu*, the competition law issue was whether a licence agreement under which Genentech was using a patented DNA enhancer in manufacturing a drug (Rituxan) placed Genentech under a competitive disadvantage in relation to its competitors who were using the enhancer for free. During the ongoing ICC arbitration, the US Court of Appeals for the Federal Circuit had held that the US patents in question did not, in fact, cover the use of the enhancer by Genentech. The CJEU found no breach of EU competition law since Genentech could simply terminate the licence agreement.

Put differently, it was in the licensee's own hands to end any competitive disadvantage.[199] The CJEU drew a parallel with case law where it had held that there may still be commercial value in a licence agreement upon expiry of the underlying patent. This must apply *a fortiori* in a case where the licensed (US) patent continued to exist, and just did not cover the use by Genentech. On this basis, the CJEU did not see any restriction on the freedom of the licensee, nor any foreclosure effects. Hence, it did not have to deal with the second question, which concerned the consequence of a breach of Article 101 TFEU for an arbitration award based on the tainted agreement.

[196] Above I B (i). But see the case law by Member State courts referred to above (see I D (ii)), implementing overriding EU mandatory rules (n 119).

[197] Regarding the latter see Chong, 'The Public Policy and Mandatory Rules of Third Countries in International Contracts' (n 147) at n 26 with further references.

[198] Case C-567/14 *Genentech Inc v Hoechst GmbH and Sanofi-Aventis Deutschland GmbH* ECLI:EU:C:2016:526.

[199] Ibid at paras 39–42.

By contrast, Advocate General Wathelet's Opinion covered this second question. The Advocate General concluded from the 'fundamental importance' of Article 101 'to the EU legal order' that Member State courts must exercise a full review of the award on this basis.[200] Under this proposal, the review by the French court would not be constrained by the limitation of flagrant or obvious breaches of public policy under domestic law. It would also be independent from the question of whether the parties had raised the competition law issue in the arbitration. In order to reach this result, the Advocate General relied heavily on the principle of effectiveness of EU (competition) law.

This may be well arguable. Nevertheless, it would go beyond the formal reasoning in *Eco Swiss*, where the Court only referred to the principle of equivalence.[201] The Court did not follow the AG's Opinion in this respect. Instead, it remained silent on the question of how far the principle of effectiveness reaches when it comes to competition law review of an international arbitration award.

We are, therefore, left with *Eco Swiss* and its progeny (EU competition law as EU public policy), as well as *CDC Hydrogen Peroxide* (narrow construction of the arbitration agreement as basis for EU constraints on arbitrability). This leaves some room for commercial parties to contract out of EU law, which ties in with the EU's limited competences in private law as will be explained in the next chapter.

[200] Opinion of the Advocate General in Case 567/14 *Genentech* ECLI:EU:C:2016:177 paras 70–71.
[201] See above n 152.

3

Contracting Out of the EU's Legal Regime

This chapter will take an EU law perspective on limits to international arbitration, understood as contracting out of a legal system. It was seen above (see chapter two, II B) that in theory, there are two such limits under the New York Convention (NYC): the doctrine of non-arbitrability and public policy. These apply to international commercial arbitration (ICA) and investment treaty arbitration (ITA) that is *not* conducted under the auspices of the International Convention on the Settlement of Investment Disputes (ICSID). In the NYC, the doctrine of non-arbitrability is linked both to the beginning (enforcement of the arbitration agreement), and the end of an arbitration (enforcement of the award); public policy only to the latter. It has already been indicated that this is the main limit in practice. This will now be examined for limits to ICA under EU law. In a second step, the analysis will turn to EU law challenges for ITA, distinguishing between ICSID and non-ICSID arbitration.

I. EU Law and International Commercial Arbitration

The EU's involvement in commercial law as part of private law has traditionally been limited. As an organisation built upon the principle of conferral (ie enumerated powers – see Article 5(2) of the Treaty on the European Union (TEU)), the EU cannot set competencies for itself beyond those established by the founding treaties (lack of 'competence–competence'). One core competency is market integration, which has been the focus of the EU and EU law since its creation.[1] Accordingly, the EU can adopt private law measures in situations with cross-border implications, the regulation of which is necessary for the proper functioning of the internal market (Article 81 of the Treaty on the Functioning of the European Union (TFEU)). This is why a substantial part of EU private law such as the Commercial Agents Directive (86/653/EEC) mentioned in chapter two is based upon the harmonisation competences of (now) Articles 114 and 115 TFEU. Although the EU's competences regarding private law have evolved considerably

[1] See ch 1 II A and ch 2, I C.

over the last decades,[2] the principle of conferred powers remains its backbone. This must be contrasted with sovereign nation states – such as the EU Member States – who are fully competent to enact legislation regarding the private dealings between its citizens, and the limits thereof. In systems theoretical terms, the (EU) market is not only structurally coupling the economic and the (EU) legal system (see chapter two II A (ii)), but also the EU and its Member States' legal systems.

In practical terms, the EU as an international actor is not only limited by subject matter, but also by the lack of general law enforcement bodies.[3] In particular, it does not have centralised lower EU courts – comparable to US federal courts – that would deal with private law claims between citizens situated in different states. This has important implications for the way in which EU law safeguards and enforces private rights: to the extent EU law creates rights, these fall under the EU guarantee of access to justice,[4] following from the EU's foundational values such as democracy and the rule of law (Article 2 TEU). Nevertheless, the EU relies heavily on Member State authorities, in particular courts, when it comes to the actual enforcement of EU rights. In procedural terms, EU case law requires that private rights deriving from EU law be treated no less favourably than the corresponding rights deriving from national law (the principle of equivalence). Additionally, EU case law postulates that Member State courts enforcing EU rights do this in a way that does not render EU-law-based claims practically impossible or exceedingly difficult (the principle of effectiveness). Both principles have already been encountered in chapter two II B. In addition, there is the overarching principle of mutual trust. This figures often on a jurisdictional level, ensuring that Member State courts generally presume that other Member State courts apply EU law correctly. These principles play an important role in the interplay between EU law and international commercial arbitration.

A. The Brussels (Recast) Regulation and its Arbitration Exception: A Contractual Paradigm?

It was seen that arbitration can be understood as a contractual construct (see chapter one, III B); and that this contract could be said to constitute its own legal (sub-)system (see chapter two, I D). The following part will illustrate the extent to which the Brussels Regulation reflects such understanding.

[2] See Xandra E Kramer, 'Judicial Cooperation in Civil Matters' in Pieter J Kuijper et al (eds), *The Law of the European Union* (The Netherlands, Kluwer, 2018) 721. For the discussion of an EU competence regarding a comprehensive European Civil Code, see Jakobien W Rutgers, 'European Competence and a European Civil Code, a Common Frame of Reference or an Optional Instrument' in Arthur S Hartkamp et al (eds), *Towards a European Civil Code*, 4th edn (The Netherlands, Wolters Kluwer, 2011), 311.

[3] There are limited exceptions to this, such as the crucial role of the EU Commission as the principal enforcement authority of EU competition law.

[4] Right to an effective remedy and to a fair trial (now Article 47 EU Fundamental Rights Charter), see Case 222/84 *Johnston* ECLI:EU:C:1986:206.

(i) The Brussels Regulation as Regulatory Instrument?

So far as horizontal relationships are concerned, the EU's interest in effective judicial protection has been confined to organising the cross-border cooperation of courts. In this sense, the EU works like a typical international organisation, employing traditional concepts of public and private international law: determining international jurisdiction, and providing conflicts-of-law rules to define the applicable law. The latter is subject to the Rome Regulations, the former – which is of particular interest here – falls under the Brussels Regulation (recast).[5] The origin of the Brussels Regulation lies in a typical international convention between the Member States of the European Community at the time.[6] This was converted into a piece of EU legislation,[7] following an increase of EU competences by virtue of the Treaty of Amsterdam (then Article 65 EC Treaty, now Article 81 TFEU). This Article integrated judicial cooperation and private international law into then-Community affairs, as opposed to intergovernmental affairs.[8] Nevertheless, the change of form from Convention to Regulation did not affect the content: the Brussels Regulation remained focused on facilitating litigation with cross-border elements, based on the principle of mutual trust between the Member States.[9] Mutual trust here translates into mutual recognition of civil and commercial judgments within the EU. One specific purpose of the Brussels Regulation is to enhance the enforceability of those judgments in all Member States in order to foster the proper functioning of the internal market. This is achieved by setting uniform rules for judicial cooperation,[10] based on concepts like effectiveness,[11] and *lis pendens* in order to avoid concurrent proceedings or irreconcilable judgments.[12] The other specific overall purpose is to facilitate

[5] Council Regulation (EC) No 44/2001 of 22 December 2000 on jurisdiction and the recognition and enforcement of judgments in civil and commercial matters [2001] OJ L12/1 (Brussels Regulation); now in its amended version Regulation (EU) No 1215/2012 of the European Parliament and of the Council of 12 December 2012 on jurisdiction and the recognition and enforcement of judgments in civil and commercial matters (recast) [2012] OJ L351/1.

[6] 1968 Brussels Convention on the recognition and enforcement of judgments in civil and commercial matters (consolidated version), [1972] OJ L299/32. Similarly, the Rome I Regulation (EC) No 593/2008 of the European Parliament and of the Council of 17 June 2008 on the law applicable to contractual obligations [2008] OJ L177/6 originates in an international law instrument, the Rome Convention, and was later converted into EU legislation. See Arthur S Hartkamp, *EU Law and National Private Law: Effect of EU Law and European Human Rights Law on Legal Relationships between Individuals*, 2nd edn (Cambridge, Intersentia, 2016), 166–67.

[7] Brussels Regulation (n 5). See Kramer, 'Judicial Cooperation in Civil Matters' (n 2).

[8] Hartkamp, *EU Law and National Private Law* (n 6).

[9] Brussels Regulation (n 5), Recital 26 states: 'Mutual trust in the administration of justice in the Union justifies the principle that judgments given in a Member State should be recognised in all Member States without the need for any special procedure … As a result, a judgment given by the courts of a Member State should be treated as if it had been given in the Member State addressed.' See further II 1 on mutual trust below.

[10] Brussels Regulation (n 5) Recitals 1, 3, and 6.

[11] Ibid Recitals 20 and 22 regarding the enforcement of choice-of-court agreements or judgments rendered in another Member State (abolishing any need for a special declaration of enforceability ('exequatur'), Recital 26.

[12] Ibid Recitals 21–22.

access to justice,[13] which relates to the substantive fairness of these uniform rules: this is addressed through principles like predictability,[14] but also flexibility in the interest of proper administration of justice.[15] Fairness is also pursued by an overall approach aimed at balancing the interests of plaintiffs and defendants.[16]

Underlying the Brussels Regulation is a strictly territorial approach,[17] which requires a connection between court proceedings and the territory of the relevant Member State. This is guaranteed by vesting general jurisdiction in the courts of the defendant's domicile (Article 4(1)); exclusive jurisdiction over immovable property (Article 24(1)); or certain corporate disputes (Article 24(2)) in the courts either at the seat of the corporation or at the location of the property. This corresponds with a classic public international law concept of linking sovereignty with territory and jurisdiction over this territory.[18] At the same time, the Brussels Regulation is an international private law instrument. It starts with the default rule of party autonomy (Recital 19), leading to robust rules on contractual jurisdiction (Article 7(1)) and enforcement of choice-of-court agreements ((Recital 20), Article 25 (prorogation)). This contractual approach is subject to exceptions motivated by EU regulatory concerns. So insurance, consumer, and employment contracts are being carved out in order to provide adequate protection for – typically – weaker parties,[19] and setting out detailed rules on specific jurisdiction in these areas.[20] Finally, there is a reference to fundamental rights[21] and public policy as barrier to enforcement of judgments rendered in another EU Member State (Article 45(1)(a)). The latter is reminiscent of the NYC[22] (ie of traditional regulatory techniques in international law).

[13] Ibid Recital 1.

[14] Ibid Recital 15.

[15] Ibid Recital 23.

[16] For the need for such balance (in the abstract) see Roy Goode, Herbert Kronke, Ewan McKendrick, *Transnational Commercial Law: Texts, Cases and Materials*, 2nd edn (Oxford, Oxford University Press, 2015) para 18.21; more specifically, regarding the Brussels (Recast) Regulation, see, eg, Recital 22 (addressing abusive litigation tactics – in particular, minimising the risk of the defendant taking action in notoriously slow jurisdictions so as to protract proceedings initiated by the plaintiff in the contractually agreed court – known as an 'Italian torpedo'). See, on the other hand, Recital 16 (especially non-contractual jurisdiction to be based on reasonable foreseeability for the defendant) and Recital 29 (enforcement mechanism subject to respect of the rights of the defence).

[17] Ibid Recitals 13–14.

[18] Hannah Buxbaum, 'Territory, Territoriality, and the Resolution of Jurisdictional Conflict' (2009) 57 *American Journal of Comparative Law* 631 at 632 refers to this as 'triangular relationship' between territory, sovereignty, and jurisdiction (relying on FA Mann).

[19] Recitals 18–19.

[20] Article 10 et seq., Article 17 et seq., and Article 20 et seq. Recital 19 explicitly departs from party autonomy as an absolute principle by providing that in insurance, consumer or employment contracts 'only *limited autonomy* to determine the courts having jurisdiction (is) allowed …' (emphasis added).

[21] In particular, fair trial principles, including the rights of the defence, see note 16 (end).

[22] See ch 2, II B (ii). The same is true with regard to the Hague Judgment Convention, the role of which for future international dispute settlement in courts as opposed to arbitration remains to be seen. See Alcolea, Lucas C, 'The 2005 Hague Choice of Court and the 2019 Judgments Convention versus the New York Convention: Rivals, Alternatives or Something Else?' (2019–2020) 6 *McGill Journal of Dispute Resolution* 187. Available at: https://ssrn.com/abstract=3624791.

The combination of the subject matter (civil and commercial matters) with regulating jurisdiction and enforcement can lead to completely different overall assessments: one can either stress party autonomy as the Brussels Regulation's point of departure and focus, together with its purpose of enhancing the proper functioning of the internal market. This would tally with private law programming (see chapter two, I B), in particular with party autonomy as a tool for achieving efficiency[23] and thereby legitimacy (see chapter two, I D (i)). From this perspective, the Brussels Regulation would ultimately remain a commercial law instrument. Alternatively, one can concentrate on its public international law tradition and regulatory purpose of allocating international jurisdiction, together with its second aim of fostering fairness in judicial administration. This would be a public law perspective.

This indicates that the public/private divide is not necessarily the result of an exercise that can always clearly distinguish between different areas of law or even different sets of norms: one and the same Regulation can be understood as part of either public or private law. This is best captured by a transnational law approach (see chapter two), focusing on different processes or functions. At its heart, therefore, the difference between private and public law is here understood to lie simply in perspective. They should not be seen as legal (sub-) systems of their own, but as different approaches to the same things. To recall the terminology of systems theory, there is the overall legal system, which follows the code legal/illegal (see chapter two). What distinguishes the public law perspective from the private law perspective is their respective programming,[24] without going so far as to constitute operational closure vis-à-vis each other or vis-à-vis other legal sub-systems. In private law, 'legal' is normally connected with upholding party autonomy (contractual freedom), dealing with irritations in particular from the economic system through, say, the concept of contract (see chapter two, I B (iii)). In public law, 'legal' is generally connected with the controlled exercise of state powers (legality of state action), distinguishing and structurally coupling the political system via the rule of law.[25]

The conclusion from this for the Brussels Regulation is that it is both a contractual and a regulatory instrument. As contractual instrument, it is distinguishing and structurally coupling the economic system. As regulatory instrument, it is dealing with irritations from the political system. Depending on perspective, the meaning and reach of its arbitration exception differs.

[23] Xandra E Kramer, Alina Ontanu, and Michiel de Rooij et al (eds), 'The Application of Brussels I (Recast) in the Legal Practice of EU Member States: Synthesis Report', Erasmus University/TMC Asser Institute 2016–2018. Available at: www.asser.nl/media/5018/m-5797-ec-justice-the-application-of-brussels-1-09-outputs-synthesis-report.pdf, 11 with further reference.

[24] For the difference between code and programming see ch 2, I B (ii) and (iii).

[25] See chapter two, I B (iii). Regarding the development of German public law, compare Michael Stolleis, *Öffentliches Recht in Deutschland* (Munich, CH Beck, 2014), 67, 71. For a US perspective see also Alexander Somek, *The Cosmopolitan Constitution*, paperback ed (Oxford, Oxford University Press, 2016), 51–53.

(ii) The Arbitration Exception before and after West Tankers

Article 2(d) of the Brussels Regulation has always excluded arbitration from its scope.[26] This arbitration exception can be understood in different terms, depending on the chosen angle. If one sees the Brussels Regulation as a contractual instrument (above (i)), the arbitration exception is both an underlying premise and a necessary consequence: party autonomy reigns. By contrast, if one understands the Brussels Regulation as a regulatory instrument, it is just what its name infers: an exception from the rule that it is ultimately the Regulation that determines international jurisdiction, and not automatically or exclusively the will of the parties.

It is precisely this transnational nature of the Brussels Regulation (see (i) above) that gives rise to the controversy about its exact reach. This will be shown by the example of *West Tankers* and its progeny.

The *West Tankers* case[27] involved a dispute over a vessel – owned by West Tankers and chartered by Erg – that had been damaged in a collision with another ship. After Erg's insurer (Allianz and Generali) had paid out under the insurance, Erg brought arbitration proceedings in London against West Tanker for the excess damage, relying on an arbitration clause in the charterparty. Allianz and Generali sued West Tankers for the sums payed out to Erg before an Italian court. West Tankers denied liability for Erg's claim regarding (excess) damages and defended itself against the Italian case by claiming lack of jurisdiction based on the arbitration agreement. West Tankers also brought a suit against the insurers in the London Commercial Court as the court at the seat of the arbitration, asking for an anti-suit injunction in aid of the arbitration. The anti-suit injunction was granted, and the case progressed to the House of Lords.

The House of Lords considered EU case law regarding the (in)compatibility of antisuit injunctions in support of jurisdiction clauses with the Brussels Regulation. It was of the opinion that this could not be extrapolated to arbitration clauses, since arbitration was excluded from the Brussels Regulation. However, upon preliminary reference, the CJEU did not agree. The decision is well-known for the proposition that EU Member State courts are, as a matter of EU law, prevented from enforcing arbitration agreements by way of an anti-suit injunction.

This could mean that the arbitration exception of the Brussels Regulation was being limited or even disregarded.[28] Strictly speaking, however, the Court did not really opine on the arbitration exception. Instead, it focused on the proceedings before the Italian court as relevant 'subject matter', which brought the case within reach of the Brussels Regulation: it was this Regulation-based jurisdiction

[26] Art. 2 provides that: 'This Regulation shall not apply to … (d) arbitration.'

[27] Case C-185/07 *Allianz SpA et Generali Assicurazioni Generali SpA v West Tankers Inc* ECLI:EU:C:2009:69 (*West Tankers).*

[28] Critically Jacob Grierson, 'Comment on West Tankers Inc v RAS Riunione Adriatica di Sicurta S.p.A. (The Front Comor)' (2009) 26 *Journal of International Arbitration* 891 with extensive references at fn 40.

of the Italian courts that an anti-suit injunction would interfere with. So, it did not matter whether this interference was in support of an arbitration or a jurisdiction clause.

The dogmatic differentiation notwithstanding, the effect of *West Tankers* was to apply the Brussels Regulation to the London court's attempt to enforce the arbitration agreement. What mattered was that another Member State court has been first seised, even though this may have been in breach of the arbitration agreement. This followed from the *lis pendens* rule, which is laid down in Articles 27 and 28 of the Brussels Regulation. It requires a court to stay its proceedings until the court first seised has ruled on its own jurisdiction. In an ideal world, from the perspective of the party wishing to arbitrate, the court first seised will promptly find a lack jurisdiction and refer the parties to arbitration.

The respect for the court first seised follows a strict interpretation of the Brussels Regulation's *lis pendens* rule by the CJEU, notably in the *Gasser* case.[29] The expectation that this court will find itself not competent and refer the parties to arbitration follows from the NYC as incorporated into the relevant national law. Because of its arbitration exception, the Brussels Regulation does not interfere with this. Nevertheless, the question is whether this expectation is indeed warranted in real-life scenarios,[30] because the court first seised may either take too long to decline jurisdiction or assume jurisdiction incorrectly.

The *first in time rule* was therefore understood as setting a wrong incentive for potential defendants in arbitration.[31] They could start judicial proceedings in slow-moving jurisdictions – often referred to as the *Italian torpedo* – in order to delay or even avoid proceedings in the contractually agreed forum. Commercial sense would favour a more prominent role for the contractually agreed courts in the case of exclusive jurisdiction agreements, or the arbitral tribunal and courts at the contractually agreed seat of the arbitration in the case of arbitration agreements.

The question is, hence, whether we favour commercial sense over international comity in the form of respect for courts of other sovereign states. In other words, how do we balance party autonomy and enforcement of the parties' (original) bargain – the contractual paradigm of the Brussels Regulation – with international comity and its regulatory paradigm? Put this way, *West Tankers* is about a more general issue than the reach of the arbitration exception of the Brussels Regulation. The answer in theory affects both arbitration and choice-of-court agreements.[32] Technically, the issue could have been phrased as inquiring whether

[29] Case C-116/02 *Erich Gasser GmbH v MISAT Srl.* ECLI:EU:C:2003:657.

[30] J Grierson, 'Comment on West Tankers' (n 28), 900 calls this '(at best) naïve'.

[31] The EU Commission addressed the potential abuse of *lis pendens* in its impact assessment of *West Tankers*, Impact Assessment, Accompanying document to the Proposal for a Regulation of the European Parliament and of the Council on jurisdiction and the recognition and enforcement of judgments in civil and commercial matters (Recast), SEC(2010) 1547 final, 37–38.

[32] *West Tankers* concerned the attempt by an EU Member State court to enforce an arbitration agreement. Under *Gasser* (Case C-116/02 *Gasser*, n 29), the situation would not have been different had there been a choice-of-court agreement providing for exclusive jurisdiction of that court.

lis pendens – incentivising a race to the courthouse – makes sense even if it is being abused in practice. The Court would then have had a chance to re-consider its existing case law in light of criticism of an unconditional *first in time* rule.[33] Instead, *West Tankers* concerned the arbitration exception in the Brussels Regulation, hence focusing on its role as contractual instrument.

Under *West Tankers*, the arbitration exception does not strip a Member State court of its competence to determine its own jurisdiction, even if this means deciding – incidentally – upon the validity and applicability of an arbitration clause.[34]

One might ask: how could it? An EU Member State's competence to decide upon its own jurisdiction does not originate in EU law.[35] It follows from the principle of equal sovereignty of nation states under general international law. The Brussels Regulation coordinates the exercise of this sovereignty by its Member States as a matter of EU law, stopping short of including arbitral jurisdiction. Put differently, the arbitration exception is not limiting sovereignty, it is embracing it. Despite EU coordination of Member State jurisdiction on the basis of mutual trust (see below), national sovereignty reasserts itself the moment the conditions for mutual trust are disproved.[36]

The CJEU in *West Tankers* also stressed a litigant's entitlement to a judicial forum in case it deemed the arbitration clause void, inoperative, or incapable of being performed.[37] This adds the perspective of the defendant in the arbitration, who – either rightly or opportunistically – insists on its fundamental right to judicial protection. This is an EU fundamental right, but it is also recognised internationally and within the EU Member States. The CJEU did not pronounce on the limits of this right, as a matter of EU law, in case of potential abuse. Not engaging

[33] Case C-116/02 *Gasser* (n 29). Criticism of this strict reading of *lis pendens* has led to revisions with respect to exclusive jurisdiction clauses in Article 31(2) and 31(3) of Regulation (EU) No 1215/2012 of the European Parliament and of the Council of 12 December 2012 on jurisdiction and the recognition and enforcement of judgments in civil and commercial matters (recast) [2012] OJ L351/1. This is still open to critique from a practical point of view, see, eg, Chrispas Nyombi, Tom Mortimer, Rhidian Lewis, 'Italian Torpedoes in the Shadow of the Recast Brussels Regulation 2012' (2015) 36 *European Competition Law Review* 263. For a further revision proposal, see below ch 4.

[34] Case C-185/07 *West Tankers* (n 27) paras 26–27.

[35] Despite the Court's reference to the practical effectiveness of the Brussels Regulation, Case C-185/07 *West Tankers* (n 27) para 24.

[36] This is the case, for example, where the basis of a claim that has been upheld in one Member State falls away under the (so far applicable) law of the Member State that is then asked to enforce the other Member State's judgment. This was the scenario in Case 145/86 *Hoffmann v Krieg* ECLI:EU:C:1988:61: A German court had granted maintenance to a wife against her husband, based on an ongoing matrimonial relationship. However, the marriage was divorced in the Netherlands. The maintenance claim remained enforceable in Germany since there was no obligation to recognise the Dutch divorce decree under the Brussels Regulation (exempting the status of natural persons from its scope). Upon request, the CJEU confirmed to the Hoge Raad that the Dutch courts need not now enforce the German maintenance judgment, which did technically fall under the Brussels Regulation: 'the [Brussels Regulation] does not preclude the court of the State in which enforcement is sought from drawing the necessary inferences from a national decree of divorce when considering the enforcement of the foreign maintenance order.' Ibid at para 17.

[37] *West Tankers* (n 27) at para 31.

with potential limits may well have been warranted in the individual case. To recall, it was the insurers who sought indemnification from West Tankers. So, the factual circumstances were distinct from the typical Italian torpedo where one party starts litigation in a slow-moving jurisdiction although it has apparently agreed to arbitration. Allianz and Generali were not originally parties to the agreement containing the arbitration clause; as insurers they were bound on the basis of legal succession through surrogation.[38] Looking ahead, it would be useful to reflect on the circumstances under which a party may have forfeited its right to judicial protection. In any event, there is so far nothing in *West Tankers* that would not also follow from general international law.

This analysis changes when it comes to the principle of mutual trust between Member State courts that lies at the heart of the Brussels Regulation.[39] The reasoning starts from the point of view of the Italian court with jurisdiction for claims in tort with a cross-border element under Article 5(3) of the Brussels Regulation. As a matter of EU law, we assume that the Italian court correctly engages with this case. For this assumption to work, it does not matter whether there is an arbitration agreement. Consequently, *West Tankers* left no room for other courts to enforce what they saw as the clear will of the parties. Under *West Tankers*, we simply trust EU courts with jurisdiction based on EU law to get it right.[40] Phrased this way, two things become clear: first, the CJEU approaches the Brussels Regulation as a regulatory instrument, emphasising international comity over commercial needs. Second, trust lies with Member State courts and not – as is the case under the NYC[41] – arbitration tribunals. Trust in the EU judiciary appears to conflict with trust in arbitration, and the former prevails over the latter.

West Tankers caused a profound shock in the London arbitration practice, which had been proceeding on the presumption that an arbitration clause in the relevant contract would automatically get rid of the Brussels Regulation.[42] It is only from this commercial perspective that party autonomy, and hence the arbitration exception, appeared as *the* one thing that needed to be reinforced.

One of the EU Commission's reform proposals for the Brussels Regulation was therefore a specific rule clarifying its relationship with international arbitration:

This Regulation does not apply to arbitration save in the limited case provided for therein. In particular, it does not apply to the form, existence, validity or effects

[38] It depends on national (here: English) law whether arbitration clauses are seen as binding upon legal successors. This would also be the case, eg in Germany, see *BGH judgment of 03.05.2000*, XII ZR 42/98 with further references. Available at: http://juris.bundesgerichtshof.de/cgi-bin/rechtsprechung/document.py?Gericht=bgh&Art=en&nr=24146&pos=0&anz=1.

[39] *West Tankers* (n 27) at para 30.

[40] The CJEU had clarified that the proceedings before the London Commercial Court did not come within the scope of the Brussels Regulation. See ibid paras 22–23, stressing that this depends upon the nature of the rights thereby protected. Although often criticised in the literature, this makes sense since the jurisdiction of the London court was based on the English Arbitration Act, hence a subject matter explicitly carved out from the Brussels Regulation.

[41] See ch 2, I D (ii).

[42] See Thomas Panighetti, 'Has London Outmaneuvered the Italian Torpedo?' (2013) 5 *Arbitration Law Review* 276, 280.

of arbitration agreements, the powers of the arbitrators, the procedure before arbitral tribunals, and the validity, annulment, and recognition and enforcement of arbitral awards.[43]

The Commission then proposed to strengthen both choice of court and arbitration agreements by focusing on the court designated by the parties and leave the question of whether this choice was valid to the designated forum. Regarding arbitration agreements, this meant enhancing the role of the court at the seat of the arbitration. Accordingly, the proposed Article 29(4) reversed the *first seised* rule to the effect that, even if first in time, that court should stay its proceedings to the benefit of the court at the seat of an arbitration, or the arbitral tribunal respectively, charged with the – even incidental – question of whether there is a valid and applicable arbitration agreement. It also provided that if the applicability of an arbitration agreement was established, the seised court had to decline jurisdiction. Furthermore, Article 33(3) of the Commission's proposal clarified when an arbitral tribunal is seised of a dispute. Effectively, this would have inserted some regulation of arbitration, albeit in a pro-arbitration way following a contractual paradigm.

Nevertheless, in the Brussels Regulation (recast), there is no reference to arbitration in either Article 29 or Article 33. Instead, Recital 12 reinforces the rule that arbitration is *not* covered: EU law presents itself as neutral towards commercial arbitration.[44] Consequently, ICA is presumed not to be subject to any form of regulation. The new Recital 12 attempts to clarify what this exclusion means:

> first, the Brussels Regulation (recast) does not intend to interfere with the NYC, in particular, the Member States' obligation to recognise and enforce arbitration agreements as well as arbitral awards.[45]

Second, any ruling as such on 'whether or not the arbitration agreement is null and void, inoperative, or incapable of being performed' need *not* be recognised and enforced under the Brussels Regulation (recast).[46] This is independent from the question of whether the validity and applicability of the arbitration agreement

[43] Commission Proposal for a Regulation of the European Parliament and of the Council on jurisdiction and the recognition and enforcement of judgments in civil and commercial matters (Recast) COM(2010) 748 final.

[44] This coincides with a divide between EU and private international law as seen by George Bermann, 'Reconciling European Union Demands with the Demands of International Arbitration' (2011) 34 *Fordham International Law Journal* 1193 at 1194. But it becomes clear from the above discussion on limited EU competencies in private law that this divide extends to private law more generally.

[45] The Brussels Regulation (recast) states in Recital 12 that: '(N)othing in this Regulation should prevent the courts of a Member State, when seised of an action in a matter in respect of which the parties have entered into an arbitration agreement, from referring the parties to arbitration, from staying or dismissing the proceedings, or from examining whether the arbitration agreement is null and void, inoperative or incapable of being performed, in accordance with their national law. … This should be without prejudice to the competence of the courts of the Member States to decide on the recognition and enforcement of arbitral awards in accordance with the Convention on the Recognition and Enforcement of Foreign Arbitral Awards, done at New York on 10 June 1958 ('the 1958 New York Convention'), which takes precedence over this Regulation.'

[46] Ibid, Recital 12 (para 2).

was the main object or an incidental question. It means that another Member State court is *not* bound to interpret the same arbitration agreement in the same way.

Third, nevertheless, where a Member State court has proceeded to a decision on the merits, this judgment falls under the Brussels Regulation (recast) in the usual way.[47] This last scenario logically means that the court has found the arbitration agreement was invalid or inapplicable.

In principle, therefore, ICA remains carved out from the Brussels Regulation on recognition and enforcement of commercial judgments within the EU. This arbitration exception, however, is qualified in an ambiguous way. Rulings regarding the validity of the arbitration agreement (even incidental ones) seem to fall outside the scope of the Brussels Regulation (recast), at least in principle. At the same time, decisions on the merits are *always* covered, *even* if there originally was an agreement to arbitrate. In the latter case, claims brought outside the seat jurisdiction do not guarantee the abstinence of the EU Member State court seised under the Brussels Regulation. This is clear from the rejection of the respective part of the Commission's proposal that would have amended the *first seised* rule. Thus, where a Member State court holds an arbitration agreement invalid and inapplicable and proceeds (as it then typically will) to the merits, that substantive judgment must be recognised and enforced within the EU – even if the court wrongly assumed its own jurisdiction.

Conversely, if a Member State court finds that an arbitration agreement is valid and applicable, this ruling would not have to be recognised in other Member States. In such a case, the court will not proceed to a judgment on the merits since the dispute must then be arbitrated. *De facto* this means that there is mutual respect for judicial findings on the merits that have – correctly or incorrectly – sidestepped the arbitration agreement. However, there is no mutual respect for decisions that *uphold* the arbitration agreement. In the language of mutual recognition, this would be a disguised form of negative mutual recognition.[48]

From an EU law perspective, this makes sense: mutual trust between Member State courts is limited to decisions on the merits. By contrast, the EU is not interested in a correct finding on the jurisdictional question of arbitrability. This is seen from the fact that as long as there is no judgment on the merits, another Member State court could revisit the question of the invalidity or inapplicability of the arbitration agreement, hold it void, inoperable, or incapable of being performed and proceed to a substantive decision. The lack of EU interest in the issue of arbitrability can be explained by its lack of a general competence in this respect.[49]

From the point of view of international arbitration, this can have unfortunate consequences: it sets an incentive for Member State courts to side-step arbitration

[47] Ibid at para 3.

[48] This technique is (openly) used in EU asylum law, where EU Member States are bound to recognise decisions to deny asylum by other Member States, but not decisions to grant it. The same technique can be said to underly the (ambiguous) explanation of Recital 12 of the Brussels Regulation (recast).

[49] As explained by the principle of conferral above and illustrated by the arbitration exception. See also ch 2, II B.

agreements and to proceed to the merits of a case, knowing that this final decision will then fall under the Brussels regime. The Commission proposal would have better reflected commercial interests by strengthening party autonomy and creating a special role for the seat court. This will be considered again in chapter four.

For the time being, it should be noted that the revision of the Brussels Regulation failed to reinforce its contractual angle regarding arbitration agreements in a way similar to jurisdiction agreements.[50] In any event, the Brussels Regulation (recast) illustrates the continued attempt by the EU to distance itself from arbitration. Trust lies with EU Member State courts, not with arbitration tribunals.

Notwithstanding the lengthy clarifications regarding the arbitration exception in Recital 12 (recast), there are substantial ambiguities. It remains particularly unclear whether a Member State court which has upheld an arbitration agreement can enforce it by all means available under national law. One could read Recital 12 (recast) both as confirming or overruling *West Tankers*. From a commercial law perspective, it was hoped that the Court would soon get an opportunity to address this issue.

(iii) Gazprom: *Cutting off Arbitration Tribunals from the EU Legal System*

The *Gazprom* case[51] was a failed attempt to clarify things. It had a distinctive factual setting since it was essentially a shareholder dispute. It concerned a Lithuanian company, 'Lietuvos dujos' AB, its general manager, and a couple of board members whom the Lithuanian state, as one of the shareholders, sought to judicially investigate. The state had also applied for certain corrective measures under the Lithuanian Civil Code, in case the investigation found any improper conduct on behalf of the officers. Gazprom, together with E.ON Ruhrgas and the Lithuanian state, was a major shareholder in the company under investigation, and Gazprom had appointed the (Russian) board members now under scrutiny. There was a shareholder agreement in place, which provided for arbitration of '[a]ny claim, dispute, or contravention of this agreement, or its breach, validity, effect or termination'. Gazprom initiated arbitration before the Arbitration Institute of the Stockholm Chamber of Commerce, claiming that the state's application for judicial investigative measures breached the arbitration agreement. It obtained an arbitral decision (named 'final award') in its favour, which ordered the Ministry, acting for the Lithuanian state, to withdraw some of its court claims ('arbitral anti-suit injunction'). Gazprom sought to enforce this anti-suit injunction in the Lithuanian courts. Meanwhile, the court had decided to proceed with

[50] See above n 33.
[51] Case C-536/13 *Gazprom OAO v Lietuvos Respublika* ECLI:EU:C:2015:316.

the investigation, holding that the claims underlying the investigation proceedings were *not* arbitrable under Lithuanian law. It hence regarded the arbitral anti-suit injunction as a breach of Lithuanian sovereignty and (international) public policy. The case reached the CJEU by way of preliminary reference from the Lietuvos Aukščiausiasis Teismas (the Lithuanian Supreme Court), asking whether recognition and enforcement of the arbitral decision breached the national court's competence to determine its own jurisdiction under the Brussels Regulation.

This case is peculiar for various reasons. First, it concerned an arbitral order, not an award that could be subject to recognition and enforcement under the NYC. The latter requires a ruling on the merits (eg an award of damages that can be enforced). There is authority to the effect that also non-monetary (eg purely declaratory) awards or injunctive relief may be enforceable under the NYC.[52] But for arbitration agreements, the NYC provides a specific form of enforcement in Article II: as seen in chapter two, it is up to any court with international jurisdiction either to send the parties to arbitration on the basis that the subject matter is capable of arbitration (Article II(1)), and the agreement is not void, inoperative or incapable of being performed (Article II(3)); or to refuse to do so. In this case, the request of enforcement of the decision by the Stockholm Arbitration Institute reached the very same court that had already been charged with the substance of the matter, the arbitration agreement notwithstanding. But in any event, dogmatically this still falls under Article II of the NYC. The fact that the parallel arbitration had by that time resulted in an arbitral finding that the dispute was covered by the arbitration agreement does not necessarily change this into an Article V scenario; and it does not change the nature of the arbitral order into an award on the substance.[53]

Second, the *Gazprom* case is remarkable since the Lithuanian court asked the CJEU for guidance on a matter that had nothing to do with EU law. It concerned a Lithuanian company and a request for investigation under Lithuanian law. The only cross-border nexus was the fact that the two board members appointed by Gazprom were Russian nationals. So, Advocate General Wathelet correctly raised the question of whether the Brussels Regulation was applicable under the circumstances.[54] He concluded that the Court could refuse to answer the question. Alternatively, the Court would have to ground its jurisdiction in the general provision of the Brussels Regulation stating that 'persons domiciled in a Member State

[52] See the references by Gary B Born, *International Commercial Arbitration*, Vol III, 2nd edn (The Netherlands, Wolters Kluwer, 2014), § 26.03[B][7].

[53] For a similar conclusion see Pietro Ortolani, 'Anti-Suit Injunctions in Support of Arbitration under the Recast Brussels I Regulation' (2015) *Max Planck Institute Luxemburg Working Paper Series* 1 with further references Available at: www.mpi.lu/research/working-paper-series/2015/wp-2015-1/.

[54] Opinion of Advocate General Wathelet in Case C-536/13 '*Gazprom OAO v Lietuvos Respublika*' ECLI:EU:C:2014:2414 paras 53–57. At stake was the original version of the Brussels Regulation, not the recast, which did not apply *ratione temporis*. However, this does not matter for this question of jurisdiction.

shall, *whatever their nationality*, be sued in the courts of that Member State' under Article 2(1) (emphasis added).

The Court did not explain on what basis it found its own competence. There is no reference to the said Article 2(1) of the Brussels Regulation in its judgment. Instead, the Court quoted Recital 11. This states that, for the sake of predictability, general jurisdiction is based on the defendant's domicile. So, the Court may implicitly have followed the Advocate General's reasoning, but this is far from clear.[55] On its face, the case looks like one that is internal to an EU Member State, and the Court could have declined jurisdiction on this basis. Moreover, the case had arisen under the original version of the Brussels Regulation.[56] Nevertheless, the Court used it as a reason to opine on the Brussels Regulation (recast) which by the time of the judgment in May 2015 had become applicable to future cases. These two instances (ie the question mark over EU jurisdiction generally and the specific lack of applicability of the Brussels Regulation (recast)), suggest a strong interest by the CJEU in clarifying the scope of the latter.

It was shown in section (ii) above that the Brussels Regulation (recast) kept the general arbitration exception, but included a longer Recital 12, ostensibly guiding the relation between EU law and international arbitration. Both the Advocate General and the Court thus took the opportunity to interpret it. The former even went as far as considering what implication Recital 12 (recast) had for anti-suit injunctions in the *West Tankers* scenario – an issue that was not at stake here. Advocate General Wathelet concluded that the EU legislature had intended to correct the boundary between the Brussels Regulation and arbitration as drawn by the *West Tankers* judgment.[57] For him, this meant that *West Tankers* had been overruled: if the same scenario occurred today under the Brussels Regulation (recast), the Italian court would only be 'seised' from the moment it found the arbitration agreement null and void, inoperative or incapable of being performed as per Article II(3) of the New York Convention.[58]

By contrast, the Court confined itself to the issue at hand, leaving open the question of whether the Brussels Regulation (recast) had any impact on the judgment in *West Tankers*. Instead, it relied on the distinction between anti-suit injunctions issued by the courts and those issued by an arbitral tribunal. Advocate General Wathelet had already argued in the alternative that the latter fell outside the Brussels Regulation since the principle of mutual trust does not extend to

[55] An alternative basis may have been the one presented in Joined Cases C-279/88 and C-197/89 *Massam Dzodzi v Belgian State* ECLI:EU:C:1990:360 para 30: if a national law provision puts EU law in contention (in that case, by providing for treatment of a spouse as if he or she were an EU citizen) the Member State court can have an interest in clarification by the CJEU even in internal scenarios so as to avoid divergences developing between the Court's case law on EU law and that of Member State courts. But, again, there is no indication in the Court's *Gazprom* decision that this concern was at stake.

[56] Regulation No 44/2001 of 22 December 2000 (n 5).

[57] AG Opinion in Case C-536/13 *Gazprom* (n 54) para 132.

[58] Ibid at para 133 with reference to the European Parliament resolution of 7 September 2010 on the implementation and review of Council Regulation (EC) No 44/2001 (P7TA(2010)0304, recital M).

arbitration tribunals.[59] EU law obligations are for the Member States (and their courts), not arbitrators. The Court looked at the enforcement proceedings as relevant subject matter – just noting that there was also a parallel investigation – and agreed with the Advocate General's alternative argument on this basis. The enforcement proceedings as 'arbitration matter' were except from the Brussels Regulation – similarly to the London Commercial Court proceedings resulting in the anti-suit inunction in *West Tankers* (see above ii) – and arbitral tribunals were not bound by the principle of mutual trust.[60]

In short, the arbitration exception in the Brussels Regulation remains ambiguous as shown above, but it means at least that arbitration tribunals remain unregulated by EU law. From the point of view of the EU legal system, they are treated as outside players. This could be considered a pro-arbitration approach. It will be revisited below (see B (iii)) and in the discussion of legitimacy in chapter four.

B. The Reach of EU Public Policy: What is Left of Party Autonomy?

The CJEU has, so far, refrained from directly addressing the arbitrability of competition law claims. There is a similar reluctance on part of the Court to use the principle of effectiveness in order to give extra weight to the public interest in undistorted competition vis-à-vis private interests in commercial arbitration. By contrast, the CJEU relies heavily on EU public policy. This translates into a prominent role for the EU Member State court at the end of an arbitration when it needs to decide on annulment or enforcement of an arbitral award. It raises the question of whether party autonomy is not, ultimately, lost. This will be considered in the context of consumer law and arbitration.

(i) Consumer Protection as EU Public Policy

The potential link between consumer arbitration and EU law became clear in 2006, when the Court of Justice had to adjudicate the *Mostaza Claro* case.[61] Ms Claro and Móvil had concluded a mobile telephone contract containing an arbitration clause. When Ms Claro failed to comply with the minimum subscription period provided for in the telephone contract, Móvil initiated arbitration proceedings in the contractually agreed forum. These resulted in an arbitral award against Ms Claro which she challenged before a Spanish court. Ms Claro argued that the

[59] AG Opinion in Case C-536/13 *Gazprom* (n 54) paras 153–54.
[60] Judgment of the Court in Case C-536/13 *Gazprom* (n 51) paras 36–39.
[61] Case C-168/05 *Mostaza Claro v Centro Móvil Milenium SL* ECLI:EU:C:2006:675.

award should be annulled since the arbitration clause was an unfair contract term, therefore null and void under Spanish law implementing EU consumer law.[62]

The question referred by the Spanish court was whether Ms Claro could make this argument for the first time in court when she had failed to raise an objection to the arbitrator's jurisdiction in the arbitration, defending herself on other grounds. Spanish law provided for possible annulment where there was no valid arbitration agreement or the award breached public policy.

The Court started with the issue as presented by the national court (ie the potential invalidity of the arbitration agreement and its examination *ex officio*). It went through its own case law and even Spanish law in order to demonstrate that effective consumer protection required an affirmative answer. However, it then acknowledged the efficiency of arbitration as a competing interest, quoting *Eco Swiss*.[63] It seemed only logical to follow this up with a reference to the actual holding in that case, which relied not on the invalidity of the arbitration agreement due to a breach of EU competition law, but on public policy (see chapter two, II A (ii) and B (ii)). The CJEU transferred this reasoning to consumer protection, drawing an explicit analogy between the EU prohibition of cartels (then Article 81 EC) and the public interest underlying consumer protection.[64]

Mostaza Claro eventually holds that as a matter of EU law, a Member State court must determine whether the arbitration clause constitutes an unfair term and is, therefore, void, irrespective of belated pleading to that effect. This holding rests on *Eco Swiss* and hence consumer protection as EU public policy. But it differs from the competition law cases (chapter two, II A (ii) and B) in its explicit reference to the EU principle of effectiveness.

(ii) Practical Implications for the Enforcement Court

In subsequent case law regarding consumer arbitration the Court clarified the obligations of EU Member State courts when implementing EU public policy. By the time of the decision in *Pannon GSM*,[65] the Court deemed its own jurisprudence sufficiently obvious so as to constitute a duty for national courts to examine *ex officio* whether a contractual term was unfair.[66] For consumer arbitration clauses, this meant that a Member State court charged with the enforcement of an arbitral award had to consider the potential unfairness of the arbitration agreement *ex officio*.

[62] Council Directive 93/13/EEC of 5 April 1993 on unfair terms in consumer contracts [1993] OJ L95/29.

[63] Case C-168/05 *Mostaza Claro* (n 61) para 34 with reference to Case C-126/97 *Eco Swiss China Time Ltd v Benetton International NV* ECLI:EU:C:1999:269. Regarding the latter, see ch 2, II A (ii).

[64] Case C-168/05 *Mostaza Claro* (n 61) para 37.

[65] Case C-243/08 *Pannon GSM Zrt. v Erzsébet Sustikné Győrfi* ECLI:EU:C:2009:350.

[66] Case C-168/15 *Milena Tomásová v Slovenská republika* ECLI:EU:C:2016:602 paras 30, 33.

This was the situation in *Asturcom*, another Spanish mobile phone case.[67] Ms Rodríguez Nogueira defended herself against the enforcement of an arbitral award rendered in her absence. Unlike Ms Claro, she had not tried to have the award set aside by way of annulment action. As a consequence, the time limit for a judicial remedy under Spanish law had passed. The Court found that time limit (in *casu* two months from notification of the award) not too short so as to constitute an issue under the EU principle of effectiveness. Nevertheless, the Court relied on the principle of equivalence and stressed that if national mandatory rules amounting to public policy were able to set aside *res judicata*, then the same must be true of EU consumer protection. This is an outright application of *Eco Swiss* to the context of consumer law. It illustrates that in practice, there is an overlap between contractual and regulatory limits to party autonomy: protecting the weaker party can at the same time amount to a public interest (chapter two, II A).

(iii) A Regulated Pro-Arbitration Approach?

The EU cases above can be understood as being pro-arbitration, but within certain limits. This will be referred to as regulated pro-arbitration approach. The judgment in *Eco Swiss*[68] is commonly understood as – implicitly – acknowledging the arbitrability of EU competition law.[69] *Mostaza Claro* stressed again the importance of efficiency for international arbitration (see (i) above). The *CDC* case[70] concerned the choice of court – prorogation – for litigating EU competition law claims. The Court allowed prorogation, if the relevant jurisdiction agreement explicitly includes such claims, the principle of EU effectiveness notwithstanding. As explained in chapter two, II (B (i)), the Court did not opine on arbitration agreements. This tallies with the EU's overall attempt to present itself as neutral towards arbitration, which also underlies the Brussels Regulation (above A).[71]

Nevertheless, after *CDC*, the contractual principle of party autonomy can outweigh the EU public interest in effective application of its competition laws – at least for jurisdiction agreements. This is remarkable as such and would allow for the general argument that the EU is processing irritations from ICA

[67] Case C-40/08 *Asturcom Telecomunicaciones* ECLI:EU:C:2009:615.

[68] Case C-126/97 *Eco Swiss* (note 63). See also ch 2, I A (ii).

[69] See, eg, Assimakis P Komninos, 'Arbitration and EU Competition Law' (19 April 2009). Available at: http://ssrn.com/abstract=1520105.

[70] Case C-352/13 *Cartel Damage Claims (CDC) Hydrogen Peroxide SA v Akzo Nobel NV* ECLI:EU:C:2015:335 (ch 2, II B (i)).

[71] It should be stressed already that this attempt is ill-fated. Neutrality cannot do away with the need to make value judgments when private and public interests clash. See further ch 4. Also, there may still be negative effects for arbitration. For example, the party trying to avoid arbitration can litigate in an EU forum that it considers most likely to proceed to the merits, the arbitration agreement notwithstanding. It was seen above (I A (ii)) that in this case, the final judgment on the merits needs to be recognised by all other EU Member State courts (referred to there as negative mutual recognition). Here, EU law appears to run counter to the interest of international arbitration, the aim of which must be to ensure the widest possible safeguard of the arbitration agreement.

mostly according to private law programming. Arbitration tribunals could invoke the strong role of party autonomy in EU commercial law and translate it into a pro-arbitration position generally.

There are other pro-arbitration elements in EU law. It was seen that the EU public interest in consumer protection can be outweighed by *res judicata*:[72] EU law in principle accepts a defence of preclusion if the EU issue has not been raised before the expiry of a two-month time limit following notification from the arbitral award.[73] Also the *Gazprom* case (see above A (iii)) can be read as pursuing a pro-arbitration approach since it explicitly refrains from regulating arbitration tribunals. Again, this could be more clearly communicated as a pro-arbitration approach in principle.

However, when a party seeks enforcement of an award within the EU, there are limits to this. In particular, EU law generally insists on strict abidance with EU public policy. This is unsurprising if one acknowledges that EU law is generally characterised by a mix of public and private law programming. In chapters one and two, this was explained theoretically as transnational law approach, which has led to EU contract law being labelled 'regulatory'.[74]

For the sake of efficiency of international arbitration, it would be preferable to take account of EU public interest limits at an earlier stage of the arbitration. The trigger point available for this in EU law is a careful construction of the agreement to arbitrate (see the discussion of the decisions in *CDC Hydrogen Peroxide* and *Genentech* in chapter two, II B). Member State courts have also drawn on the *Ingmar* decision to scrutinise the arbitration agreement (see chapter two, I D (ii)).

It is worth including these cases into a cautious EU doctrine of non-arbitrability: where EU public interests are at stake – such as important social standards like consumer protection or protection of the weaker party generally, or crucial features of market integration such as undistorted competition – there remains a risk that the individual case is deemed to be non-arbitrable by an EU Member State court. These regulatory limits would be developed case by case, considering the concrete factual circumstances (eg how weak is the position of the consumer here in relation to the business partner; or what is the range of possible damages of potential anticompetitive behaviour). In addition to specifying EU public interest limits, it would be necessary to clarify whether these are treated as a question of non-arbitrability of the subject matter or of invalidity or a narrow construction of the arbitration clause.

[72] Case C-40/08 *Asturcom Telecomunicaciones* (n 67). See ch 3, I B (ii).

[73] At least, this is the position with regard to the principle of effectiveness of EU law. Only where national procedural law provides for an exception for a defence amounting to national public policy, the same must account for EU public policy (*in casu*, consumer protection). See ch 3, I B (ii).

[74] Hugh Collins, 'The Hybrid Quality of European Private Law' in Robert Brownsword, HW Micklitz, Leone Niglia and Stephen Weatherill (eds), *The Foundations of European Private Law* (Oxford, Hart Publishing, 2011), 453. See also Stephen Weatherill, *Contract Law of the Internal Market* (Cambridge, Intersentia, 2016).

For actors in international arbitration, the choice is between risking an award that is unenforceable within the EU for public policy reasons, and involving the EU judiciary at an earlier stage, considering the arbitrability of the individual case. This is already going on in the case law, although unnoticed. For example, *West Tankers* (see A (ii) above) involves questions such as whether a claim in tort (ie a statutory claim) is covered by an arbitration clause in a charter contract, and whether the insurance companies as non-signatories are bound by it. These issues would fall under the heading of arbitrability in its broader sense (see chapter two, I D (ii) and II).

If EU law were to favour the protection of public interests generally by a narrow construction of arbitration agreements, parties could still ensure through careful drafting that *any claim whether contractual or not* shall be submitted to arbitration. It was seen that this was the solution by the Court in *CDC* (chapter two, II B (i)). It leaves party autonomy intact but does not give parties certainty regarding the enforceability of the ensuing award. Phrasing this explicitly as arbitrability issue would have the advantage of signalling that there may be enforceability issues. It would make the EU's concern about public interests more transparent. This concern could be heeded by arbitrators when construing arbitration clauses, and this would lay the ground for trust in both the EU and international arbitration (see further chapter four).

II. EU Law and Investment Treaty Arbitration

The relationship between EU law and investment treaty arbitration (ITA) is characterised by public law programming which focuses on the legality of state action, including state contracting (see chapter one, III A). This means that the room for party autonomy is much more limited from the start; and the regulatory aspects of EU law take over as will be illustrated below.

A. EU Autonomy and Mutual Trust as Pillars for EU Self-Preservation

The EU case law claiming that the EU comprises a new, autonomous legal order has already been referenced in the preceding chapters. It created the EU legal system, rendering the EU independent from unilateral Member State action. So, EU law cannot be undone or changed by the Member States.[75] From one

[75] In reality, there is interdependency between the EU and Member State legal orders, as the Court acknowledged in Joined Cases C-402/05P & C-415/05P *Kadi and Al Barakaat v Council* [2008] ECR I-06351 at para 167. But EU autonomy can be understood as the theoretical benchmark determining the stopping point at which this interdependency would result in undermining the very purpose (integration) of the EU.

angle, this purpose is achieved by the principle of EU primacy, and from a slightly different angle, by the doctrine of direct effect. It was also pointed out above (see chapter two, I C (i)) that nowadays, the EU's self-understanding as a legal system is found in the notion of EU autonomy. This includes independence not only from the national legal systems of its Member States (*internal autonomy*), but also from the international legal system (*external autonomy*).

The EU's self-understood independence from the international legal order has been illustrated by case law regarding EU external relations (see chapter two, I C), ie the realm of EU public law. To recall, autonomy in a systems theoretical sense is consisting of those elements that formally shield the EU legal order against irritations from the outside (see chapter two, I C (ii)). Such irritations not only originate from the overall international legal system. Regarding ICA, they also include irritations from the economic system; regarding ITA those from the political system.

EU law deals with these irritations differently. The preceding part on ICA and the Brussels Regulation exemplifies an attempt at neutrality by minimising EU regulation to avoid collisions.[76] Nevertheless, as shown by the unfolding of *West Tankers* and its progeny, simply not regulating or refraining from addressing the interface between party autonomy and EU public policy does not resolve the underlying tensions.

Essentially, the question is how to balance commercial with EU regulatory interests. As to the latter, mutual trust (in national courts within the EU) has been emerging as one increasingly important element. It was the rock on which *West Tankers* stood and potentially still does. By contrast, the lack of mutual trust with regard to arbitration tribunals in *Gazprom* de-coupled the EU from ICA, which is based – under the NYC – on trust in arbitration, not the courts. It will be seen below that mere de-coupling of ITA does not work since the Member States, as the main actors in ITA, are squarely bound by EU law.

(i) EU Regulation of State Contracting

First, it is important to note that, from an EU perspective, there is nothing wrong with regulating public actors, in particular, the Member States themselves. That is the whole point of EU integration: defining specific international law obligations for its members. From the perspective of EU Member States, obligations under EU law *de facto* take precedence not only over their national, but also over their international law obligations. The niche for exceptions regarding treaties that the Member States had concluded *prior* to the founding of the EC/EU – or, respectively, *prior* to their accession to the EC/EU – does not exist when it comes to the EU's 'very foundations'. *Kadi*, in this respect, excluded recourse to then Article 307

[76] One could compare this to the more general divide between EU and private law. See above n 44.

EC, now 351 TFEU.[77] Member State obligations extend to their respective organs. So, there is also nothing remarkable about the EU regulating public courts, as illustrated above by the jurisdictional rules of the Brussels Regulation.

Any regulation of private actors, by contrast, requires much more circumspection: in the Brussels Regulation, this led to the continuous carve-out of ICA. There is no such carve-out of ITA. This makes sense since ITA, by definition, involves state action. The origin of the arbitration lies in a contract between states, and the measure under legal review is an act by the host state (see chapter two, I D (iii)). The Court was therefore correct in holding in *Achmea* that a distinction must be drawn between ITA and ICA.[78] But how far does the regulation of EU Member States' contracting reach?

(ii) Strict Obligation for EU Members to use the EU Judicial System under Achmea

The *Achmea* case concerned an arbitration brought by a Dutch insurance group (formerly 'Eureko', then 'Achmea') against Slovakia under the bilateral investment treaty (BIT) between the Netherlands and Slovakia. Since both are EU Member States this is a so-called *intra*-EU BIT. Generally speaking, the case raised the question of whether *intra*-EU investment arbitration is compatible with EU autonomy:[79] the privileged treatment of foreign investors protected under the BIT may run counter to the EU principle of equal treatment, and arbitration between an investor and an EU Member State may conflict with the latter's duty to bring EU law-related disputes before the CJEU. The CJEU focused on the latter problem. It scrutinised the offer to arbitrate by Slovakia in the BIT, which constituted the relevant state action and is, as such, subject to the EU treaties. This was irrespective of the fact that this offer must subsequently be taken up by the investor as a non-state actor. (On the hybrid nature of ITA see chapter one, III and chapter two, I D (iii)).

[77] This provision starts from the rule that the rights and obligations under international treaties concluded by the Member States prior to 1 January 1958 (or, respectively, prior to their accession to the EU) shall not be affected by EU law. It then sets out a duty of the EU Member States to eliminate any incompatibilities. For a detailed discussion of this provision with regard to investment treaties see Konstanze von Papp, 'Solving Conflicts with International Investment Treaty Law from an EU Law Perspective: Article 351 TFEU Revisited' (2015) 42 *Legal Issues of Economic Integration* 325.

[78] Case 284/16 *Slowakische Republik (Slovak Republic) v Achmea BV* ECLI:EU:C:2018:158 para 55 (contrasting the jurisdiction of an arbitral tribunal in commercial cases, which derives from an agreement between private parties, with arbitral jurisdiction in ITA, which is ultimately based on a treaty between Member States).

[79] For more detail see, eg, Cristina Contartese and Mads Adenas, 'EU Autonomy and Investor-state Dispute Settlement under *inter se* Agreements between EU Member States: *Achmea*' (2019) 56 *Common Market Law Review* 157; Burkhard Hess, 'The Fate of Investment Dispute Resolution after the Achmea Decision of the European Court of Justice' (2018) *Max Planck Institute Luxemburg Working Paper Series* 3. Available at: www.mpi.lu/research/working-paper-series/2018/wp-2018-3/.

The Member State's offer to arbitrate is then subject to the prohibition in Article 344 TFEU to solve EU law disputes outside the EU's judicial system.[80] Until *Achmea*, the legal community was split over the question of whether Article 344 TFEU applied to ITA. One problem concerned the actors. In particular, the question was posed as to whether only state-to-state disputes were covered.[81] The other concerned the subject matter, as Article 344 TFEU only covers EU law-related disputes.

In *Achmea*, the Court used a broad approach to both issues. It clarified that Article 344 TFEU can also cover disputes between a Member State and a private party, at least where the basis for consent originates in a treaty between states. And it found that a dispute arising under investment treaties can 'concern the interpretation or application of the (EU) treaties'. As to the latter, the Court relied heavily on its Opinion 2/13 regarding ECHR accession,[82] which stresses the operational closure of the EU legal system (see chapter two, I C (i)).

The argument went as follows: the specific nature of EU law – its independent source, its primacy and direct effect – justifies both its *internal* and *external* autonomy. EU law has evolved into 'a structured network of principles, rules and mutually interdependent legal relations binding the EU and its Member States reciprocally and binding its Member States to each other'.[83] It followed that, under the applicable clause of the BIT, EU law must be qualified as both the 'law in force of the contracting party' and a 'relevant agreement between the contracting parties'.[84] This combines a constitutional with a contractual approach to international law treaties.[85] Consequently, an arbitral tribunal deciding a dispute under this BIT must take EU law into consideration (ie interpret or apply EU law).[86]

The dispute was therefore caught by the prohibition of Article 344 TFEU, unless it could be subject to the preliminary reference mechanism under Article 267 TFEU. It was seen above that this article provides for the referral of EU law questions by EU Member State courts to the CJEU. In the language of systems

[80] Article 344 TFEU states: 'Member States undertake not to submit a dispute concerning the interpretation or application of the Treaties to any method of settlement other than those provided for therein.' See Case C-459/03 *Commission v Ireland* (*Mox Plant*) ECLI:EU:C:2006:345. For the possible repercussions of an EU Member State's offer to arbitrate commercial cases see ch 4, I A (iv).

[81] The majority view of German commentators, for example, was that Article 344 TFEU only applied to disputes between EU Member States, not between one Member State and one private party. The Frankfurt Appellate Court in *Achmea* (under the name of *Eureko* at the relevant time) had followed that strand of literature. See Decision of 10 May 2012 in Case 26 SchH 11/10 of the *Oberlandesgericht (OLG)* Frankfurt, openJur 2012, 68499 at paras 88–106. Available at: https://openjur.de/u/399128.html. See also Konstanze von Papp, 'Clash of "Autonomous Legal Orders": Can EU Member State Courts Bridge the Jurisdictional Divide between Investment Tribunals and the ECJ? A Plea for Direct Referral from Investment Tribunals to the ECJ' (2013) 50 *Common Market Law Review* 1039 at 1049.

[82] Opinion 2/13 *Accession of the European Union to the European Convention for the Protection of Human Rights and Fundamental Freedoms* (ECHR Accession) ECLI:EU:C:2014:2454.

[83] Case 284/16 *Achmea* (n 78) at para 33.

[84] Ibid at paras 40–41.

[85] For the differentiation in theory see Jan Klabbers, *Treaty Conflict and the European Union* (Cambridge, Cambridge University Press, 2009).

[86] Case 284/16 *Achmea* (n 78) at para 42.

theory, it structurally couples the national with the EU legal system (see chapter two, B (iii) and C (ii)). It represents the central point of the EU judiciary, providing the necessary structure for EU law-related questions to reach the CJEU. Art 344 TFEU adds to this an obligation for Member States to use the EU judicial system for EU law-related disputes.

The Court held that investment tribunals could not avail themselves of the preliminary reference mechanism.[87] *Achmea* confirms that Member States, vis-à-vis each other, cannot contract out of the EU judicial system, even if the actual dispute is not one between states, but between one EU Member State and one private party.

(iii) Critique

Achmea is correct insofar as it notes a difference between ICA and ITA. The question is whether it draws the right consequence from this distinction. It relies on *Eco Swiss* in stating that the Member State courts play an important role in providing a – limited – review of arbitral awards on the basis of fundamental provisions of EU law and, if necessary, the case should be referred to the CJEU.[88] The discussion should here have moved on to the question of whether or to what extent Member State courts can fulfil this role in ITA. Instead, the Court relied on the EU law principle of effectiveness.[89] This benchmark as such is noteworthy.

It was seen in chapter two (see II A (ii) and B (i)) that the Court has been rather reluctant to explicitly engage with the principle of effectiveness of EU law when it comes to regulating commercial arbitration. *Eco Swiss* formally argues the basis of equivalence between EU and national public policy (see chapter two, II A (ii)).

This reluctance remained in subsequent cases. *Mostaza Claro* did refer to the need for effective consumer protection, but quickly contrasted this with the equivalent interest in efficient commercial arbitration (see I B (i) above). Even *Asturcom* ultimately relied on the principle of equivalence and not effectiveness (see II B (ii) above). By contrast, the Court in *Achmea* simply referred to the full effectiveness of EU law, in particular, Article 19 TFEU.[90] This has a similar effect as in *Gazprom* (see I A (iii) above) in that it draws a line between the EU judiciary and arbitration tribunals. This has direct repercussions for the future of ITA within the EU since it prohibits Member States from submitting to arbitration for *intra*-EU investment

[87] Ibid at paras 43–48. This is in line with a narrow construction of 'court or tribunal of a Member State' in Article 267 TFEU, as employed for commercial arbitration tribunals in Case 102/81 *Nordsee Deutsche Hochseefischerei GmbH v Reederei Mond Hochseefischerei Nordstern AG & Co KG et al* ECLI:EU:C:1982:107. For a detailed and more generous construction of Article 267 TFEU see Opinion of Advocate General Wathelet in Case C-284/16 *Slowakische Republik (Slovak Republic) v Achmea BV* ECLI:EU:C:2017:699 paras 86–113.

[88] Case 284/16 *Achmea* (n 78) at para 54.

[89] Ibid at para 56.

[90] Ibid at para 50.

disputes. The regulatory aspect of EU law is so strong that it ultimately puts an end to *intra*-EU ITA.[91]

Another problem is that the Court in *Achmea* was not relying on the effective application of substantive EU law. Instead, it focused on its 'system of judicial remedies'.[92] This is a very formal approach. In systems theoretical terms, a formal argument concludes with reference to the system itself (self-reference), thereby preventing a substantive discussion.[93] The opposite is a discussion of the substance that incorporates considerations from the outside (the environment), which are then processed within the system. The latter (so-called *hetero*-reference) is naturally more complex in that it allows for some form of engagement with the environment. It hence prevents a system from becoming isolated.[94] While the formal argumentation in *Achmea* reduces complexity, it contributes to EU self-isolation, not only with regard to international arbitration, but also to the international legal system more generally. This will be taken up again in chapter four.

As indicated above, the Court in its *Achmea* decision should have considered the possibility of Member State courts intervening in the arbitration. *Achmea* itself was an example of this: the courts at the seat of the arbitration (Frankfurt, Germany) had got involved and finally referred EU law-related questions, amongst them the correct reading of Article 344 TFEU. The Court could have used *Achmea* as an example for the required interaction between national courts and the CJEU on EU law questions in both ICA and ITA.

On this basis, similarly to the logic displayed for commercial cases,[95] this could have led to holding that it is up to the national courts to obtain the necessary guidance from the CJEU when getting involved in an arbitration. Article 344 TFEU may then have been interpreted as not prohibiting Member States from subjecting to international arbitration – either on the basis of a contract, or on the basis of a treaty – as long as the path to the national courts during or at the end of an arbitration remained open. Such an approach would have conformed to the general approach to arbitration in commercial cases.

This would have led to the following distinction: ITA that is *not* conducted under the auspices of ICSID will typically be subject to the arbitration laws of its seat. As long as the seat of the arbitration is within the EU, the seat court will be an EU Member State court, bound by EU law and applying its arbitration laws, if necessary, under the guidance of the CJEU. Dogmatically, there would have been no reason to treat *non*-ICSID arbitration within the EU differently from ICA. The same could arguably be said for enforcement proceedings of any arbitral award as

[91] In March 2020, the EU Member States reacted by terminating their BITs, see critically Nikos Lavranos, 'Comment: When 23 Member States Terminate their Intra EU BITS' (6 May 2020). Available at: https://borderlex.eu/2020/05/06/comment-when-23-eu-member-states-terminate-their-intra-eu-bits/.

[92] Case 284/16 *Achmea* (n 78) at para 55.

[93] Niklas Luhmann, *Das Recht der Gesellschaft*, 1st edn (Frankfurt, Suhrkamp, 1995), 393.

[94] Luhmann ibid at 394.

[95] Case law since Case 102/81 *Nordsee* (n 87) paras 14–15. See also Case C-126/97 *Eco Swiss* (n 63) paras 33–40.

long as enforcement is sought before an EU Member State court. One may even include ITA under the Energy Charter Treaty (ECT) to which both the EU and its Member States are parties.[96]

In short, international arbitration (ICA and ITA) could remain unregulated by EU law as long as this interaction is structurally possible (ie as long as the correct application of EU law can be guaranteed via the involvement of an EU Member State court). Such an alternative approach would be in line with *Eco Swiss*[97] and would put the focus on scenarios that may involve EU law issues, but where the pathway to an EU Member State court is precluded (ie ITA with a seat outside of the EU or likely to be enforced outside the EU) and ICSID arbitration. For such cases, a broader reading of Article 344 TFEU, and hence a stricter limit on Member State contracting may be justified.[98]

B. The Reach of Article 344 TFEU: An Overarching EU Law Paradigm for Non-Arbitrability?

It was seen in chapter two (see II A) that arbitrability can take different forms. It can refer to the question of whether the parties have indeed agreed to arbitrate the relevant claim or dispute. Seen in this light it would be a contractual issue, best understood to be resolved by private law programming. It can also refer to the issue of whether the parties are allowed to submit their dispute to arbitration (doctrine of non-arbitrability). This may be questionable either because there is a relationship of structural subordination between the parties, or because the dispute raises an inherently public interest.

These are issues that require some form of public law programming. Nevertheless, the underlying issue is the same: have the parties validly contracted out of the judicial system? Contracting out of the EU judicial system appears much easier for private parties than for EU Member States. As stressed above, it is the latter who are always an actor in ITA based on an *intra*-EU BIT. The analytical starting point in light of Article 344 TFEU would be: Member States cannot contract out of the EU judicial system as long as the dispute raises an issue of EU law.

[96] ECT arbitration tribunals have concluded following *Achmea* that it is not up to them to extrapolate the reasoning in *Achmea* to *intra*-EU arbitration under the ECT. So, they found no obstacle to their jurisdiction. See *Masdar Solar & Wind Cooperatief UA v Kingdom of Spain* ICSID Case No ARB/14/1 (Award, 16 May 2018) paras 678–83. Available at: www.italaw.com/sites/default/files/case-documents/italaw9710.pdf; *Vattenfall AB and others v Federal Republic of Germany*, ICSID Case No ARB/12/12 (Decision on the *Achmea* issue, 31 August 2018) paras 163–64.

[97] Case C-126/97 *Eco Swiss* (n 63). See also ch 2, II A (ii).

[98] This is also the argument by Advocate General Wathelet in Case C-284/16 *Achmea* (n 87) who after careful analysis at paras 237 et seq suggests that Article 344 TFEU may preclude Member States from submitting to ICSID arbitration, where no equivalent involvement of national courts is possible (para 253), but concludes that for a *non*-ICSID case like *Achmea* the same judicial safeguards apply as for ICA (para 254).

The question then becomes where the benchmark lies for qualifying a dispute as EU law related. The lower it is, the better the claim that there is an overarching paradigm for non-arbitrability of disputes involving EU Member States.

(i) Distinguishing EU Law-Related Disputes from Cases Involving EU Law as Fact

The *Achmea* case (see A (ii) above) indicated that the threshold for qualifying a dispute as being about the interpretation or application of EU law is extremely low. This is at least true in a scenario where the consent for ITA between one EU Member State and a foreign investor derives from an *intra*-EU BIT.

What about ITA involving an EU Member State and investors from a non-EU state (third country)? This concerns multilateral treaties such as the Energy Charter Treaty,[99] or *extra*-EU BITs.[100] The latter are now being replaced, since the Lisbon Treaty in 2012 added a new EU investment competence as part of its foreign commercial policy (Article 207 TFEU).[101] In practice, the EU and its Member States are now concluding mixed international investment treaties or agreements with third countries (EU investment agreements). This fits into a broader global trend of multi-lateralising investment law by including investment chapters in regional trade agreements.[102]

One must hence look at investor-state dispute settlement (ISDS) provisions in EU investment agreements in order to understand how far the EU's external autonomy reaches. It is noteworthy from the outset that the Court has shown much more leniency here, particularly in regard to the ISDS mechanism of the Comprehensive Economic and Trade Agreement between the EU and its Member States with Canada (CETA).[103]

The dispute settlement provisions in Section F of CETA's investment chapter (ie Chapter 8) provide for a two-tiered arbitration system. There is an arbitration tribunal – consisting of 15 members who will normally hear cases in divisions

[99] See Ciaran Cross and Vivian Kube, 'Is the Arbitration Clause of the Energy Charter Treaty Compatible with EU law in its Application between EU Member States?' Analysis commissioned by the Munich Environmental Institute (February 2018). Available at: www.bilaterals.org/IMG/pdf/180226_gutachten_english_b.pdf.

[100] This remains a question for arbitration under existing BITs by the EU Member States with third countries. For an argument that *extra*-EU BITs can be distinguished from *intra*-EU BITs under *Achmea* see Angelos Dimopoulos, 'The Principle of Autonomy and its Implications for Intra and Extra EU BITs' *EJIL: Talk!* (27 March 2018). Available at: www.ejiltalk.org/achmea-the-principle-of-autonomy-and-its-implications-for-intra-and-extra-eu-bits/.

[101] EU Commission, 'Towards a Comprehensive European International Investment Policy' COM(2010) 343 final, 7 July 2010. See, eg, Catherine Titi, 'International Investment Law and the European Union: Towards a New Generation of International Investment Agreements' (2015) 26 *European Journal of International Law* 639.

[102] See the edited collection by Thilo Rensmann (ed), *Mega-Regional Trade Agreements* (Cham, Springer, 2017).

[103] The CETA text is most easily accessed at: https://ec.europa.eu/trade/policy/in-focus/ceta/ceta-chapter-by-chapter/.

of three arbitrators – and an appellate tribunal, with members of both tribunals to be appointed by the CETA Joint Committee. This structure was approved by the Court in Opinion 1/17, having reviewed it against the benchmark of EU autonomy. As in previous cases, the Court focused on the EU judicial system and Article 19 TEU,[104] but chose a different angle.

It started by noting that the CETA tribunal would be acting *outside* the EU judicial system.[105] The Court implicitly endorsed the argument by the majority of governments that the CETA agreement set up a legal order that was 'wholly separate' from the EU.[106] The question became whether its provisions ensured it remained separate under all circumstances. To this effect, the Court reviewed the de-coupling mechanisms that the CETA agreement provided to make sure that both the EU legal system and the envisaged ISDS were closed vis-à-vis each other. On one level, this means that the CETA tribunal must stop short of interpreting or applying EU law. To recall, this was the hurdle that the BIT in *Achmea* failed to clear (see A (ii) above). On another level, it further must be ensured that the powers given to CETA tribunals could not lead to awards that interfere with the EU legal system.[107]

In contrast to the *intra*-EU ISDS under scrutiny in *Achmea*, the CETA agreement cleared the first hurdle: the CJEU was convinced that investment disputes thereunder would not relate to the interpretation or application of EU law. This was due to carefully drafted provisions attempting to draw clear boundaries around both CETA and EU law. For a start, CETA provisions have no direct effect (ie they cannot be relied on in the domestic courts).[108] Conversely, the ISDS provisions of CETA clarify that the CETA tribunal cannot apply the domestic law of one of the parties to the dispute.[109]

For the Court, this sufficiently distinguishes CETA from the (failed) agreement on the EU Patent Court, and from the bilateral investment treaty in *Achmea*. Instead, CETA reduces domestic law – and hence, in the Court's reading, EU law – explicitly to a fact.[110] It was seen in chapter two (I B (i)) that this allows

[104] Opinion 1/17 *Comprehensive Trade Agreement between Canada and the European Union and its Member States (CETA)* ECLI:EU:C:2019:341 at para 111.

[105] Ibid at para 113.

[106] Ibid at para 77.

[107] The CETA agreement may not 'structure the powers of those tribunals in such a way that … they may issue awards which have the effect of preventing the EU institutions from operating in accordance with the EU constitutional framework'. Ibid at para 119.

[108] See CETA Article 30.6 (under the heading of 'private rights').

[109] The Court interpreted this – correctly – as including EU law, see Opinion 1/17 *CETA* (n 104) paras 121–26. The Court did not consider the possibility that EU law, or parts thereof, may (also) come into play under Art 8.31 (1), which provides that the tribunal applies CETA as interpreted in accordance with the Vienna Convention and other rules and principles of international law applicable between the parties. See (ii) below.

[110] CETA Art 8.31(2) provides that: 'The Tribunal shall not have jurisdiction to determine the legality of a measure, alleged to constitute a breach of this Agreement, under the domestic law of the disputing Party. *For greater certainty, in determining the consistency of a measure with this Agreement, the Tribunal may consider, as appropriate, the domestic law of the disputing Party as a matter of fact.* In doing so, the

for a less normative approach, enabling a non-hierarchical view of the relationship between different systems. This is indeed what the CJEU was trying to achieve: it explained that the interpretation of (EU) international agreements by the EU judiciary is not hierarchically superior to the interpretation of international agreements by other courts.[111] For the Court, this followed from previous case law, in particular from Opinion 1/09 regarding the EU Patent Court, and Opinion 2/13 regarding ECHR Accession.[112]

Each judicial system interprets the relevant international agreement irrespective of the views of another judicial system. This formal line-drawing resembles the Court's approach in the *Gazprom* case, separating arbitration tribunals from Member State courts (see I A (iii) above). Only the latter were held to be bound by the EU principle of mutual trust. The CETA Opinion makes a similar distinction between Member States (bound by mutual trust), and third countries (not bound by mutual trust).[113] While this is correct, it leaves open the question of the potential impact, if any, of other EU principles.

(ii) Can the CETA-*Opinion be Reconciled with* Achmea?

The Court's disregard of potential EU influence in its *CETA*-Opinion is diametrically opposed to its approach in *Achmea* (see A (ii) above). In *Achmea*, the Court deduced from the specific nature of EU law that it must at the same time be understood as part of the domestic law of a Member State and of international law as applicable between EU Member States.[114] If EU law, due to its specific nature, must be understood as part of international law, this is not only true in one case (*Achmea*), but must be true more generally.

One must hence ask what this characteristic of EU law means for Article 8.31.1 of CETA, stating that 'this agreement must be interpreted in accordance with [the Vienna Convention and] other rules and principles of international law applicable between the Parties'. Couldn't this be interpreted to mean that CETA may also have to be interpreted in accordance with EU law? Canada is not an EU Member State, so normally, it cannot be bound by EU law. Hence it is not generally applicable 'as between the parties', its international law character notwithstanding.

Tribunal shall follow the prevailing interpretation given to the domestic law by the courts or authorities of that Party and any meaning given to domestic law by the Tribunal shall not be binding upon the courts or authorities of that Party' (emphasis added).

[111] '[W]ith respect to international agreements entered into by the Union, the jurisdiction of the courts and tribunals specified in Article 19 TEU to interpret and apply those agreements does not take precedence over either the jurisdiction of the courts and tribunals of the non-Member States with which those agreements were concluded or that of the international courts or tribunals that are established by such agreements.' Opinion 1/17 *CETA* (n 104) para 116.

[112] Ibid at paras 106, 117.

[113] Ibid at para 129.

[114] Case C-284/16 *Achmea* (n 78) para 41.

This would have been the easy way of distinguishing, as a matter of principle, the approach in *Achmea* from that in Opinion 1/17. Nevertheless, EU foundational or general principles may have an equivalent principle within general international law (see chapter 4, II B). Moreover, there may also be room for extraterritorial reach of EU law (eg in EU antitrust law).[115] So, the particular characteristic of EU law as part of international law should still have been considered by the Court in its CETA Opinion, with specific regard to its implications for the future interpretation of CETA.

Instead, the Court did not address any ways in which EU law could still be relevant as 'law' for the CETA tribunal and hence in an *extra*-EU scenario.[116] It was satisfied by the apparent intention of the drafters of CETA to exclude this risk. In other words, the Court trusted in a strictly textual reading of CETA (see (iii) below).[117]

This must be contrasted with *Achmea*, where there was no such trust in an EU-friendly application and interpretation of a Member State treaty. This may result from the fact that the latter is entrusted to different ad hoc tribunals appointed without central oversight equivalent to that by the Joint CETA Committee. Also, traditional ITA is being conducted without appellate oversight comparable to that envisaged by the CETA appellate tribunal under CETA's new investment court system (ICS). There is an argument that this is a *quasi*-institutionalised approach, with the necessary structures for a sufficiently consistent interpretation of CETA in place, in contrast to the typical scenario under Member State BITs.

Trust in a textual application of CETA by its ICS would also explain the Court's approach to the second hurdle. To recall, the benchmark here was that the powers given to CETA tribunals could not lead to awards that interfered with the EU legal system.[118] For example, the investment tribunal might award

[115] See the Court's approval of the qualified effects test in Case C-413/14 P *Intel Corporation Inc v European Commission* ECLI:EU:C:2017:632 paras 40–46. For a detailed analysis in the context of EU agreements see Florian Wagner-von Papp, 'Competition Law in EU Free Trade and Cooperation Agreements (and What the UK Can Expect After Brexit)' 2017 *European Yearbook of International Economic Law* 301. See also Giorgio Monti, 'The Global Reach of EU Competition Law' in Marise Cremona and Joanne Scott, *EU Law Beyond EU Borders: The Extraterritorial Reach of EU Law* (Oxford, Oxford University Press, 2019), 174, 183. Compare also the envisaged extension of certain aspects of EU state aid law to non-EU subsidies, see Commission White Paper on levelling the playing field as regards foreign subsidies, COM/2020/253 final (17 June 2020).

[116] See the hypothetical scenarios flagged up by Ingolf Pernice, 'Study on International Investment Protection Agreements and EU Law' in European Parliament, Directorate-General for External Policies of the Union (Directorate B, Policy Department), *Study: Investor-State Dispute Settlement (ISDS) Provisions in the EU's International Investment Agreements Vol 2 – Studies*, EXPO/B/INTA/2014/08-09-10, Part III, 132, 146–49 (September 2014). See also Javier Diez-Hochleitner, 'The European Union Facing Investment Arbitration' in Piet Eeckhout and Manuel López-Escudero (eds), *The European Union's External Action in Times of Crisis* (Oxford, Hart Publishing, 2016), 453, 468.

[117] See also Panos Koutrakos, (Editorial) 'More on Autonomy – Opinion 1/17 (CETA)' (2019) *European Law Review* 293 (referring to the Court's 'leap of faith').

[118] Above n 107.

damages for an EU – or Member State – act implementing EU law which is found to be in breach of investment protection standards under CETA. Classic cases would be alleged expropriation or a breach of the fair and equitable treatment standard.

If, under EU law, the EU or Member State measure was legally enacting an EU public interest, there would be a conflict between investment protection on the one hand, and the public interest on the other. The Court clarified that the standard of protection of EU public interests must not be undermined by investment protection under CETA.[119] From an EU law perspective, any conflict with investment protection must be resolved for the benefit of the EU. In particular, the central role of the CJEU under Article 19 TEU would have to be preserved.[120] The CJEU explained in some detail that CETA was carefully drafted in order to ensure this.[121]

After Opinion 1/17 (*CETA*), Member States are not, overall, prohibited from submitting to arbitration. The line is drawn between *intra*- and *extra*-EU arbitration or, more precisely, between disputes that are EU law-related and those that are not, as long as the latter do not call into question EU standards and the role of the Court in interpreting these.

(iii) Critique

The question remains whether this line, distinguishing the conclusion in the CETA-Opinion from that in *Achmea* (see A (ii) above), is convincing. The Court relied heavily on the meticulous drafting of CETA. It was hence satisfied that the degree of EU public interest protection remained unchallenged.[122] For example, the CJEU referred to Annex 8-A,[123] which is reminiscent of the police powers

[119] Opinion 1/17 *CETA* (n104) paras 148–50.

[120] Ibid at para 151. This squares with Opinion 2/13 (*ECHR Accession*) and *Achmea* (see A (ii) above).

[121] Pointing, eg, to Art 28.3.2 (carving out measures necessary to protect public security or public morals or to maintain public order or to protect human, animal or plant life or health in a way that is very similar to the *chapeau* of GATT Article XX), to Art 8.9.1 (safeguarding the state's regulatory powers concerning 'legitimate policy objectives, such as the protection of public health, safety, the environment or public morals, social or consumer protection or the promotion and protection of cultural diversity'), and to Art 8.9.2 (emphasising that 'the mere fact that a Party regulates, including through a modification to its laws, in a manner which negatively affects an investment or interferes with an investor's expectations, including its expectations of profits, does not amount to a breach of this Section [on investment protection]'). Ibid at paras 152–54. The CJEU also drew comfort from the Joint Interpretative Instrument providing that CETA 'will … not lower [the standards and regulations of each Party] related to food safety, product safety, consumer protection, health, environment or labour protection' and that CETA 'preserves the ability of the European Union and its Member States and Canada to adopt and apply their own laws and regulations that regulate economic activity in the public interest'. Ibid at para 155.

[122] Ibid.

[123] Ibid at para 157. Point 3 of this Annex states that 'except in the rare circumstances when the impact of a measure (…) is so severe in light of its purpose that it appears manifestly excessive, non-discriminatory measures (…) that are designed and applied to protect legitimate public welfare objectives, such as health, safety and the environment, do not constitute indirect expropriations'.

doctrine regarding indirect expropriation.[124] Nevertheless, this is a thin basis for the following reason:

In practice, it may be difficult to determine whether a measure is genuinely enacted for a public purpose, and at the same time applied in a manner that does not, *de facto*, discriminate against a foreign investor. The EU itself has experience with this under the *Keck* case law[125] regarding indistinctly applicable state measures that may still have to be scrutinised for disparate impact or incidental burden on foreigners. In other words, there is no absolute 'right to regulate' for Member States under EU law, so there is no reason to take this for granted under an EU (mixed) international law agreement such as CETA.

Similarly, the EU's experience with the World Trade Organisation (WTO) illustrates that the carve-out of regulatory space in certain policy areas (eg Article XX of the GATT) does not stop WTO panels and its Appellate Body from applying a more or less strict proportionality test to measures pursuing such policies, which can – as far as certain implementing measures are concerned – still result in the finding of a breach of international trade law.[126]

Also, from an ITA perspective, the police powers doctrine is no guarantee for regulatory space of host states. Even if it achieves some balance between the state's regulatory interest on the one hand, and the protection against expropriation on the other, there remain other investment protection standards, in particular fair and equitable treatment (FET). This can be illustrated by the plain packaging case against Uruguay.[127] All three arbitrators were in agreement that the police powers doctrine – applied as part of customary international law (ie even without explicit treaty language to this effect) excluded a finding of expropriation. However, one arbitrator dissented from the overall decision in favour of the state, arguing that the contradictory way in which the challenged measures had been interpreted by the domestic courts breached the FET.[128] Although the CJEU was satisfied that

[124] *Chemtura Corporation v Government of Canada* (Award, 2 August 2010), para 266. Available at: www.italaw.com/sites/default/files/case-documents/ita0149_0.pdf.

[125] Joined Cases C-267 and 268/91 *Criminal Proceedings against Bernard Keck and Daniel Mithouard* ECLI:EU:C:1993:905. For a critical appraisal of the evolution of the case law see, eg, Stefan Enchelmaier, 'The Development of the Free Movement Principles over Time' in Sacha Garben and Inge Govaere (eds), *Internal Market 2.0*, Modern Studies in European Law, 102 (Oxford, Hart Publishing, forthcoming 2020).

[126] Appellate Body Reports *European Communities – Measures Prohibiting the Importation and Marketing of Seal Products*, WT/DS400/AB/R,WT/DS401/AB/R (22 May 2014). See, eg, Rob Howse, Joanna Langille and Katie Sykes, 'Sealing the Deal: The WTO Appellate Body's Report in EC-Seal Products' (2014) 18 *American Society of International Law*. Available at: www.asil.org/insights/volume/18/issue/12/sealing-deal-wto%E2%80%99s-appellate-body-report-ec-%E2%80%93-seal-products.

[127] *Philip Morris Brands SÀRL et al v Oriental Republic of Uruguay* ICSID Case No ARB/10/7 (Award, 8 July 2016). Available at: www.italaw.com/sites/default/files/case-documents/italaw7417.pdf. To be precise, the measures challenged were certain presentation requirements (only one single presentation per brand), and the required insertion of graphic health warnings.

[128] *Philip Morris Brands SÀRL et al v Oriental Republic of Uruguay* ICSID Case No ARB/10/7 (Concurring and Dissenting Opinion by Arbitrator Gary Born, 8 July 2016). Available at: www.italaw.com/sites/default/files/case-documents/italaw7428.pdf.

investment protection under CETA's FET clause was sufficiently circumscribed,[129] this would not help in a similar scenario where it could be argued that EU or Member State regulation, as interpreted by the courts, remains unclear or even contradictory.

The Court's confidence in a strictly textual interpretation of CETA can only partially be explained by the distinction between an *intra*-EU and an *extra*-EU scenario. One could argue that an EU agreement with third countries would lead to irritations for EU law from the outside, which could ultimately be dealt with under the rules set out by the Court in *Kadi* (chapter two, I C (i)). By contrast, irritations originating in an agreement between Member States irritates the EU from within. In a worst-case scenario, this could lead to the non-acceptance of EU primacy by the Member States, and ultimately a break-up of the union. This is a risk the Court could never take.

Another likely explanation for the generous approach in the CETA Opinion is a genuine desire by the Court to sell itself and the EU as a reliable international player. This works only if the EU itself believes in an international law agreement, negotiated and drafted by the EU. One could justify this by referring to the ICS established under CETA (ie the *quasi*-institutionalised approach to ITA) (see (ii) above). Arguably there is a real chance that the future CETA tribunals will take a moderate stance and balance investors rights and the public interest in a way that is not biased towards business.

In any event, the Court only opined on the draft agreement as such, not on any arbitration case arising thereunder. The CETA Opinion could, therefore, be understood as saying that ITA under CETA is unproblematic from an EU law perspective, but only as long as the safeguards for the EU public interest above, as well as the Court's role under Article 19 TEU, are respected in arbitration practice. Such an interpretation is aimed at increasing the legitimacy of ITA and its interaction with EU law, which will be explained in chapter four.

[129] Opinion 1/17 CETA (n 104) at para 158.

4

Building Trust in Legal Outcomes of EU Law and International Arbitration

I. The Challenges

At the outset, this book distinguished between contractual freedom and the need for legality, in particular regarding state action. The latter is at the centre of investment treaty arbitration (ITA).[1] Accordingly, the arbitral case law in ITA has always been shifting between an emphasis on economic rights on the one hand, and state regulatory interests on the other.[2] For some time now, the cases as well as the academic debate in investment law have focused on the quest for legitimacy in investment law and arbitration. This originates in an understanding that puts legality before freedom. In this chapter, it will first be explained what legitimacy means and why it is difficult to address this in the transnational context. Secondly, potential reforms at the EU level that might alleviate its interaction with international arbitration so as to improve societal acceptance will be considered.

A. The Problem of Legitimacy in a Transnational Context

(i) What is Legitimacy?

In systems theoretical terms, legitimacy is a rather narrow issue. Luhmann first distinguishes the legitimacy of a decision's content from the procedure or process in which it was arrived at.[3] For him, the former is a non-issue or, more precisely, a question that correctly figures under the question of whether a decision is legal. So, the notion of legitimacy would not add anything here. By contrast, following Luhmann, one would have to concentrate on the latter. Legitimacy can, therefore, only be about procedure. Procedure or process is understood as yet another

[1] In international commercial arbitration, the same tension can arise when there is a state party to the proceedings (see A (iv) below) for what has been called *investomercial* arbitration).

[2] The police powers doctrine (or, the so-called 'right to regulate' referred to in ch 3, II B (iii)) would be one example of the latter. Its counterpart, the so-called 'sole effects' test for indirect expropriation would be an example of the former, see, eg *Metaclad Corp v United Mexican States* ICSID ARB(AF)/97/1 (Award, 30 August 2000). Available at: www.italaw.com/sites/default/files/case-documents/ita0510.pdf.

[3] Niklas Luhmann, *Legitimation durch Verfahren*, 3rd edn (Darmstadt, Luchterhand, 1978), 1–2.

system of its own. It achieves legitimacy if it is structured in a way that allows for the acceptance of a decision's substance independent of its correctness.[4]

What do such structures look like? Luhmann states that the search for the truth must always lie at the heart of the procedure/process. 'Truth' does not represent a value, but a *medium* of communication and hence has a specific social function. This function is to transfer complexity that has already been reduced.[5] People engage with each other based on particular certainties that everyone must be able to take for granted. Truth in this sense is only the base line of the procedure or process, since there are other *media* that could serve the same function (ie a transfer of reduced complexity). Power is an example of this: whoever is in power can induce others to comply (ie adapt their behaviour accordingly). The function of power is the same as the function of truth in that a reduction of complexity is passed on. The difference between truth and power is that there might well be a reason to try and rebel against the latter. Power hence needs further legitimisation. Legitimising factors of power are *reasons* that convince people to act in line with authority, that is, to accept the decisions of those in power.

Luhmann concludes that any legitimising factors must strive for a reduction of complexity, and create reasons for the acceptance of decisions so as to avoid a recourse to force.[6] This is why legal arguments or the reasoning of a decision play a central role under systems theory: they build structure and enhance legitimacy at the same time. For the latter, the reasoning must at least be formally convincing so as to be accepted as binding. This means that one must not be convinced of the substantive correctness of a decision – recall Luhmann's scepticism about *the* correct outcome above.[7] Instead, acceptance is generalised: complex societies can work only if everyone can expect that decisions that have been arrived at within a certain framework will be accepted. This formal or procedural definition of legitimacy from systems theory must be contrasted with a more substantive one, which is nowadays prevalent in EU law as well as in international arbitration.

(ii) The Legitimacy Debate in EU Law

As for EU law, the legitimacy question has always been linked to the EU's supranational character, in particular its increase in powers, coupled with the direct effect of EU law and its claim for primacy over national laws. It is well-known under the

[4] Ibid at 3–5. Luhmann departs from the assumption that in highly complex social systems there is never one correct decision that would be universally valid, or valid forever. Rationally acting individuals will always strive for their own benefit and seek compensation for personal losses. Societal consensus must hence be sought step by step, time and time again. So there is a learning curve over a period of time.

[5] Ibid at 23. For more detail see ch 2, I B (iv).

[6] Ibid at 25–26.

[7] See n 4.

notion of democratic deficit. This can mean various things, and thus can serve very different agendas.[8] One could approach it as a more general issue that is not limited to the EU since it applies to both the privatisation and Europeanisation of (national) industries.[9] For EU lawyers, democratic legitimacy has long presented a benchmark against which to judge EU governance,[10] with specific regard to the composition and decision-making of the EU institutions.[11] Democratic legitimacy is here generally understood in terms of formal representation and traceable connection between EU voter and EU action. This has been fleshed out by new standards such as input *versus* output legitimacy.[12]

The benchmark of democracy has subsequently been adapted to the transnational context,[13] and the focus has shifted to participation through deliberation.[14] The debate has increasingly centered on issues such as whether there is a European public in the classical form of a *demos*,[15] and through which platforms it could be mobilised. It is worth noting that the intensity of the problem is increasing with the EU's development from a market organisation into a political union. But even if one concentrates on the EU's role as economic regulator – similarly to, eg, WTO-made law – there remains a problem of legitimacy that goes to the substance of its output: to the weighing of different interests, and hence to the acceptance of the EU and its decisions.

This is where democratic deficit stands for a fair balance between economic and non-economic interests. Following the Maastricht treaty, the issue became known as social legitimacy of the EU (then the European Community),[16] which

[8] See the systematic overview and analysis by Thomas Jensen, 'The Democratic Deficit of the European Union' (2009) *Living Reviews in Democracy*. Available at: https://pdfs.semanticscholar.org/f45d/b3bdd50dd40d06df9ad974d8acf8df168a4b.pdf.

[9] Giandomenico Majone, 'The Regulatory State and its Legitimacy Problems', *Reihe Politikwissenschaft / Institut für Höhere Studien, Politikwissenschaft* 56 (Wien, July 1998). Available at: https://nbn-resolving org/urn:nbn:de:0168-ssoar-246700.

[10] Joseph HH Weiler, Ulrich R Haltern, and Franz C Mayer, 'European Democracy and its Critique' (1995) 18 *West European Politics* 4.

[11] For more recent analyses see, eg, Vivien A Schmidt, 'The Eurozone's Crisis of Democratic Legitimacy: Can the EU Rebuild Public Trust and Support for European Economic Integration?' *European Commission Directorate-General for Economic and Financial Affairs Discussion Paper* 015 (2015). Available at: http://publications.europa.eu/resource/cellar/b4f269c4-8907-11e5-b8b7-01aa75ed71a1.0001.02/DOC_2. See also Michael Shackleton, 'Transforming Representative Democracy in the EU? The Role of the European Parliament' (2017) 39 *West European Politics* 191.

[12] Fritz W Scharpf, *Governing in Europe: Effective and Democratic?* (Oxford, Oxford University Press, 1999).

[13] Critically regarding the use of democracy as a national concept see, eg, Andrew Moravcsik, 'Reassessing Legitimacy in the European Union' (2002) 40 *Journal of Common Market Studies* 603.

[14] See, eg, John S Dryzek, *Deliberative Global Politics: Discourse and Democracy in a Divided World* (Cambridge, Polity Press, 2006).

[15] Critically regarding the usefulness of traditional concepts see, eg, Daniel Innerarity, 'Does Europe Need a Demos to be Truly Democratic?' (2014) *LSE 'Europe in Question' Discussion Paper Series* 77. Available at: www.lse.ac.uk/european-institute/Assets/Documents/LEQS-Discussion-Papers/LEQS Paper77.pdf.

[16] Joseph HH Weiler, 'After Maastricht: Community Legitimacy in Post-1992 Europe' in William J Adams (ed), *Singular Europe: Economy and Polity of the European Community after 1992* (Ann Arbor, University of Michigan Press, 1992), 11.

became increasingly important in light of new EU social rights,[17] and again following the financial and the Euro crises.[18] The issue of social rights has been discussed in particular when social policies were scrutinised in light of fundamental (market) freedoms. The problem here is that the EU is not a social, but an economic organisation. Its competencies regarding social policies are limited, the general understanding being that social redistribution remains firmly in the power of its Member States. And the EU is not a nation state where solidarity amongst its citizen may have grown over a long period of time. This means that, compared to its Member States, the EU is less well equipped to achieve distributive justice.

In light of the financial and banking as well as the Euro crises, the EU has not been perceived as delivering on its promise of increased societal welfare based on free markets. The Corona pandemic illustrates that emergency health and safety policies are implemented along national lines. In short, the more profound non-economic interests get, the more superfluous an international economic organisation like the EU appears to be. People are turning to their nation state for a social safety net.

(iii) The Legitimacy Debate in ITA

The question of whether and how to solve the public interest in transnational dispute settlement has become a crucial question for the future of ITA. Here, the legitimacy debate[19] originated in problems deriving from the hybrid nature of ITA (ie the fact that public law type disputes are being judged *extra*-judicially). The question of why a 'private' arbitration tribunal should be allowed to decide on issues of public interest has triggered various suggestions for reform.[20]

[17] Eg, when fundamental (economic) freedoms clashed with workers' rights: see Mark R Friedland and Jeremias Adams-Prassl, *Viking, Laval and Beyond* (Oxford, Hart Publishing, 2016).

[18] See, eg, Sacha Garben, 'The Constitutional (Im)balance between "the Market" and "the Social" in the European Union' (2017) 13 *European Constitutional Law Review* 23, Dagmar Schiek, 'Towards More Resilience for a Social EU – the Constitutionally Conditioned Internal Market' (2017) 13 *European Constitutional Law Review* 611.

[19] Eg Susan D Franck, 'The Legitimacy Crisis in Investment Treaty Arbitration: Privatizing Public International Law through Inconsistent Decisions' (2005) 73 *Fordham Law Review* 1521. From an EU perspective, see Steffen Hindelang, 'Study on Investor-State Dispute Settlement (ISDS) and Alternatives of Dispute Resolution in International Investment Law' in European Parliament, Directorate-General for External Policies of the Union (Directorate B, Policy Department), *Study: Investor–State Dispute Settlement (ISDS) Provisions in the EU's International Investment Agreements Vol 2 – Studies*, EXPO/B/INTA/2014/08-09-10, Part II, 39 (September 2014).

[20] Dogmatically, this was addressed by defining the degree of deference owed by tribunals to the regulatory state, see Anthea Roberts, 'The Next Battleground: Standards of Review in Investment Treaty Arbitration' (2011) 16 *International Council for Commercial Arbitration Congress Series* 170. Available at: https://ssrn.com/abstract=2186208; Caroline Henckels, 'Balancing Investment Protection and the Public Interest: The Role of the Standard of Review and the Importance of Deference in Investor-State Arbitration' (2013) 4 *Journal of International Dispute Settlement* 197. See also the systematic and critical overview of reform proposals by Hindelang (n 19) 56–113.

In 2015, the public online consultation by the EU Commission regarding the envisaged Transatlantic Trade and Investment Partnership Agreement (TTIP) resulted in an overall finding of 'widespread opposition to … ISDS in TTIP or in general'.[21] The quest for legitimacy has been taken on at different levels.[22] In procedural terms, it translates into issues such as whether arbitration is sufficiently transparent (ie whether non-parties should have access to proceedings) and whether awards or other documents should be made public.[23] In substantive terms, it leads to considerations of fairness, in particular balancing investment protection and other societal concerns. Proposals to narrow the definition of protected investment (eg by way of closed lists) or to recalibrate standards of investment protection, including certain exceptions or carve-outs, belong here.[24]

Moreover, one can also look to the decision-makers in ITA. Departing from the typical background of repeat players (see chapter two, I A), this has led to requests for a larger or more mixed pool of arbitrators to exclude any systemic bias and improve impartiality especially by stricter rules regarding conflicts of interest.[25] The most significant reform – other than an outright abandonment of ITA – would be institutional.[26] This is driven by the *post*-Lisbon European agenda, which is ultimately planning institutional reform by replacing *ad hoc* tribunals with a multilateral investment court.[27]

[21] Commission Report (Staff Working Document), 'Online public consultation on investment protection and investor-to-state dispute settlement (ISDS) in the Trade and Investment Partnership Agreement' (SWD(2015) 3 final), 14.

[22] See UNCTAD IIA Issues Note (June 2019). Available at: https://unctad.org/en/PublicationsLibrary/diaepcbinf2019d5_en.pdf (categorising potential reform into 'improved procedures', 'limited ISDS', and 'standing ISDS tribunal').

[23] Resulting in the adoption of the United Nations Convention on Transparency in Treaty-based Investor-State Arbitration (the 'Mauritius Convention on Transparency') of 10 December 2014. Available at: https://treaties.un.org/Pages/ViewDetails.aspx?src=TREATY&mtdsg_no=XXII-3&chapter=22&clang=_en. See Stephan Schill, 'The Mauritius Convention on Transparency: A Model for Investment Law Reform?' *EJIL:Talk!* (8 April 2015). Available at: www.ejiltalk.org/the-mauritius-convention-on-transparency-a-model-for-investment-law-reform/.

[24] See Vera Korzun, 'The Right to Regulate in Investor-State Arbitration: Slicing and Dicing Regulatory Carve-Outs' (2017) 50 *Vanderbilt Journal of Transnational Law* 355.

[25] See James D Fry and Juan I Stampalija, 'Forged Independence and Impartiality: Conflicts of Interest of International Arbitrators in Investment Disputes' (2014) 30 *Arbitration International* 189.

[26] Gus van Harten, 'A Case for an International Investment Court' *Society of International Law* (SIEL) *Inaugural Conference 2008 Paper*. Available at: www.ssrn.com/abstract=1153424. See also, Lukasz Kulaga, 'A Brave, New International Investment Court in Context: Towards a Paradigm Shift of the ISDS' (2012) 38 *Polish Yearbook of International Law* 115. Available at: https://ssrn.com/abstract=3448233.

[27] See Chapter Eight of the EU-Canadian Free Trade agreement (CETA) and the Investment Court System (ISC) established thereunder (see ch 3, II B, text available at https://ec.europa.eu/trade/policy/in-focus/ceta/ceta-chapter-by-chapter/). Here, the EU is pursuing a permanent form of dispute settlement with an envisaged multilateral investment court (CETA Art 8.29), see also August Reinisch, 'The European Union and Investor-State Dispute Settlement: from Investor–State Arbitration to a Permanent Investment Court' (2016) *Centre for International Governance Innovation* (CIGI) *Investor-State Arbitration Series* 2. Available at: www.cigionline.org/sites/default/files/isa_paper_series_no.2.pdf.

Nevertheless, there is a deeper dimension to the legitimacy debate in ITA. This can be traced back to a sharp divide regarding the function of international investment law. On the one hand, this could be seen as protecting private investments with a view to achieving an overall higher standard of wealth in a global economy. In the literature, this is referred to as 'neoliberal theory', which embraces the free market model of the Western world.

On the other hand, from the perspective of developing countries, international investment law could be seen as a more-or-less ill-equipped development tool. This has been known as dependency theory,[28] focusing on the real impact of unregulated flows of investment in non-Western countries. This divide could be labelled as theoretical or ideological: essentially, it contrasts a belief in private investment and free markets with a belief in state regulation. This underlies the debate over investor *obligations*,[29] where the different perspectives of those who believe in free markets and those who believe in the state are most visible.

Against this background, the legitimacy debate in ITA can be seen as the sequel to the discussion of a new economic order under international law.[30] The difference is that the dichotomy between economic freedom and societal needs is no longer just playing out between developed and developing countries. The divide between winners and losers of globalisation is increasingly being felt in highly developed societies. For example, this has had wide repercussions within the European public in the wake of such mega trade agreements as the TTIP (above).

This lack of trust suggests that procedural reforms of ITA are unlikely to address the root of the problem. Even substantive or institutional reforms are facing considerable challenges, which are pointedly formulated by Sornarajah when warning that the 'same ideology preferences for investment protection may come to be stated more authoritatively by judges in court'.[31]

Seen this way, the debate is reminiscent of the EU discussion about the weighing of economic versus social integration (see above). It becomes clearest when considering the question of why multinational corporations (ie *capitalist* enterprises) and their lawyers (ie the *private elite*), should be the sole winners of an ad hoc system of adjudication with no or very limited appellate oversight.[32]

[28] Muthucumaraswamy Sornarajah, *The International Law on Foreign Investment*, 4th edn (Cambridge, CUP, 2017) 67 et seq.

[29] See, eg, Anne Peters, *Beyond Human Rights: The Legal Status of the Individual in International Law* (Cambridge, Cambridge University Press, 2016), 339 et seq.

[30] See already Michel Virally, 'Vers un droit international du développement' (1965) 11 *Annuaire Français de Droit International* 3, Jean Touscoz, *Transferts de technologie: sociétés transnationales et nouvel ordre international* (Paris, PUF, 1978). See also Alain Pellet, 'Contre la tyrannie de la ligne droite; aspects de la formation des normes en droit international de l'économie et du dévelopment' (1992) 19 *Thesaurus Acroasium* 291. For a more recent overview see Ahmed Mahiou, 'Du droit économique au nouvel ordre économique international: quelques réflexions' (2013) 27 *Revue international de droit économique* 523.

[31] Sornarajah (n 28), 323.

[32] Critically, Christian J Tams, 'An Appealing Option: The Debate About an ICSID Appellate Structure' *Beiträge zum Transnationalen Wirtschaftsrecht* 57 (June 2006). Available at: http://telc.jura.uni-halle.de/sites/default/files/altbestand/Heft57.pdf. See also the edited collection by Karl P Sauvant (ed), *Appeals Mechanism in International Investment Disputes* (Oxford, Oxford University Press, 2008).

From this perspective, it would seem only natural to phrase the issue as serving *the many* as opposed to *the few* or, more technically, as question of room for democratic choices in ITA.[33] This is where the debate has been heading over the past few years: from legitimacy to democracy, which is understood in terms of adequate protection of non-economic rights of domestic societies. In other words, like in the EU, the issue is not just how to ensure voter representation or participation in the process. Instead, it is about societal fairness of results.

(iv) Repercussions for ICA

The experience from the legitimacy debate in EU law and in ITA indicates that this question is part of a broader problem, which is likely to have repercussions for any action of public authorities or state-owned entities. This means that it can easily extend to arbitration against states or state-owned entities more generally. The issue has already been taken up by the notion of 'investomercial' arbitration.[34]

To recall, arbitration proceedings against a state cannot only be brought based on an investment treaty, but also on an investment contract. What does EU law imply for such cases? The CJEU has so far only subjected unilateral offers by Member States in investment treaties to Article 344 TFEU (see chapter three, II A (ii)). But this raises the question of whether arbitration agreements between a state and a private party could generally be understood as involving state action. Put differently, why should a Member State be hindered from offering to arbitrate in an investment treaty, but not in an investment or other commercial contract with public impact? Disputes under commercial contracts can also concern the interpretation and application of EU law in the same way as disputes under investment treaties.

Furthermore, even cases between two private parties can have obvious implications for the broader public. One of the standard cases on confidentiality, an essential feature of ICA and anathema to the critics of ITA, was a commercial arbitration between *Esso* and two public utility companies. Subsequently, the question arose of whether the material produced during the arbitration, including transcripts and evidentiary material, must be labelled as confidential and hence withheld in court proceedings.[35] The Chief Justice of the Australian High Court explained that the court must honour the difference between commercial secrecy

[33] David Schneiderman, 'Against Constitutional Excess: Toquevillian Reflections on International Investment Law' (2018) 85 *University of Chicago Law Review* 585, 586 (describing this as 'democratic backsliding' due to 'shrinking policy space').

[34] Charles N Brower used the term 'investomercial' arbitration for commercial arbitration against a state party, see Isabella Bellera Landa, 'State Parties in Contract-Based Arbitration: A Report from the 16th Annual ITA-ASIL Conference'. Available at: http://arbitrationblog.kluwerarbitration.com/2019/06/17/state-parties-in-contract-based-arbitration-a-report-from-the-16th-annual-ita-asil-conference.

[35] In *Esso Australia Resources Ltd v Plowman*, (1995) 11 *Arbitration International* 3 at 235, the Australian High Court held that confidentiality did not automatically apply to such documents, distinguishing the private nature of the hearing itself.

as the rule, and governmental secrets as an exception. Since there was a legitimate public interest in obtaining information about the affairs of the companies in question – evidenced by a likely impact of the arbitration on oil prices – the general rule of disclosure as to public affairs prevailed.[36]

This illustrates that the public interest is not necessarily a non-issue in ICA. It just plays out differently. In *Esso* it arose in the form of a flexible approach to the often-assumed principle of confidentiality in commercial arbitration.[37] It can also arise with a view to determining whether the subject matter is arbitrable in the first place. Cases involving competition law have been pointed out before in this respect (see chapter two, II).

Moreover, in ICA, there are other levels beyond both procedural issues and arbitrability where the public interest might come into play. One concerns the question of which courts have the jurisdiction to intervene. The French *Ryanair* case can serve as an example in this respect. It concerned two contracts between SMAC, a French state-owned entity responsible for the operation of a local airport (Angoulême), and Ryanair, together with one of its subsidiaries. The agreements provided for the establishment of a regular air link between London and Angoulême as well as related marketing services.

Ryanair terminated the contracts and instituted LCIA arbitration proceedings pursuant to contractual arbitration clauses. By contrast, SMAC brought court proceedings before the Poitiers Administrative Tribunal, relying on public procurement rules and issues arising from the occupation of public law. When the London arbitrator confirmed its jurisdiction, the case reached the ordinary French courts by way of enforcement proceedings.

This led to the question of whether the administrative or the ordinary French courts – if any[38] – were competent to serve as enforcement courts for the arbitration. Commercial tradition would speak in favour of the ordinary courts, any elements of mandatory public law notwithstanding. However, this may be questioned from the point of view of an administrative court that, in principle, has jurisdiction over the subject matter under national law.

The jurisdictional conflict went through all instances in both the ordinary and the administrative courts, finally reaching a specialised court, the *Tribunal des Conflits*. This found in favour of the administrative courts, reasoning that the agreements were public services contracts under French public law (the *Code de marchés publics*) and hence subject to mandatory public procurement rules.[39] By contrast, it stated that ordinary French courts would have jurisdiction over the

[36] Ibid at 247–49.

[37] Dogmatically, however, this depends on the applicable arbitration law and – if any – institutional rules under which an arbitration is being conducted.

[38] The *Conseil d'État* sympathised with the argument that the supervisory function was for the London court (as seat court) to fulfil, Conseil d'État No 352750 (19 April 2013) ECLI:FR:XX:2013:352750.20130419.

[39] *Tribunal des Conflits No C 4075* (24 April 2017). Available at: https://beta.legifrance.gouv.fr/ceta/id/CETATEXT000034478477.

enforcement of foreign awards relating to contracts concerning international trade interests.

In conclusion, if there is an argument that the contract goes beyond commercial interests and raises issues of mandatory public law or the occupation of public land, the administrative courts will have jurisdiction regarding the enforcement of ensuing awards.[40]

This distinction between trade and public interests is remarkable, especially since its timing coincided with the peak of the legitimacy debate in investment law and arbitration. It illustrates that mandatory rules in ICA have a public law connotation that can be so strong as to divest ordinary courts of their jurisdiction – provided there are special administrative courts to fill the void, as would be the case in some civil law jurisdictions such as France or Germany.

From a commercial lawyer's perspective, it is highly relevant to consider that it may not be a civil or commercial court that functions as a supervisory court for an arbitration, but rather as administrative court. The latter will typically be much more open to arguments that the ultimately prevailing legal principle is that of legality, and not necessarily *pacta sunt servanda.*

Compliance with mandatory public law can also reach the substance of the transaction. This can be illustrated by the case of *Neckarpri GMBH v EDF International SAS (v Baden-Württemberg as Additional Party)*,[41] which concerned a share deal regarding a stake in the German energy company *Energie Baden-Württemberg* (EnBW). Neckarpri, a private limited liability company wholly owned by the German land Baden-Württemberg, claimed that the contract with which it had purchased EDF's stake in EnBW was excessively priced and hence contained state aid that was illegal under EU law.

State aid must normally be notified to the EU Commission. If the Commission finds that it is incompatible with the internal market, it orders that the aid must be abolished or altered (Article 108(2) TFEU). If the aid has already been paid out, it must be recovered by the state. This can be achieved under national law by rendering the respective contract null and void. Accordingly, the claimant in the *EDF* case (and the Baden-Württemberg state) argued that the state-aid element of the share price had to be recovered; alternatively, that the share purchase agreement was null and void.

[40] An equivalent approach applies to the division of competencies between French ordinary and administrative courts regarding the annulment of domestic arbitration awards, see the *Inserm* decision by the *Cour de Cassation* No 09-10198 (26 January 2011). Available at: https://beta.legifrance.gouv.fr/juri/id/JURITEXT000023495292. This shows its general validity, including both national and international arbitration and the enforcement and annulment of awards.

[41] ICC 18519/GFG; the facts here reported are taken from Commission Opinion of 19 September 2014, which the EU Commission provided to one of the arbitrators. Available at: https://ec.europa.eu/competition/court/neckarpri_en.pdf). See also the summary by Gaillard, Emmanuel, Darrigade Coralie, Reich, Daniel, 'Shearman & Sterling Secures Victory for EDF in Dispute Over German Power Company Sale'. Available at: www.shearman.com/en/newsinsights/news/2016/05/secures-victory-for-edf-in-dispute-over-german (Shearman summary).

The arbitration tribunal was divided over the question of whether there was indeed any state aid, in the absence of a notification to the EU Commission.[42] But it held unanimously that the state-owned entity could not rely on the state's own failure to notify the aid in the first place. So the share purchase agreement and the price agreed remained valid, irrespective of (potential) state aid.

From a contractual perspective, this reasoning is perfectly sound. It can be based on the relevant contract, in particular – as was the case here – if it contains a compliance clause that can be read as assurance of the necessary notification (or the fact that this is unnecessary under the circumstances). It can also rely on the *venire contra factum proprium* principle, in particular, the fact no one should be allowed to benefit from his/her own previous wrongdoing. In the world of ICA, this was, therefore, a sound decision.

Nevertheless, the Commission in its above-mentioned opinion[43] suggested a very different outcome. The Commission relied on the principle of effectiveness in the Court's case law, and especially in EU state aid law: the purpose of EU state aid law is to prevent – or, as the case may be, remedy – the distortion of competition by strengthening the position by a specific economic operator to the detriment of others. To this end, it must be ensured that state measures – including payments agreed in contracts concluded by state-owned companies – are notified to the Commission if they may distort competition by granting a price that could not be achieved on the market. It is then the Commission's responsibility to scrutinise the measure for compatibility with the internal market.

Based on EU state aid law, the Commission is clearly taking a regulatory perspective, focusing on the legality of state action. This means that the moment a state aid issue is raised by the parties, the case arguably follows public law programming. This explains why reference to principles of contract law and the question of who should be allowed to rely on what is no longer sufficient. What matters is that the state aid issue is properly dealt with.

The problem is reminiscent of the ITA cases that first brought to light potential conflicts between EU state aid law and *intra*-EU investment protection.[44]

[42] One arbitrator was of the view that there was a state aid component of which the Commission should have been notified. See the Shearman summary above (n 41). It should be noted that unnotified state aid is generally unlawful, but not necessarily incompatible with the internal market.

[43] See n 41 above.

[44] See *AES Summit Generation Limited and AES-Tisza Erömü Kft v Hungary* ICSID Case No ARB/07/22 (Award, 23 September 2010). Available at: www.italaw.com/sites/default/files/case-documents/ita0014_0.pdf; *Electrabel SA v Hungary* ICSID Case No ARB/07/19 (Award, 25 November 2015). Available at: www.italaw.com/sites/default/files/case-documents/italaw4495.pdf (both arbitrations under the Energy Charter Treaty). A well-known example of EU state aid issues arising in an ITA based on a bilateral investment treaty between EU Member States (*intra*-EU BIT) is *Ioan Micula et al v Romania* ICSID Case No ARB/05/20 (Award, 11 December 2013). Available at: www.italaw.com/sites/default/files/case-documents/italaw3036.pdf. This award, however, could not settle the arbitration, in particular the state aid issue. Romania brought an action for annulment under ICSID and the EU Commission formally declared the damages awarded to the plaintiffs to constitute (new) State aid (Commission Decision (EU) 2015/1470 of 30 March 2015 on State aid SA.38517 (2014/C) (ex 2014/NN) implemented by Romania – Arbitral award *Micula v Romania* of 11 December 2013 (notified

The Commission has been consistently arguing from an EU regulatory perspective, which will typically benefit the state whose measure is under scrutiny. By contrast, it is the contractual view that matters for the other party. These two perspectives are equally valid, but the opposing interests need to be balanced against each other in a way that remains respectful of both. Adding the protection of democratic choices to the side of the state whose measures are under scrutiny upsets this balance.

B. Fundamental Risk for the International Legal System

(i) Democracy as a Benchmark?

There are several problems with democracy as a benchmark for decision-making in individual cases. For a start, democracy does not fit a transnational structure. Legally scrutinising a state measure while making way for democratic choices means looking to the *national* public interest.[45] In a transnational context, however, there is no place for a purely national interest. And why should there be? States have entered international obligations limiting their national choices in the first place. For example, the aim of the EU as a market organisation was to counter protectionism. Hence, it is not enough to now stress the democratic choice to protect one's own industries to the detriment of foreign ones.

National democracies remain free to push for changes to these international obligations. Nevertheless, while they are in place, using democracy as a defence is akin to using domestic laws to defend against international treaty obligations. Put pointedly, democracy remains a national concept,[46] and hence it falls short of accounting for the public interest in a transnational context. What started out as dichotomy between private and public interests becomes a strain on internationalism and *international* scrutiny of state action.

under document C(2015) 2112) [2015] OJ L232/43. The General Court quashed this decision in Cases T-624/15, T-694/15 and T-704/15 *European Food SA et al v European Commission* ECLI:EU:T:2019:423 para 91, holding that the Commission had overstepped its competencies. The General Court left open the question of whether an arbitration award that orders compensation for withdrawal of tax incentives in breach of EU state aid law (for the time after EU accession) could constitute new state aid. At the time of writing, the case was pending on appeal under C-638/19P *Commission v European Food and Others.*

[45] This can be illustrated by the reasons with which the European Court of Human Rights (ECtHR) justifies deference to states by employing the margin of appreciation doctrine: 'Because of their direct knowledge of their society and its needs, the national authorities are in principle better placed than the international judge to appreciate what is "in the public interest". Under the system of protection established by the Convention, it is thus for the national authorities to make the initial assessment both of the existence of a problem of public concern warranting measures of deprivation of property and of the remedial action to be taken.' *James and Others v The United Kingdom (Application no 8793/79)* ECtHR Judgment of 21 February 1986 para 46. Available at: http://hudoc.echr.coe.int.

[46] This is well recognised in the literature on legal pluralism and global governance, see, eg, Peer Zumbansen, 'Defining the Space of Transnational Law: Legal Theory, Global Governance and Legal Pluralism' (26 September 2011) *Osgoode CLPE Research Paper No 21/2011*. Available at: www.ssrn.com/abstract=1934044.

The other problem with democracy as a benchmark when scrutinising state measures is that it sits uneasily with the rule of law. Democracy is both a legal and a political concept for the nation state. In a democracy, it is the majority (in parliament) that makes and changes the laws. It is part of the political system insofar as political choices are being made. These political choices are then (in the form of laws) processed via the legal system, which uses its own programmes.[47] Democratic law-making provides irritations for the modern legal system, which focuses on the law as set – legal positivism – and vice versa. At the same time, the democratic state structurally couples the legal with the political system, thereby excluding other irritations such as corruption, political terror or abuse of economic power for driving general politics.[48]

On the upside, this means that discussing the 'democratic deficit' can engage both political scientists and lawyers. It is the nation state in which ordinary people have a voice by way of voting and representation. The downside, however, is that an additional differentiation enters the picture. It was seen in chapter two (I D (i)) that ICA is about squaring law with economics. ITA – and arbitration involving states more generally – adds to this the task of processing irritations from the political system: in other words, it needs to connect law with both economics and politics.

Irritations from the political system lead to the well-known question of how to justify *legal* review of state action (ie scrutiny under the law of decisions originating in the political process).[49] This question has, over time, been more or less hotly debated in the national context.[50] For example, in the process of US independence, James Otis started to conceptualise the people as the supreme power, so as to build a Constitutional (law) argument against the binding power of certain acts of the English parliament.[51]

In a transnational context, such an argument is much more difficult to run, given the fact that there is no global *pouvoir constituant* or global polity. On the contrary, international law-making could be described as executive governance,[52] so it would appear logical for Constitutionally bound national democracies to not follow suit. From this perspective, the critique is ultimately about applying – international – legal limits at all.

[47] Such as norms, theories, interpretative methods etc. See ch two, I B (iii).

[48] See Niklas Luhmann, *Das Recht der Gesellschaft* (Frankfurt, Suhrkamp, 1995) 470–71, 480.

[49] American lawyers would generally refer to this as judicial review (starting with the US Supreme Court case of *McCulloch v Maryland* 4 Wheat (17 US) 316, 4 LEd 579 (1819)). I will here use the broader notion of legal review, since the term judicial review is more narrowly understood in the UK. In any event, this review is characterised by the fact that it applies the legal code; it does not necessarily involve state judiciaries, but includes arbitration that decides a case based on the law.

[50] See also (iv) below.

[51] James Otis, *The Rights of the British Colonies* (Boston/London Repr, J Almon, 1764).

[52] Damian Chalmers, Markus Jachtenfuchs and Christian Joerges, *The End of the Eurocrats' Dream: Adjusting to European Diversity* (Cambridge, Cambridge University Press, 2016).

(ii) Risk of Re-Politisation and Re-Nationalisation

This is where the legitimacy debate can be difficult to grasp for lawyers since this is what the law is about: applying the code lawful/unlawful, including to democratic action by states.[53] The underlying assumption is that it is lawful to do so and that the finding of state action to be lawful or unlawful in any given case is, in itself, lawful. This was referred to as basic legal paradox.[54] The legitimacy debate challenges the question of whether it is always justified to merely employ the rule of law, meaning that it emphasises the legal paradox.

This challenge weighs more heavily in the transnational context. The absence of a global polity (see (i) above) means that the law is the integrative factor for the international community.[55] Respect for democratic choices therefore fosters the political role of the nation state. The role of democracy in a transnational context can hence be stressed only while acknowledging that this involves two differentiations: that between the national and the international system; and that between the legal and the political system. This produces a 'double' risk for international law.

To illustrate this, there has been a tendency over the past decade to foster the role of the state in ITA.[56] This is unproblematic if done with a view to strengthening an international rule of law while balancing the remaining regulatory space of the state.[57] Nevertheless, it is susceptible to an opposite effect. As stressed above, emphasising the role of the state reinforces the tendency to understand the public interest as the *national* interest. This can feed resentment against *foreign* investors: why should foreigners be able to hold a national society accountable for its (democratic) choices?

From an *international* law perspective, the answer to this would start with the historical protection of the alien, on the assumption that the democratic majority in each nation state can take care of itself. From a non-legal perspective, the

[53] Michael Stolleis, *Öffentliches Recht in Deutschland: Eine Einführung in seine Geschichte* (Munich, CH Beck, 2014), 67 explains the evolution of German public law as process of de-politisation.

[54] See ch two, I B (ii).

[55] In particular, for the EU, see ch two, I C (i).

[56] One topical example of this is the return to domestic litigation requirements under Art 14.D.5 of the US-Mexico-Canada-Agreement (USMCA). Available at: https://ustr.gov/sites/default/files/files/agreements/FTA/USMCA/Text/14-Investment.pdf. Other suggestions include Jarrod Hepburn, 'In Accordance with which Host State Law: Restoring the "Defence" of Investor Illegality in Investment Arbitration' (2014) 5(3) *Journal of International Dispute Settlement* 531–59, available at https://ssrn.com/abstract=2428859 (taking 'legitimacy' clauses regarding foreign investment seriously); Ankita Ritwik, 'Tobacco Packaging and the State's Ability to Legislate' (2013) 54 *Harvard International Law Journal* 523 (suggesting an option for the state to either repeal the relevant law, or to compensate the investor); Robert Wisner and Neil Campbell, 'Bringing the Home State Back In: The Case for Home State Control in Investor-State Dispute Settlement' (2018) 19 *Business Law International* 5 (prior review of ICSID claims by host state and permission to proceed).

[57] Markus Wagner, 'Regulatory Space in International Trade and International Investment Law' (2014–2015) 36(1) *University of Pennsylvania Journal of International Law* 1–87. Available at: https://ssrn.com/abstract=2403959. See also Schneiderman, 'Against Constitutional Excess' (n 33).

ITA critique can, however, be embraced by both the Political Left – interested in regulatory space for non-economic interests such as health, environment or social policies – and the Political Right – interested in traditional values. In combination, they put a significant strain on the binding force of the rule of law.

The law may even be completely abandoned, depending on the degree to which the (national) societal interest is elevated to the state interest. This means that the original aim of de-politicising international investment law and disputes would have to be given up. The legitimacy debate would, together with the public distrust in international (investment) arbitration, ultimately lead to re-politicising investment disputes or even international law disputes. From a legal perspective, this can only be done within legal limits. From an international law perspective, formulating such legal limits cannot just be left to domestic law.

(iii) Implications for Reform Suggestions

Against this background, reform suggestions for investment law and arbitration would have to address the question of how to strengthen societal (non-economic) interests while upholding the rule of law, without reverting to nationalism. In systems theoretical terms, the challenge is to structurally couple ITA to the overall international legal system, and – in the absence of a global polity – to the national political systems.

In part, this is similar to the issues that have been addressed under the heading of global governance and, more specifically, global administrative law.[58] From a slightly different angle, the challenge might also be tackled within global constitutionalism, in particular by construing the UN Charter as something akin to a global constitution.[59]

It is here suggested to focus on the reality that social policies are a domestic issue, which would tally with the acknowledgment from transnational legal orders (TLO) theory that there is an enduring role for the nation state.[60] Nevertheless, the perspective needs to be an international one; ideally starting with the law, but also looking beyond it.

[58] Benedict Kingsbury et al, 'Foreword: Global Governance as Administration – National and Transnational Approaches to Global Administrative Law' (2005) 68 *Law and Contemporary Problems* 1. Available at: https://scholarship.law.duke.edu/lcp/vol68/iss3/1.

[59] Bardo Fassbender, 'Sources of Human Rights Obligations Binding the UN Security Council' in Pieter HF Becker, Rudolf Dolzer and Michael Waibel (eds), *Making Transnational Law Work in a Global Economy: Essays in Honour of Detlev Vagts* (Cambridge, Cambridge University Press, 2010), 71, 86.

[60] See ch 2, II. On this basis, there have been wake-up calls for social inclusion within national democracies without which there would be no future for the global economy. See, eg, Dani Rodrik, *Straight Talk on Trade: Ideals for a Sane World Economy* (Princeton, Princeton University Press, 2018), 222–27. Similarly, Gregory Shaffer, 'How Do We Get Along? International Economic Law and the Nation State' (2019) 117 *Michigan Law Review* 1229. Available at: www.ssrn.com/abstract=3249249. This does not exclude the – desirable – possibility of engaging some form of social safety or security on the transnational level. For the EU, see Konstanze von Papp, '"Benefit Tourism" Post-Brexit: Tackling the Ghost by More EU Social Engagement' (2018) 69 *Northern Ireland Legal Quarterly* 271.

To recall the broader view of systems theory, it was the constitutionally bound *state* that structurally coupled law and politics on the national level, not the Constitution as such (see chapter 2, I B (iii)). In other words, lawyers need to make room for the possibility that the law alone is no longer sufficient to integrate transnational or global problems under the heading of international law. It must be accompanied by a carefully crafted role for the democratically legitimated nation state as regards social fairness.

At the same time, non-lawyers and lawyers alike need to acknowledge that the reference to democracy alone cannot be sufficient to remove a situation with transnational elements from enforcement of the rule of law. Put differently, there must be limits to democratic decision-making in a transnational context that withstand political pressure.[61]

The same is true regarding commercial interests (ie economic pressure). Like the EU, ICA and ITA have traditionally been frameworks established by and following the logic of economic interests. Accordingly, ICA has been continuously judged against the benchmark of utility for its users[62] and it will continue to be of commercial relevance for investments made while the relevant investment treaty was in place, or even later in the case of sunset clauses.[63] The difficulty of enforcing legal limits to economic freedom while respecting democratic choices is well known to EU lawyers. EU law on fundamental market freedoms can serve as an example (see (iv) below).

(iv) Squaring the Law, the Market, and Democracy: The Example of EU Fundamental Freedoms

In EU law, the fundamental freedoms exemplify the tensions between an ordo-liberal concept that favours free trade – and hence economic interests and rights of

[61] From the point of view of the legal system, this must be the ideal. It is acknowledged that, in reality, states will continue to threaten the exit from, or indeed leave, international organisations and treaties. For the importance of *jus cogens* against this background see below.

[62] See the empirical surveys conducted regularly amongst arbitration users by the University of London, in particular the 2018 International Arbitration Survey: The Evolution of International Arbitration (in partnership between White & Case LLP and the Queen Mary School of International Arbitration). Available at: www.arbitration.qmul.ac.uk/research/2018/. Interestingly, efficiency aspects such as cost or length of arbitration proceedings have declined, while enforceability of the award and aspects of party autonomy such as the ability to avoid or choose a specific jurisdiction rank high among the benefits of arbitration for its users. This illustrates that law is still seen as something that can be bargained for (see ch 2, I D (i)) but, at the same time, the expectation is that the bargain will be legally enforceable. For challenges to the commercial mainstream view, arguing that the perceived benefits of arbitration could be absorbed by efficient cross-border litigation, see, eg, Jens Dammann and Henry Hansmann, 'Globalizing Commercial Litigation' (2008) 94 *Cornell Law Review* 1 and, more recently, Paul Stephan, 'Nothing to Say for the FAA: Why Arbitration Does Not Offer Unparalleled and Mutual Benefits' *University of Memphis Law* Review (forthcoming). Available at: https://ssrn.com/abstract=3580227. The impact of the Hague Judgments Convention (see ch 3, I A (i)) remains to be seen.

[63] See further Catherine Titi, 'Most-Favoured Nation Treatment, Survival Clauses and Reform of International Investment Law' (2016) 33 *Journal of International Arbitration* 425.

individuals – and state intervention for the public good. Since rights are enforced by the judiciary, this translates into a question mark over the competencies of courts and lawmakers in relation to each other (ie the respective forces of the rule of law and democracy).

This tension will always remain as a problem that is likely to be resolved depending on perspective. Under a national constitution, it is addressed by theories of representation reinforcement: the judicial protection of minorities making up for democratic failure, in particular, a potential 'tyranny by the majority'.[64] In a transnational context, the minorities typically under-represented in the democratic process would be foreigners. The theoretical analogy works insofar as the quest for democracy will concentrate on form, which means making up for the lack of representation of foreigners in the political process. Nevertheless, it stops working the moment we move beyond discrimination.

In the EU, protection under the fundamental freedoms moved on from *de jure* to *de facto* discrimination (ie judicial scrutiny of state measures that were facially neutral towards foreigners or foreign products). This further enhanced the role of the judiciary to the detriment of domestic policies.[65] The evolution of EU law teaches us that the broader the protection of economic rights, the bigger the problem of finding regulatory space for the nation state in non-economic matters.[66] This is true at least if there is an emphasis on market freedoms as deregulatory tools.[67]

If one were to criticise the deregulatory aspects of fundamental freedoms law by reference to democracy, the latter would take a different shape: democratic decision making would stand for a sense of community in the respective smaller unit.[68] Ideally, such a sense of community leads to the general acceptance of objective law. The pursuit of democracy here goes beyond formal representation. Instead, it includes issues such as what community are we addressing,[69] what are its needs, and how much solidarity is there?

[64] From this perspective, there remains scepticism regarding democratic input. This is why the legal system often processes laws as legal limitations on individual freedom or private property. See Luhmann (n 48), 467. Majoritarian decision making is here understood as an irritating factor for economic rights (contract, property, ie concepts that structurally couple the economic system).

[65] Miguel P Maduro, *We The Court: The European Court of Justice and the European Economic Constitution* (Oxford, Hart Publishing, 1998) 160 et seq.

[66] Critically, eg, Stephan Leibfried, 'Social Policy Left to the Judges and the Market?' *in* Helen Wallace, Mark A Pollack, Alasdair R Young (eds), *Policy-Making in the European Union*, 7th edn (Oxford, OUP, 2014), 263. See also above A (ii).

[67] Iannis Lianos, 'In Memoriam Keck (…)', CLES *Research Paper Series* 5/2014 10, 20 et seq. (available at www.ucl.ac.uk/cles/research-paper-series). US lawyers will know the equivalent problem of reducing state police powers from the *Lochner* era's wide reading of the (dormant) Commerce Clause.

[68] See Morton J Horwitz, 'Republicanism and Liberalism in American Constitutional Thought' (1987–1988) 29 *William & Mary Law Review* 57, 72 (re-reading the Antifederalists' call for small republics as constituting the (homogenuous) social basis for modern democratic societies).

[69] In particular, empirical issues such as belonging and identity become most important, see generally Francis Fukuyama, *Identity: The Demand for Dignity and the Politics of Resentment* (London, Profile Books, 2018).

In the EU literature, the debate has, over time, shifted to this latter perspective, exemplified by the focus on social legitimacy following the financial and Euro crises.[70] This is less about form, and more about substance in the form of fairness of outcome. It is this struggle for social legitimacy that best corresponds to the contemporaneous ITA critique. The EU experience indicates that societal acceptance of the rule of law within a transnational community requires socio-political elements to be taken on board of economic rationales.[71] This means that there must be room for the consideration of different interests in judicial processes and legal reasoning. Only then can they fulfil their legitimising role, hence fostering societal acceptance (see A (i) above) and, ultimately, trust in the system (see chapter two, I B (iv)).

II. Ensuring Critical Self-Reflection through Outward Engagement

It was seen above (I B) that the legitimacy debate in the transnational context of EU law, ITA and – although less salient – ICA contains a risk for the (international) legal system: the law may no longer be accepted as a limit to democratic decision making by sovereign states. For the relationship between EU and international arbitration, this means that any reform suggestion must ensure that it is based on and accepted as international law.

There is a clear commitment to the EU's role in the wider international community in Article 3(5) of the Treaty on European Union (TEU).[72] This could be read as constitutional dimension of the EU's duty to strictly observe and develop international law.[73] The EU's respect for international law is regularly stressed by the CJEU.[74] So, in principle, some form of outward engagement must

[70] See eg the edited volume by Frank Vandenbroucke (ed), *A European Social Union After the Crisis* (Cambridge, Cambridge University Press, 2017). See also Jotte Mulder, *Social Legitimacy in the Internal Market: A Dialogue of Mutual Responsiveness*, Modern Studies in European Law (Oxford, Hart Publishing, 2018); and for the role of the judiciary in particular Alicia Hinarejos, 'Social Legitimacy and the Court of Justice of the EU: Some Reflections on the Role of the Advocate General' (2012) 14 *Cambridge Yearbook of European Legal Studies* 615.

[71] See, eg, the interdisciplinary collection edited by Georg Menz and Amandine Crespy *Social Policy and the Eurocrisis: Quo Vadis Social Europe?* (London, Palgrave Macmillan, 2015).

[72] Art 3(5) TEU states: 'In its relations with the wider world, *the Union* shall uphold and promote its values and interests and contribute to the protection of its citizens. It *shall contribute* to peace, security, the sustainable development of the Earth, solidarity and mutual respect among peoples, free and fair trade, eradication of poverty and the protection of human rights, in particular the rights of the child, as well as *to the strict observance and the development of international law*, including respect for the principles of the United Nations Charter' (emphasis added).

[73] See, eg, Katja Ziegler, 'The Relationship between EU Law and International Law', University of Leicester School of Law Research Paper No 15-04. Available at: https://ssrn.com/abstract=2554069.

[74] For the precedence of international treaties ratified by the EU over EU secondary law see, eg, Case C-308/06 *Intertanko* ECLI:EU:C:2008:312 para 42; for international customary law see Case C-162/96 *Racke v Hauptzollamt Mainz* ECLI:EU:C:1998:293 paras 52–60 and, more controversially,

be required.[75] At the same time, the discussion so far has shown that a transnational, market-driven approach must be coupled with socio-political elements to be perceived as legitimate (see I above). This means that any outward engagement by the EU must ensure sufficient consideration for the public interest that is not already addressed by the economic or political systems respectively. This means that EU law must add the discussion of non-economic interests as well as the rule of law – in particular, the legality of state action – to the debate.

The question then becomes: What is the best way to put this into effective action with regard to ICA and ITA? The remainder of this chapter will consider the possibility of an institutionalised dialogue between EU law and international arbitration as well as improvements to legal reasoning by reference to common concepts.

A. Institutionalised Dialogue

As discussed above (see I A (i)), trust is achieved by fostering legitimacy. This requires a structured framework which transfers reduced complexity. The basic operation for this in the (EU) legal as a social system is communication (see chapter two, I B (ii)). Such communication must be accompanied by reasons that enable, in general, acceptance of decisions by the public. The easiest way to do this would be to improve the existing judicial structures of the EU so as to enable a dialogue with international arbitration via the Member State courts (see (i) below). Additionally, new structures that directly link arbitration tribunals with the CJEU should remain under consideration (see (ii) below).

(i) Improving the Indirect Link between the CJEU and Arbitral Tribunals via Member State Courts

Regarding ICA, it was seen that the Brussels Regulation (recast) has remained on a path aiming for regulation of dispute settlement of civil and commercial matters only insofar as this involves the EU Member State courts. By contrast, arbitration tribunals are seen as standing outside the EU legal system.[76] This

Case C-366/10 *Air Transport Association of America v Secretary of State for Energy and Climate Change* ECLI:EU:C:2011:864 para 101. For a critical assessment of the direct effects test(s) used by the Court to establish the judicial reviewability of EU secondary law against the benchmark of international law see Nicolas AJ Croquet, 'The Import of International Customary Law into the EU Legal Order: The Adequacy of a Direct Effects Analysis' (2013) 15 *Cambridge Yearbook of European Legal Studies* 47.

[75] I would even go further than Ziegler's suggestion (n 73) that the strict observance of international law by the EU be better be served by engagement than by closure, and argue that this can *only* be done by way of dialogue.

[76] See ch 3, I A (iii). In particular, the principle of mutual trust only applies to Member state courts, not arbitration tribunals, Case C-536/13 "*Gazprom*" *OAO v Lietuvos Respublika* ECLI:EU:C:2015:316.

divide is further stressed by the fact that EU law refrains from regulating arbitration agreements.[77] The EU presents itself as a neutral bystander regarding commercial arbitration. This is reminiscent of the EU's traditional approach to private law more generally.[78]

However, drawing a line between EU law and commercial arbitration cannot achieve public trust. Value judgments are constantly being made in the presumably neutral area of private law relationships.[79] The separation of the EU from (commercial) arbitration merely signals a lack of interest in or control of the settlement of 'private' disputes within the EU that are mostly driven by economic interests. In short, the EU's refusal to engage with commercial arbitration reinforces its social legitimacy problem (see I A (ii) and B (iv) above) and will not solve the underlying tension between public and private interests. From a public interest perspective, it may expose the EU to criticism of under-regulation, illustrating another instance of a purely market-driven ideology.

At the same time, the full force of EU regulation returns in the form of EU public policy the moment an EU Member State court is faced with the enforcement of an arbitral award (see chapter two, II A (ii) and chapter three, I B). Reliance on EU law becomes the technique of the losing party in arbitration, who either wants to have the award annulled or its enforcement resisted. This has led to a negative perception of EU law as causing delay on the way to an enforceable award, or helping to avoid obligations under international law. This can be illustrated by the *Micula* case, where it is now up to the CJEU to decide whether the Commission's finding of state aid in the award itself can stand, and whether this means that the award in unenforceable in the EU for breach of public policy.[80]

From the point of view of arbitration, this risks removing its very benefits,[81] situating the EU as an irritating, over-regulating factor. EU law can only satisfy the public and the commercial community by adopting an openly positive stance towards arbitration while at the same time clarifying legal limits. This was developed in chapter three (I B (iii)) under the notion of regulated pro-arbitration approach. Such a regulated pro-arbitration approach in the EU can be developed

[77] See ch 2, II B (i) and ch 3, I A (ii).

[78] See ch 3, I A (ii).

[79] Daniela Caruso, 'The Missing View of the Cathedral: The Private Law Paradigm of European Legal Integration' (1997) 3 *European Law Journal* 3. Caruso focuses on general obstacles to private law harmonisation within the EU, distinguishing between legislative resistance, judicial inertia, and combinations of both in the Member States. Daniela Caruso persuasively attributes these obstacles to a reluctance to engage with value choices underlying seemingly neutral private law relationships.

[80] *Micula et al v Romania* ICSID Case No ARB/05/20 (n 44), see above I A (iv). The CJEU could avoid holding the award to be unenforceable under EU law if it followed the General Court and found that there was no state aid. This would square with its approach in *Genentech* (see ch 2, II B (ii)) where it interpreted the licence agreement in a way that denied a breach of Art 101 TFEU, with the result that it did not reach the question of whether the award could be unenforceable for breach of EU competition law.

[81] See, in particular, n 62 above.

through the usual interaction between Member State courts and the CJEU (ie by way of preliminary references under Article 267 TFEU).[82]

It is here suggested that this indirect dialogue between the EU and international arbitration could be rendered more efficient by accelerating the clarification of EU law. This could be achieved by setting incentives to consider potential EU law issues at the outset of an arbitration. The basis for this could be an expedited preliminary reference procedure, which would be offered only before or during an ongoing arbitration, but not if the arbitration has already been concluded. In other words, efficiency would speak in favour of making EU-law based arguments at the beginning of an arbitration, not at the end. Arbitration lawyers would hence have an incentive to translate any public policy-related caveats at the outset of an arbitration into arguments against the arbitrability of the dispute – either in its stricter sense (non-arbitrability of the subject matter) or in the broader sense directed at the validity or reach of the arbitration agreement.

Ideally, EU law would thus become a potential winning strategy in an arbitration. *De lege ferenda*, this could be accompanied by a minor form of regulation of the role of the seat court in arbitration along the lines of the original proposal by the Commission when recasting the Brussels Regulation: the *first in time rule* would be reversed for the benefit of the designated court in an arbitration agreement, in the same way as it now is for exclusive jurisdiction agreements.[83]

Under the current EU framework, there is already the possibility of an expedited procedure to bring EU law questions before the CJEU.[84] More specifically for the area of freedom, security and justice,[85] there is also the urgent preliminary ruling procedure under Articles 107 et seq. of the Rules of Procedure of the Court of Justice.[86] The Court itself provides some guidance as to the circumstances under which it will agree to such expedited or urgent procedures.[87] The category that could be made fruitful for EU law questions arising in an arbitration is the one labelled by the Court as the 'particular severity of the legal uncertainty to which the reference for a preliminary ruling relates'.[88]

[82] Under EU law as it stands, the possibility that an arbitral tribunal could make a preliminary reference to the CJEU under Art 267 TFEU is precluded (case law since Case 102/81 *Nordsee Deutsche Hochseefischerei GmbH v Reederei Mond Hochseefischerei Nordstern AG & Co KG et al* ECLI:EU:C:1982:107 paras 10–13). See also above ch 3, II A (iii) and (ii) below.

[83] See ch 3, I A (ii).

[84] Art 23a of the Statute of the Court of Justice of the EU, Arts 105 et seq of the Rules of Procedure of the Court of Justice (available since 2000).

[85] This would apply to the regime set out under the Brussels Regulation, see Recital 3 of Regulation (EU) No 1215/2012 of the European Parliament and of the Council of 12 December 2012 on jurisdiction and the recognition and enforcement of judgments in civil and commercial matters (recast) [2012] OJ L351/1.

[86] This is also based on Art 23a of the Statute (n 84) and has been available since 2008.

[87] Court of Justice of the European Union, Research and Documentation Directorate, 'Fact sheet: Urgent Ruling Procedure and Expedited Procedure' (April 2019). Available at: https://curia.europa.eu/jcms/upload/docs/application/pdf/2019-10/tra-doc-en-div-c-0000-2019-201906086-05_00.pdf.

[88] Ibid at 14.

In other words, the need for legal certainty must be exceptionally strong. This category consists of certain landmark cases in EU constitutional matters, but also asylum cases involving key operating principles of the Dublin Regulation and hence the overall workability of the EU's asylum regime.[89] On this basis, an argument could be made that the overall functioning of the EU's mutual recognition regime in civil and commercial matters is equally important. The regime under the Brussels Regulation (recast) can only function properly if the arbitration exception – ambiguous as it is[90] – is being implemented in the EU regulatory interest, while at the same time fostering the efficiency of arbitration.

This would send a welcome signal to businesses and private law firms. It embraces party autonomy as a crucial feature of the Brussels Regulation (recast),[91] reinforced by the exemption from the *lis pendens* rule for the benefit of the contractually agreed forum.[92] The EU's strong recognition of party autonomy could at least serve as an argument as to why EU law might prioritise questions if they are brought before the seat court and from there referred to the CJEU.

In any event, efficiency concerns translate into offering timely certainty on EU law questions for Member State courts involved in an arbitration, which might otherwise lead to an award that is unenforceable in the EU. Efficiency is also recognised in practice by the EU cases described in chapter three, I B (i), and dogmatically via party autonomy.[93]

(ii) Building a Direct Link between the CJEU and Arbitral Tribunals

The suggested expedited procedure would apply to both EU-based commercial arbitration and *non*-ICSID investment arbitration (ie treaty-based investment arbitration under the UNCITRAL rules or rules of commercial institutions such as the International Chamber of Commerce (ICC) or the London Court of International Arbitration (LCIA)). As long as these arbitrations are seated within the EU, there will always be an option for the parties to seek judicial assistance by a Member State court. This option should be incentivised as per the suggestion at (i) above of an expedited preliminary reference procedure at the start of, or during, an ongoing arbitration.

[89] See the Court's own examples ibid.

[90] See ch 3, I A (ii).

[91] Xandra E Kramer, Alina Ontanu, Michiel de Rooij et al, 'The Application of Brussels I (Recast) in the Legal Practice of EU Member States: Synthesis Report', Erasmus University/TMC Asser Institute 2016–2018. Available at: www.asser.nl/media/5018/m-5797-ec-justice-the-application-of-brussels-1-09-outputs-synthesis-report.pdf, 11 with further reference.

[92] Recital 22 and Art 31(2) and 31(3) of the Brussels Regulation (recast) (n 85). This applies only to jurisdiction clauses not to arbitration agreements (see ch 3, I A (ii)) for the Commission's unsuccessful proposal to have the same exemption from *lis pendens* for arbitration tribunals or designated seat courts in arbitration agreements, respectively).

[93] For the link between party autonomy and efficiency see Kramer et al, 'The Application of Brussels I (Recast) in the legal practice of EU Member States' (n 91).

By contrast, involvement of an EU Member State court before or in an ongoing arbitration is not possible in ICSID arbitration, and therefore not in all arbitrations under EU investment agreements (such as the Canada–EU Comprehensive Economic and Trade Agreement (CETA) discussed in chapter 3, II B). At least in this respect, it is advisable to keep under consideration proposals to include arbitration tribunals within the preliminary reference procedure by way of a generous reading of Article 267 TFEU.[94]

The Court has refused to take this path in the *Achmea* decision,[95] which is again illustrating the attempt at a clear boundary between arbitration and the EU judicial system. Nevertheless, *Achmea* can also be understood as a refusal by the Court to intrude into the domain of the Member States as masters of the EU treaties. In other words, if one concludes that the wording of Article 267 TFEU cannot be stretched so as to include arbitration tribunals in the preliminary reference mechanism, an intervention by the Member States in the form of a treaty amendment to this effect is required. Put differently, it is up to the Member States whether they want to keep the separation between the EU judicial system and arbitration. The alternative is to explicitly include arbitration tribunals generally – or ICSID tribunals in particular – within Article 267 TFEU. It is not just efficiency arguments that would speak in favour of such a direct link between international arbitration and the EU. Building arbitration tribunals into the EU's judicial structures would also acknowledge the fact that arbitrators remain indirectly regulated by EU law when looking to the actual enforceability of their awards within the EU.

The *Micula* arbitration can serve as an example here.[96] This concerned changes to Romanian regulations providing certain tax incentives for the food and drink industry on the basis of which the claimants had made substantial investments in Romania before its EU accession. From an EU law point of view, the question was whether these tax reductions were subsequently caught by the EU state aid regime, with the effect that any award in favour of the plaintiffs could be said to constitute illegal state aid.

The tribunal indicated that it would have been open to the argument that EU law obligations in the process of accession might have excluded the wrongfulness of Romania's action under the International Law Commission's (draft) articles on state responsibility (ILC articles on state responsibility).[97] However, this was not pleaded. It was just agreed, therefore, that EU state aid law constituted part of the factual matrix under which Romania's amendments to the relevant domestic regulations in light of its preparation to join the EU had to be judged.[98]

[94] Opinion of Advocate General Wathelet in Case C-284/16 *Slowakische Republik v Achmea BV* ECLI:EU:C:2017:699 paras 86–113 with further references.

[95] Case 284/16 *Slowakische Republik (Slovak Republic) v Achmea BV* ECLI:EU:C:2018:158 paras 43–48. On *Achmea*, see also ch 3, II A (ii) and (iii).

[96] *Micula et al v Romania* ICSID Case No ARB/05/20 (Award, 11 December 2013) (above nn 44 and 80) – *Micula* award.

[97] Ibid at para 329.

[98] Ibid at para 328.

The EU state aid issue had been on the table from the beginning, where Romania phrased it potential obstacle to the tribunal's jurisdiction regarding the claimants' plea for restitution. The tribunal disposed of this by holding that its jurisdiction to award restitution under both ICSID and the Swedish–Romanian bilateral investment treaty was in no way limited.[99] It also drew a clear line between remedies and enforcement, which it repeated in the final award – hinting at the fact that ICSID awards are self-executing and not subject to public policy concerns as under the New York Convention (NYC).[100] The tribunal ultimately awarded the claimants a substantial sum.

This prompted a Commission decision finding that the award itself constituted illegal state aid. The decision was subsequently quashed by the General Court and is now pending before the CJEU.[101] This means that the enforceability of the award in the EU is still an open question.[102] One could disregard this as a fault that can be overcome by enforcing the award in non-EU jurisdictions. It was pointed out in chapter one, II B that forum shopping is only a problem from a regulatory point of view, whereas it embraces commercial freedom. From an EU point of view, such forum shopping is undesirable at least in an *intra*-EU arbitration. Nevertheless, it cannot be avoided.

The question then becomes what EU law could contribute to getting timely clarity on the reach of EU public policy (ie the enforceability of awards within the EU). Were (ICSID) arbitration tribunals able to make a preliminary reference to the CJEU, the *Micula* tribunal could have referred the state aid issue to the CJEU at the time of its decision on jurisdiction in September 2008. Nevertheless, the problem remains that the tribunal had no inclination to make the future enforceability of its award an issue in the arbitration.[103]

This is where the law of international arbitration is in charge of contributing to a better engagement with EU law. It is generally recognised that arbitrators have some form of duty to ensure that their award will be enforceable. A textual interpretation of arbitration rules such as the ICC or the LCIA would suggest that this method is perceived as a – soft – duty to use best efforts.[104] In arbitrations without

[99] *Micula et al v Romania* ICSID Case No ARB/05/20 (Decision on Jurisdiction and Admissibility, 24 September 2008) paras 166–68. Available at: www.italaw.com/sites/default/files/case-documents/ita0530.pdf. The plea for restitution appears to have been dropped later, when the potential impact of EU state aid law focused on compensation as a remedy.

[100] *Micula* award (n 96) paras 340–41, with explicit reference and a full quote of Art 54 of the ICSID Convention (see also below n 106). By contrast, the Commission had relied on *Eco Swiss* (ibid paras 334–36) in order to flag up potential enforcement problems in the EU, suggesting an accordingly narrower interpretation of the BIT.

[101] See above n 44.

[102] Enforcement proceedings in various EU jurisdictions have so far been unsuccessful, see in particular the Swedish Decision of the Nacka District Court in Stockholm of 23.01.2019 (Ä 2550-17). Available at: www.italaw.com/sites/default/files/case-documents/italaw10319.pdf. By contrast, it was seen in ch 2, II A (ii) that enforcement proceedings in the US and in the UK have been successful.

[103] Above n 100 and accompanying text.

[104] Art 42 of the 2017 ICC Rules states under the heading of 'General rule': 'In all matters not expressly provided for in the Rules, the Court and the arbitral tribunal shall act in the spirit of the Rules and

such explicit rules, it could be argued that this soft duty follows from the spirit of arbitration, the very aim and practical benefit of which is to have an enforceable award in the end.[105]

The latter is even more true for ICSID arbitration, where awards are self-executing (ie not subject to recognition and enforcement proceedings and hence the public policy of the forum) under the NYC.[106] The *Micula* tribunal seems to have concluded from this that there cannot be any risk for the later enforcement of its award.[107] However, at the very least there is now a huge delay in clarifying this for the EU. In *Micula*, being an *intra*-EU arbitration, it was also predictable that enforcement may be sought within the EU.[108] Arguably, there was hence a best efforts duty on the tribunal to do everything it could to avoid the enforcement problem within the EU. Arbitration case law could build on such best-efforts duties, which could, in the future, provide the necessary link to the EU judiciary – provided that the EU integrates (ICSID) arbitration tribunals in its judicial system.

(iii) CJEU Capacity?

From an EU institutional perspective, the main concern regarding the suggested expedited preliminary reference procedure or the proposed direct link with arbitration tribunals would be an increasing workload. Would the CJEU have the capacity to deal with this? However, this question arises less from these proposals than from the fact that the CJEU's jurisdiction over EU law is exclusive, and the scope of EU law has been steadily increasing[109] – most notably for current

shall make every effort to make sure that the award is enforceable at law.' Art 32.3 of the 2020 LCIA Rules contain a similarly worded clause, providing that: 'For all matters not expressly provided in the Arbitration Agreement, the LCIA, the LCIA Court, the Registrar, the Arbitral Tribunal, any tribunal secretary and each of the parties shall act at all times in good faith, respecting the spirit of the Arbitration Agreement, and shall make every reasonable effort to ensure that any award is legally recognised and enforceable at the arbitral seat.'

[105] See, eg, Julian Lew, 'The Law Applicable to the Form and Substance of the Arbitration Clause' in Albert Jan van den Berg (ed), Improving the Efficiency of Arbitration Agreements and Awards: 40 Years of Application of the New York Convention, *ICCA Congress Series* 9 (The Netherlands, Kluwer Law International, 1999), 114.

[106] ICSID Art 54(1) states: 'Each Contracting State shall recognize an award rendered pursuant to this Convention as binding and enforce the pecuniary obligations imposed by that award within its territories as if it were a final judgment of a court in that State.'

[107] This is a very theoretical approach. Practical hurdles may still arise as there arguably remains room for narrow exceptions under national laws when contracting states enforce ICSID awards as final judgments, see Edward Baldwin, Mark Kantor and Michael Nolan, 'Limits to Enforcement of ICSID Awards' (2006) 23 *Journal of International Arbitration* 1.

[108] Compare also Art 32.3 of the 2020 LCIA Rules (above n 104) that provide for a duty of the arbitrators to ensure the enforceability of the award *at the seat* of the arbitration. While the *Micula* case as an ICSID arbitration did not have a seat at all, one can argue that, as an *intra*-EU arbitration, it already has strong links with the EU.

[109] Marie-Pierre Granger and Emmanuel Guinchard, 'Introduction' in MP Granger and E Guinchard (eds), *The New EU Judiciary: An Analysis of Current Judicial Reforms*, European Monographs Series Set 102 (The Netherlands, Wolters Kluwer, 2018), 1, 9. For the CJEU's monopoly regarding the interpretation of EU law see above ch 2, I C (ii).

purposes by the Treaty of Lisbon's addition of investment policy to the EU's external competencies.

In other words, the difficulty lies in combining the dynamic nature of EU integration and hence the growth of EU law with the Court's judicial monopoly. Nevertheless, this is a problem that cannot be resolved by preventing EU law-related cases from reaching the CJEU in a timely manner. It must be resolved by ongoing judicial reforms. The workload of the CJEU has been an issue for consideration and reform on a regular basis. This is especially true regarding amendments to the EU treaties,[110] although the most recent reform did not originate in a treaty revision but was instigated at management level, by the then-President of the CJEU.[111] It enlarged the General Court by 28 judges.

It is suggested to handle any increasing pressure on the Court's docket based on past experiences and new arrangements that could be made readily available. For example, during the run-up to the Nice treaty, it was suggested that the preliminary reference procedure which makes up most of the Court's workload could be outsourced to what is now the General Court.[112] Even though this proposal was not taken up at the time, it has survived in the form of Article 256(3) TFEU. This provides that the Statute of the CJEU could, in specific areas, transfer jurisdiction to the General Court to make preliminary rulings.[113] The EU legislature has not made use of the possibility to amend the Statute accordingly. There is a question mark about how this would impact on the uniformity of EU law, but Article 256(3) TFEU contains safeguards to address this concern.[114]

If the EU Member States were to open the preliminary reference procedure to (ICSID) arbitration tribunals, this could be managed in terms of resources by making use of Article 256(3) TFEU: transferring all or a specified part of the preliminary ruling requests originating in arbitration to the General Court.

[110] Most noteworthy here are the reforms following the Single European Act that led to the creation of what is now the General Court (1988); the possibility of creating specialised courts (*specialised panels)* introduced by the Nice Treaty (which resulted in the setting-up of the Civil Service Tribunal (2004)); and the Lisbon reforms (including the replacement of the need for unanimity by the ordinary legislative procedure with regard to the creation or abolition of such specialised courts).

[111] See the documentation by Franklin R Dehousse, 'The Reform of the EU Courts (II): Abandoning the Management Approach by Doubling the General Court' *Egmont Paper* 83, The Royal Institute of International Relations (March 2016).

[112] See the joint report by the CJEU and the (then-) Court of First Instance, 'The Future of the Judicial System of the European Union (Proposals and Reflections)', Court of Justice and Court of First Instance (1999), May 25–26. Available at: www.alanuzelac.from.hr/Pdf/eu-postdip/Buducnost%20suda%20Europskih%20zajednica%20-%20ave.pdf.

[113] Art 256(3) TFEU states: 'The General Court shall have jurisdiction to hear and determine questions referred for a preliminary ruling under Article 267, in specific areas laid down by the Statute.'

[114] Art 256(3)(2) and (3) TFEU provide for further referral to the CJEU (and, exceptionally, judicial review of the General Court's decision) if there is a risk (or, respectively, a serious risk) for the unity and consistency of EU law.

B. Building Structure through Common Concepts

The dialogue between the EU and international arbitration can also be improved without institutionalised bridges either between courts or between courts and arbitral tribunals. This would focus on the substance of the reasoning behind court and arbitral decisions. It was seen above (I A (i)) that legal reasoning serves a central purpose in that it builds structure and fosters the legitimacy of the legal system. Improving the legal reasoning of courts and arbitral tribunals can, therefore, work alongside or without the suggested institutionalisation of dialogue.

In any event, it was seen that there is substantial distrust vis-à-vis 'private' arbitration of disputes involving public interests. The mutual indifference between EU law and international arbitration does not help to tackle this. Moreover, the lack of outward engagement adds a layer of distrust between different transnational actors: on one side, there are EU and Member State judges as well as judges from very diverse third countries (both developing and developed). On the other side, there are arbitrators from the commercial world or those with a background in public international law. If all continue to operate in a self-referential way, there is no structure for trust to evolve.

Distrust can only be managed by engagement, with an emphasis on facilitating a (formal or informal) dialogue between these different decision makers.[115] They will be in a better position to take note of or engage with each other's reasoning if they all refer to basic concepts that are common to the specialised regimes of international law.[116] In systems theoretical terms, the purpose is to structurally couple the relevant legal (sub)systems (ie ICA, ITA, and EU law)(see (i) below). Ideally, this will be done while acknowledging that the overall legal system is differentiated against and structurally coupled with its environment, in particular the economic and political systems (see ii below).

(i) Baseline and Core Legal Concepts

At its core, the point of legal reasoning as suggested above (see I A (i)) must be to prevent a recourse to force. The aim is, therefore, to settle disputes peacefully on the basis of the legal code, not the code of either the economic or political system.

[115] This has been argued in comprehensive detail by Thomas Wischmeyer, 'Generating Trust Through Law? Judicial Cooperation in the European Union and the Principle of "Mutual Trust"' (2016) 17 *German Law Journal* 339 (analysing different contexts in which mutual trust plays a role as an EU principle, relying on sociological theory).

[116] See, eg, Eyal Benvenisti, 'Reclaiming Democracy: The Strategic Uses of Foreign and International Law by Domestic Courts' (2008) 102 *American Journal of International Law* 241 ('common communication tools' deriving from comparative and international law to facilitate a dialogue and hence cooperation between national courts in international law matters generally). For the need for more cross-fertilisation between the CJEU and other international courts see, eg, Tobias Lock, *The European Court of Justice and International Courts* (Oxford, Oxford University Press, 2015).

In other words, actors in EU law and international arbitration must first ask what is legal and not what is possible, either because one can afford it or has the power to do it anyway.

The baseline of peaceful dispute settlement under the legal code means an important role for a principle such as *res judicata*: the rule of law may have to stand back in individual instances so as to enable the law to fulfil its peace-enhancing function. *Res judicata* is one common concept that could be further developed in EU law and arbitration. It has already played an important part in EU commercial arbitration cases: as seen above, the EU accepts a defence of preclusion with the effect that the EU public interest in consumer protection can be outweighed by *res judicata*.[117] There is no reason why, in principle, the counterweight of *res judicata* should not be extrapolated into other areas of EU public policy in arbitration.

The CJEU and EU Member State courts (involved in arbitration) could continue to cooperate with a view to developing an EU doctrine on *res judicata* and its limits regarding EU public interests in international arbitration. Such a regulated pro-arbitration approach,[118] based on *res judicata*, would be in the EU's own interest. It would help to integrate EU law into international law disputes, and it would present the EU, in principle, as being pro-arbitration.

A regulated pro-arbitration approach is also inherent in the EU's new investment agreements with third countries such as CETA.[119] For this approach to work in *extra*-EU investment disputes, two things should be flagged up here. First, EU-specific concepts, in particular EU autonomy,[120] need to be used restrictively and, if possible, replaced by general international law concepts. The *Kadi* case illustrates how this could work. It was stressed in chapter two (I C (i)) that the General Court's approach in *Kadi* in the first instance was much more open than that of the Court on appeal. The General Court had relied on *jus cogens* as basis for EU scrutiny of an act based on international law. *Jus cogens* as a – limited – basis for EU judicial review in such a case would have structurally coupled EU with general international law.

Second, the EU needs to fully engage with the international law concept of state responsibility. As seen in chapter two, the CJEU has used the 'allocation of responsibilities' between the EU and its Member States as an EU-specific concept, without distinguishing between competencies under EU law, and state responsibility under

[117] Case C-40/08 *Asturcom Telecomunicaciones* ECLI:EU:C:2009:615. See ch 3, I B (ii) and (iii).

[118] See ch 3, I B (iii).

[119] The EU could well have given in to the public resentment against ITA and abandoned ad hoc arbitration entirely. Instead, it has continued on the traditional path, but sought to better institutionalise ITA, eg through a dominant role of state parties and introduction of an appellate mechanism. See the discussion of the CJEU's *CETA* Opinion in ch 3, II B.

[120] The discussion in ch 3 showed that the *CETA* Opinion can hardly be reconciled with the restrictive interpretation of autonomy regarding *intra*-EU cases in *Achmea* (see ch 3, II B (ii)).

international law.[121] Such a distinction between internal liability in the relationship between the EU and its Member States, and external responsibility is now envisaged for future ISDS under EU investment agreements.[122] The CJEU needs to build state responsibility issues into its case law more broadly, since this also has an impact on ITA under existing treaties,[123] and even ICA. Under Article 2 of the ILC Articles,[124] state responsibility requires a breach of international law that is attributable to the respondent. The latter part (questions of attribution of conduct) can become relevant in ICA against states.[125] This is especially the case when the state's obligation – under an investment treaty or even a commercial contract – is said to be impossible to perform due to the state's overarching duty to act in accordance with EU law.[126]

In order to tackle this efficiently, it must be possible to keep the question of whether Member State action or inaction is required by EU law out of any arbitration against EU Member States. Arbitrators could then limit themselves to judging whether the scrutinised conduct is attributable to the respondent under international law[127] or, respectively, whether attribution of conduct under international law fosters the private law-based argument that the state should not be allowed to bear the fruits of its own wrongdoing.[128] In cases where the Member State has been found responsible for the breach, the internal division of liability between Member State and EU could then be left to be decided under EU law.[129]

[121] See, in particular, Opinion 2/13 *ECHR Accession* discussed in ch 2, I C (i) and the critique by Piet Eeckhout, 'Opinion 2/13 on EU Accession to the ECHR and Judicial Dialogue – Autonomy or Autarky?' *Jean Monnet Working Paper 01/15*. Available at: http://jeanmonnetprogram.org/paper/opinion-213-on-eu-accession-to-the-echr-and-judicial-dialogue-autonomy-or-autarky/.

[122] Regulation (EU) No 912/2014 of the European Parliament and of the Council of 23 July 2014 establishing a framework for managing financial responsibility linked to investor-to-state dispute settlement tribunals established by international agreements to which the European Union is party [2014] OJ L257/121.

[123] For an analysis of Regulation (EU) No 912/2014 and its impact on arbitration under existing agreements see Philipp Stegmann, 'The Application of the Financial Responsibility Regulation in the Context of the Energy Charter Treaty: Case for Convergence or "Square Peg Round Hole"?' (2017) *Beiträge zum Transnationalen Wirtschaftsrecht*, 145. Available at: http://telc.jura.uni-halle.de/de/forschungen-und-publikationen/beitr%C3%A4ge-transnationalen-wirtschaftsrecht.

[124] International Law Commission, Report on 53rd session including *draft articles on responsibility of States for internationally wrongful acts* (General Assembly Official Records 55th session (2001), Supplement No. 10 (A/56/10)). Available at: www.un.org/law/ilc.

[125] The argument that an EU Member State's hands are tied as a consequence of its EU law obligations has been a regular feature of international arbitration involving states. See the case law examples in I A (iv) and II A (ii). The necessary distinction between public and private acts in the context of ITA is well explained by Alex Mills, 'Antinomies of Public and Private at the Foundations of International Investment Law and Arbitration' (2014) 14 *Journal of International Economic Law* 469, 494–98.

[126] This can even lead to the argument that the contract itself is void, as illustrated by the state aid issue in the *EDF* case (see I A (iv) above). Such arguments embody the operational closure of EU law (see ch two, I C).

[127] For a comprehensive analysis of Member State and EU liability see Armin Steinbach, *EU Liability and International Economic Law*, Modern Studies of European Law (Oxford, Hart Publishing, 2017) 141–50 (including a discussion of joint and several liability).

[128] In a commercial arbitration such as the *EDF* case (seeI A (iv) above).

[129] For ISDS under EU agreements this is now provided for in Regulation (EU) No 912/2014 (n 123). See also A Steinbach, *EU Liability and International Economic Law* (n 127), 151–56.

The above solution would also conform with the ILC's (draft) Articles on Responsibility of International Organisations.[130] Its Article 63 allows for special rules to govern the situation of an international organisation and its members. This could provide the point of departure for the development of a more general EU doctrine of state responsibility.[131] It would require a focus in the EU case law on questions such as how much discretion Member States have when implementing, for example, EU state aid or any other EU law that may be an issue in the arbitration. EU law should specifically refer to this question as attribution of conduct. The more discretion there is, the more likely that Member State action under scrutiny in an arbitration can be attributed to the Member State. Respectively, if arbitral proceedings were brought against the EU, if the Member State act must be attributed to the Member State, the EU can recover internally from the Member State.[132] This separation between attribution of conduct and internal liability could then also prove fruitful for contractual cases against EU Member States.

It was stated above with reference to *Kadi* that the CJEU should also openly engage with a concept such as *jus cogens*. This is not meant to suggest strict hierarchies. Rather, this is a process of establishing what can or cannot give way in a particular case from the viewpoint of one tribunal or court. This can then be criticised, on the same conceptual basis, by another court or tribunal. *Jus cogens* is codified in Articles 53 and 64 of the Vienna Convention on the Law of Treaties as a peremptory (non-derogable) rule of international law. This shows an overlap between *jus cogens* and rules with *erga omnes* effect (ie rules that remain valid notwithstanding any agreement *inter partes*). *Jus cogens* can be understood as a narrower sub-set of rules with *erga omnes* effect.[133] The concept of *erga omnes* as the opposite of *inter partes* is, in turn, something that could be used more in international arbitration, and EU law could then draw on it.

For example, one main point of focus in the preceding chapters was arbitrability. This has been broadly understood as gateway into arbitration, be it in application of the doctrine of (non-) arbitrability, or as a consequence of review of the validity or reach of the arbitration agreement.[134] Arbitrability, as the ability to contract out of the law or out of a legal regime, could also be referred to as

[130] International Law Commission, General Assembly Official Records 63rd session (2011) (A/66/10). Available at: www.un.org/law/ilc.

[131] See also Jean Aspremont, 'A European Law of State Responsibility? The Articles on the Responsibility of International Organizations and the European Union' *Amsterdam Law School Legal Studies Research Paper* No 2013–19. Available at: https://ssrn.com/abstract=2236070.

[132] In the case of ISDS against the EU under EU agreements, see Regulation (EU) No 912/2014 (n 123) where recovery is made readily enforceable for the EU in Arts 19 and 20. This could be criticised as being heavily one-sided if it is compared to the much more onerous way for Member States to recover from the EU, see, eg, Steinbach (n 127), 160–62.

[133] See, eg, Erika de Wet, 'Jus Cogens and Obligations Erga Omnes' in Dinah Shelton (ed), *The Oxford Handbook on Human Rights* (Oxford, Oxford University Press, 2013), 555.

[134] See ch 2 I D (ii) and II, and ch 3 I A (ii) and B, where it was suggested the strict approach to EU public policy could be reconsidered by developing an EU doctrine of non-arbitrability that could be used before the very end of an arbitration.

law-making *inter partes*.[135] Arbitrability may thus have to be circumspect, at least for legal outcomes with *erga omnes* effect.[136] This more widely understood concept could then guide future application of (EU) mandatory rules or public policy by the CJEU and Member State courts.

The CJEU must ultimately clarify which of these possible limits to arbitrability amount to public policy for the purpose of refusing the enforcement of an arbitral award within the EU. This needs to be done beyond the formal parameters expressed by *Eco Swiss* (the principles of equivalence and effectiveness). First, they are again too EU-centered. Second, the increase in EU competencies especially in the realm of international investment means that there will increasingly be true EU policies. Third, EU public policy limits must be clearly communicated as such in order for EU law and international arbitration to be perceived as fair, see (ii) below.

(ii) Looking Beyond the Law

It was suggested above that the modern understanding of legitimacy goes beyond a formal understanding and relates to some form of social fairness (see I A (ii) and B (iv) above). This means looking at the output of legal decisions from a broader societal point of view, which requires that non-lawyers can engage with the reasoning.

Public policy would be one example of a concept that is understood in both the legal and the political system. In order to enable a dialogue between law and politics it would thus be helpful if complex legal terms such as mandatory rules[137] could be referred to as (also) being part of public policy in any give case (or not).

In the economic system, efficiency ranks high, which is another concept that can be processed by the law, in particular within the legal concept of party autonomy.[138] Concepts such as efficiency or public policy may well be given

[135] Stavros Brekoulakis has correctly observed that the doctrine of non-arbitrability is concerned with formalising third-party interests: only those kinds of disputes the effects of which typically remain *inter partes* are arbitrable. Those that typically have effects *erga omnes* are not. In his words, non-arbitrability addresses commercial arbitration's failure to 'break its bilateral restraints', see Stavros Brekoulakis, 'The Relevance of the Interests of Third Parties in Arbitration: Taking a Closer Look at the Elephant in the Room' (2009) 113 *Pennsylvania State Law Review* 1165, 1178 with further ref.

[136] An example of this is the reasoning in the line of judgments by the German Federal Supreme Court (*Bundesgerichtshof*) regarding the arbitrability of corporate disputes. Compare the decision in 1996 in BGHZ 132, 278 (no arbitrability of corporate disputes) with subsequent decisions in 2009 (BGHZ 180, 221), and of 6 April 2017 (I ZB 23/16) ECLI:DE:BGH:2017:060417BIZB23.16.0 (setting out the precise conditions under which third-party interests will be safeguarded and corporate disputes could hence be arbitrated). For an English summary and comment on the 2009 decision see Hilmar Raeschke-Kessler in James H Carter (ed), *The International Arbitration Review*, 5th edn (London, Law Business Research, 2014), 250, 256–58.

[137] See ch 2, II A (i) (distinguishing between internal and international mandatory rules) and (ii) (introducing EU mandatory rules).

[138] See ch 2, I D (i) and ch 3, I A (i).

different weight by EU law, depending on whether arbitration cases are being processed under its private or public law programming.[139] The same may be true for commercial arbitrators when dealing with cases against state parties.[140] Nevertheless, it is important to refer to such shared concepts where possible, in order to enable a different court or tribunal, or the economic or political systems, or broader society to take this up.

Regarding democracy as a concept that structurally couples the legal and the political system, the discussion has suggested caution insofar as this may put the binding force of international law at risk (see I B above). It needs to be taken on board, however, in order to craft a role for the democratically legitimated nation state – not in a merely formal sense, but with a view to achieve social fairness (see I B (iii) and (iv) above). Even if this fails, communication flagging the preservation of community space as one aim of EU law and international arbitration would at least manage remaining distrust in these transnational actors. A suitable concept for this may be the margin of appreciation from the case law of the European Court of Human Rights (ECHR),[141] which has been established for much longer than a state's so-called right to regulate.[142] Alternatively or additionally, one could upgrade international social rights such as the right to water for the benefit of domestic societies.[143] These would also provide a common international law basis that can be used across specialised regimes and be heeded by non-legal commentators.

In any event, the EU Commission has moved in the right direction when engaging in a dialogue with the users of arbitration and the broader public, as in the run-up to the TTIP,[144] but also the recasting of the Brussels Regulation.[145] A court or tribunal's use of concepts that are well understood beyond the legal world can only enhance such dialogue in the future.

[139] See ch 3, I A (i) and B (iii).

[140] See the discussion of the *EDF* case above at I A (iv).

[141] See I B (i) above.

[142] See n 2 above and ch 3, II B (iii).

[143] An example of this is *Urbaser and CABB v Argentina* ICSID Case No ARB/07/26 (Award, 8 December 2016). Available at: www.italaw.com/sites/default/files/case-documents/italaw8136_1.pdf. This case concerned a foreign-owned company that had contracted to optimise and expand water and sewage services in the province of Greater Buenos Aires. The tribunal acknowledged the right to water as part of the human right to adequate living standards (paras 1196–99). This right by the local population played a crucial part throughout the whole award. In particular, the tribunal accepted the argument that the Argentine province had to guarantee the continuation of a basic water supply as a universal human right, with the consequence that this constituted the framework for the investor's (legitimate) expectations from the beginning (paras 622 and 624).

[144] See I A (iii) above.

[145] See the Commission's report on the application of the Brussel's Regulation (COM (2009) 174 final, 21 April 2009) and the Green paper with the Commission's suggestions (COM (2009) 175 final, 21 April 2009). See ch 3, I A (ii) for the Commission's final proposal following this consultation.

5

Summary and Key Theses

There is a divide between EU law and international arbitration (both commercial (ICA) and investment treaty arbitration (ITA)). This is illustrated by attempts on all fronts to minimise exposure and mutual irritations. This is understandable from the respective internal perspectives: in the EU, the internal logic is built around EU autonomy; in international arbitration, it is the consent between the parties that matters most. Nevertheless, there needs to be more engagement between the EU and international arbitration in order to build trust not only between the respective systems and their actors, but also with regard to the broader public.

For ease of reference, the following short summaries set out the key theses developed in each chapter.

Chapter One

The divide between EU law and international arbitration is deepened by the EU's supranational character, the strong role of its Court of Justice, and the EU-specific principles it has developed. These clash with the idea of international arbitration as consensual ad hoc adjudication outside the court system, based on party autonomy.

The clash is particularly salient in ITA involving EU Member States because EU law strictly regulates state action.

There are also problems that are independent from the supranational character of the EU. These concern the dichotomy between public and private law, which regarding arbitration manifests itself as tension between contractual freedom and legality of state action.

The difficulty of tallying economic rights with the public interest leads to legitimacy problems. For EU-related arbitration this can only be solved by way of dialogue between the EU judiciary and international arbitration.

Chapter Two

The divide between EU law and international arbitration can be explained theoretically. EU law, ICA and ITA are specialised regimes of international law. The problem of a regime theoretical approach is that it is defined by reference to the fact that each regime claims precedence over the other. The – unresolvable – issue of normative hierarchies can be alleviated by using systems theory as point of departure.

This adds a sociological lens (ie an external perspective) which allows for law to be understood as a fact. Under a systems theoretical approach, the legal system would be one among other sub-systems of the social system, characterised by the basic distinction (code) legal/illegal.

EU law, as well as ICA and ITA, can be understood as an operationally closed sub-system of the international legal system – EU law on the basis of self-referential principles such as primacy and autonomy; ICA and ITA on the basis of arbitration agreements, to the extent these function as self-validating contracts.

Another advantage of systems theory is that it shifts the focus from the divide between the sub-systems to the question of what kind of interaction is still possible. The divide is unavoidable, by definition, since the point of systems theory is to draw distinctions between the system (eg the EU) and its environment (eg ICA or ITA), and vice versa. Any interaction takes the form of irritations that, ideally, are channelled and thus limited by so-called structural coupling via shared concepts.

The basic operator of the legal system as a social system is communication. Its function is to reduce social complexities (the 'unknown') and thereby achieve trust. This is done by generalised mechanisms – in particular, truth – as mediums that communicate complexity that has already been reduced (something like basic assumptions, or common ground).

Regarding arbitration as a purely contractual construct, some caveats are in order. This is mainly due to the arising paradox the moment one of the parties denies being bound by the agreement to arbitrate. The concept of arbitrability – broadly understood as encompassing both the validity or reach of an arbitration clause and the doctrine of non-arbitrability – addresses this. As soon as the parties are no longer in agreement to arbitrate, the purely contractual theory of arbitration is at an end. Courts are getting involved, and the question becomes whether jurisdiction over arbitrability in the broad sense lies with arbitrators or national judges.

Courts of state parties to the New York Convention (NYC) are bound by its pro-arbitration objective, which is here understood as trust in arbitration. This trust may be misplaced in individual cases involving public interests (eg undistorted competition). Protection of the weaker party in typical constellations of unequal bargaining power (such as consumer cases) can also be regarded as a public interest. Arbitrability serves as the basis for bridging the public/private divide.

The public/private divide is best approached from a transnational law perspective, in particular, on the basis of transnational legal order theory. This means understanding public and private law not as separate fields or clearly distinct areas of law. Instead, it means applying different perspectives on legal problems that arise in cross-border scenarios, while acknowledging that there is a continuing role for the nation state.

Arbitrability can either follow a contractual paradigm, concentrating on whether the parties have actually agreed to arbitrate their dispute. To this, one can add a more regulatory lens, asking who the parties are, and whether they are on an equal footing. Alternatively, one can start from a public interest perspective (eg by applying the non-arbitrability doctrine to a certain subject matter or by disapplying it, as illustrated by the US development of antitrust cases).

In practice, there is a focus on the contractual paradigm of arbitrability, whereas the doctrine of non-arbitrability has played a minor role. Its function of protecting a specific public good has been taken up by public policy at the end of an arbitration, when it comes to the enforcement of an award.

Chapter Three

The relationship between EU law and ICA is characterised by the EU presenting itself as neutral which can, in part, be explained by the lack of a general EU competence in private law matters. However, ICA focuses on the arbitration exception of the Brussels Regulation in order to defend itself against EU interference. This is justified insofar as the Brussels Regulation emphasises party autonomy.

Nevertheless, understanding the Brussels Regulation as a purely commercial instrument fails to take account of its regulatory elements, in particular its aim of ensuring the proper functioning of the market, judicial fairness, and international comity. It is this regulatory aim that underlies the *West Tankers* judgment. From an ICA perspective, however, *West Tankers* cuts off anti-suit injunctions as one way to enforce arbitration agreements. In other words, it challenges an important attempt to safeguard ICA against irritations from the outside world, and has hence been perceived as undue interference with the contractual paradigm of arbitration.

The recasting of the Brussels Regulation has subsequently fostered party autonomy with regard to choice-of-court agreements. This was essentially achieved by reversing the *first seised* rule in favour of the contractually agreed forum. Nevertheless, the proposal by the EU Commission to protect arbitration agreements in a similar way failed.

Instead, the arbitration exception remains, but is now accompanied by an ambiguous recital explaining that mutual recognition does not extend to a Member State court's ruling – incidental or otherwise – on an arbitration agreement. By contrast, a Member State court remains bound to recognise another Member State court's judgment on the merits, should the latter proceed there. This results in (disguised) negative mutual recognition: a Member State's (positive) decision upholding an agreement to arbitrate need not be recognised, while the (negative) decision regarding the applicability of an arbitration agreement, which necessarily underlies a judgment on the merits, must be recognised.

Gazprom must be understood as a failed attempt to clarify the fate of *West Tankers* under the Brussels Regulation (recast). It reinforces the divide between

EU law and ICA by strictly separating arbitration tribunals and the EU judicial system. This tallies with the EU's attempt at neutrality regarding ICA (or private law more generally).

Nevertheless, this position changes when it comes to enforcement of an award within the EU: the EU insists upon Member States implementing EU public policy strictly in line with the EU principles of equivalence and effectiveness. Case law involving EU competition law or consumer protection illustrates this, and can be labelled as the EU's *regulated* pro-arbitration approach.

The late stage at which the EU public interest comes into play (annulment or, respectively, enforcement of an award) can jeopardise the efficiency of arbitration. It would be preferable to develop an EU doctrine of arbitrability and address limits to private contracting – such as protecting the weaker party (eg a consumer or commercial agent) or the public interest in undistorted competition – at the outset or during the arbitration.

ITA is different from ICA in that the arbitration is not conducted between two private parties, but between one private and one state party. Therefore, ITA has never followed the private law programming that underlies ICA but has been characterised as a hybrid. Contractual freedom has to give way to the principle of legality of state action. From an EU point of view, Member State contracting is fully subject to EU regulation. EU neutrality towards international arbitration is hence replaced by public law programming.

According to the landmark *Achmea* judgment, *intra*-EU arbitration under a bilateral investment treaty (BIT) is subject to the prohibition for EU Member States to resolve any EU-law related disputes outside the EU judicial system (Article 344 TFEU). In other words, these are non-arbitrable under EU law. While Member States have now agreed to terminate their *intra*-EU BITs, *Achmea* creates problems for *intra*-EU arbitration under the sunset clauses of *intra*-EU BITs as well as investment agreements such as the Energy Charter Treaty (ECT). Nevertheless, arbitration tribunals have already distinguished *Achmea* on the basis that it did not concern the ECT, which is a treaty to which the EU and its Member States are parties. This illustrates an attempt by the world of ITA to minimise any EU impact.

Regarding *extra*-EU ITA, the picture is different. This will be increasingly dominated by investment agreements concluded by the EU and its Member States on the one hand, and third countries on the other (EU investment agreements). The emerging prototype of such EU investment agreements continues to provide for investor-state-dispute-settlement (ISDS) but introduces a new model. This contains explicit safeguards for regulatory interests of states, as well as an appellate mechanism. Moreover, it specifies that EU law must only be regarded as fact.

The Court deems these features sufficient to alleviate any concerns that arbitration tribunals might issue awards containing any binding statement on EU law, hence jeopardising EU autonomy. This is illustrated by the Court's Opinion regarding the Comprehensive Economic and Trade Agreement between Canada and the EU (CETA), which again evidences an attempt to neatly separate the world of the EU from international arbitration.

Both *Achmea* and the CETA Opinion are subject to criticism. Whereas *Achmea* overly regulates EU Member State contracting and appears to distrust arbitration conducted under Member State BITs, the CETA Opinion too readily trusts in a restrictive interpretation of CETA in future arbitration, with no EU law implications. It is difficult to reconcile these different approaches, formally drawing the line between *intra-* and *extra-*EU scenarios.

Preferably, the Court would have synchronised its reasoning in *Achmea* with the approach based on EU public policy in ICA (*Eco Swiss*). This would add overall flexibility, while at the same time acknowledging the fact that an EU Member State's contracting may also have to be regulated in purely commercial matters, or in arbitration based on an investment contract.

It could then have limited the prohibition for Member States to submit to arbitration in EU law-related matters to cases in which there is no involvement of EU Member State courts. The latter add the necessary regulatory layer in ICA, and there is no reason why this should not also work for ITA.

This would lead to another line than that between *intra-* and *extra-*EU scenarios: it would distinguish international arbitration under the International Convention for the Settlement of Investment Disputes (ICSID) from non-ICSID arbitration.

As to the Court's approach in the CETA Opinion, this should be understood as saying that ITA under CETA is unproblematic from an EU law perspective, but only as long as the safeguards for the EU public interest as well as the Court's role under Article 19 TEU are respected in actual arbitration practice.

Chapter Four

The divide between the EU and international arbitration cannot address the public distrust vis-à-vis 'private' arbitration. The lack of outward engagement also increases distrust between different transnational decision makers.

There are different versions of legitimacy or trust. Under systems theory, structured processes of communication reduce complexities in that they limit risks (managing the unknown). This, in turn, builds trust and leads to acceptance of decisions as legitimate.

Discussion in both EU law and ITA have moved away from such a formal understanding of legitimacy. Modern-day legitimacy means fairness of outcome, particularly in terms of a balancing of economic with non-economic interests. The recent trend exemplifies this under the notion of respect for democratic choices. This is better understood as social fairness; it applies in the same way to commercial arbitration against states.

An emphasis of democracy puts international law at a double risk. First, democracy is a national concept since there is no global polity. This means that the pursuit of democracy could be used as an argument against the international order based on *equal* (democratic) sovereigns. Second, majoritarian decision making also belongs to a political system which follows the code of power, not of legality. This means that arguments based on democracy re-politicise international law and dispute settlement.

The pursuit of legitimacy and trust from the perspective of the legal system can, by definition, only take the rule of law as a starting point. Nevertheless, the legal structures need to be built in such a way as to enable outward engagement (ie a dialogue between specialised legal sub-systems as well as the legal and, in particular, the economic and political systems).

As to the first point (dialogue between different legal regimes), it is suggested that the EU should incentivise an engagement with actors in international arbitration by presenting itself more explicitly as pro-arbitration in principle. In this respect, the Commission's original proposal to include the same safeguards for arbitration agreements as for choice-of-court agreements into the Brussels Regulation should be reconsidered.

An expedited preliminary ruling procedure for EU law-related questions that reach an EU Member State court at the outset or during an ongoing arbitration would serve as an incentive to engage with EU law before the enforcement of an award.

Arbitration tribunals should consider more seriously their best-efforts duty to ensure the enforceability of an EU law-related award in the EU. Such a duty, which should be further developed in arbitral case law, would also suggest seeking early clarification of EU law issues.

At least in arbitration where involvement of an EU Member State court is not possible – in particular, ICSID arbitration – previous reform suggestions to enable a direct dialogue between arbitration tribunals and the CJEU should remain under consideration. Following *Achmea*, this can only be done via treaty amendment, so it is up to the Member States to revise the preliminary reference mechanism accordingly.

Any capacity issues could be dealt with by statutory transfer of some or all arbitration-related preliminary ruling requests to the General Court, a possibility provided for by Article 256(3) TFEU. This would also be a practically realistic option, particularly since the doubling of the number of General Court judges in the latest round of court reform.

Finally, even in the absence of such structural amendments, courts and arbitration tribunals should manage distrust by engaging in an informal way. Engagement in any form would be facilitated if specialist and non-specialist lawyers would use basic legal concepts that are common to all legal sub-systems. Selected examples are *res judicata*, attribution of conduct, and obligations *erga omnes* as opposed to *inter partes*.

More restrictive use of system-specific concepts such as, for example, EU autonomy, should be made. Also, the CJEU needs to develop EU public policy beyond the EU-specific principles of equivalence and effectiveness. There is a need for true EU public policies, given the fact that EU competencies increase. Furthermore, making EU public policies transparent is necessary to achieve social legitimacy.

As to the second point (dialogue between lawyers and non-lawyers), lawyers need to be aware that the rule of law will only be accepted externally if the legal system is perceived as legitimate. Legal reasoning will be more convincing for non-lawyers if it uses concepts that non-legal systems can also process. An example of a concept shared by law and politics is democracy, but this should be used as a starting point rather than a value in itself. For example, democracy can be referred to as carving out regulatory space for the state in order to achieve social fairness. The margin of appreciation doctrine by the European Court of Human Rights, or international human rights in the form of social rights could also be used as shared concepts.

In terms of wider engagement, the EU Commission's public consultations regarding the recasting of the Brussels Regulation or the Transatlantic Trade and Investment Partnership (TTIP) have been steps in the right direction.

Overall Conclusion

To conclude, outward engagement between the EU and international arbitration would work on a theoretical as well as a practical level. In theory, different societal systems (and different sub-systems of the legal system) remain linked to each other. In practice, existing structures could be used to engage in a more fruitful dialogue between decision makers, involving national courts in particular. This would enhance the legitimacy of international arbitration in light of its perception as 'private' or 'elitist'. The EU, with its own legitimacy problems, would be well advised to encourage such a dialogue. Instead, it has been drawing lines between international litigation and arbitration, between Member State courts and arbitration tribunals, and between ISDS in Member State treaties and its own EU trade and investment agreements. These lines can be justified, but they do not resolve conflicts between obligations under international law and EU law; and they are unlikely to present either the EU or the world of international arbitration in a more positive light.

As to the latter, the ideal of arbitration as an efficient method of international dispute settlement has already lost its appeal. It must now be ensured that it can at least live up to its other major promise: that it leads to an enforceable award, including in the EU. This could be achieved by addressing any EU law issues as early as possible, using judicial assistance from the Member State courts as EU courts and the Court of Justice of the EU.

The EU, on the other hand, should reconsider its apparently neutral attitude towards ICA, which is better understood as a *regulated* pro-arbitration approach. In particular, the original Commission proposal for the recast of the Brussels Regulation should be reconsidered. Regarding ITA, the EU should pursue a more coherent approach in both *intra-* and *extra-*EU scenarios. Limits to arbitrability of EU law-related cases could well be developed by way of analogy to ICA cases (ie by accepting the availability of Member State courts in arbitration proceedings as the necessary regulatory tool).

For the future, it would be advisable to consider including international arbitration tribunals, at least in ICSID arbitration, in the EU's preliminary ruling mechanism. Capacity issues could be practically resolved by outsourcing arbitration-related preliminary references to the General Court.

An ongoing dialogue involving the EU courts could well build trust in international arbitration. Such trust would work in favour of the law of the EU, ICA, ITA and ultimately international law generally.

BIBLIOGRAPHY

Albert, Mathias, 'Governance and Democracy in European Systems: On Systems Theory and European Integration' (2002) 28 *Review of International Studies* 293.

Alcolea, Lucas C, 'The 2005 Hague Choice of Court and the 2019 Judgments Convention versus the New York Convention: Rivals, Alternatives or Something Else?' (2019–2020) 6 *McGill Journal of Dispute Resolution* 187. Available at: https://ssrn.com/abstract=3624791.

Aspremont, Jean, 'A European Law of State Responsibility? The Articles on the Responsibility of International Organizations and the European Union' *Amsterdam Law School Legal Studies Research Paper* No 2013-19. Available at: https://ssrn.com/abstract=2236070.

Avbelj, Matej, *The European Union under Transnational Law: A Pluralist Appraisal* (Oxford, Hart Publishing, 2018).

Baetens, Freya, 'Agents of Cross-Fertilization: Abusive Forum Shopping or Legitimate Forum Choice?' in Giorgetti, Chiara and Pollack, Mark (eds), *Beyond Fragmentation: Competition and Collaboration Among International Courts and Tribunals* (Cambridge, Cambridge University Press, 2020).

Baldwin, Edward, Kantor, Mark and Nolan, Michael, 'Limits to Enforcement of ICSID Awards' (2006) 23 *Journal of International Arbitration* 1.

Basedow, Jürgen, *The Law of Open Societies: Private Ordering and Public Regulation in the Conflict of Laws*, Hague Academy of International Law Monographs 9 (The Netherlands, Brill Nijhoff, 2015).

Benvenisti, Eyal, 'Reclaiming Democracy: The Strategic Uses of Foreign and International Law by Domestic Courts' (2008) 102 *American Journal of International Law* 241.

Bermann, George, 'Navigating EU Law and the Law of International Arbitration' (2012) 28 *Arbitration International* 397.

Bermann, George, 'Reconciling European Union Demands with the Demands of International Arbitration' (2011) 34 *Fordham International Law Journal* 1193.

Binder, Christina and Hofbauer, Jane, 'The Perception of the EU Legal Order in International Law: An In- and Outside View' (2017) 8 *European Yearbook of International Economic Law* 139.

Blackaby, Nigel and Partasides, Constantine, *Redfern and Hunter on International Arbitration*, 6th edn (Oxford, Oxford University Press, 2015).

van Bochove, Laura Maria, 'Overriding Mandatory Rules as a Vehicle for Weaker Party Protection in European Private International Law' (2014) 3 *Erasmus Law Review* 147.

Bonnitcha, Jonathan, Poulsen, Lauge and Waibel, Michael, *The Political Economy of the Investment Treaty Regime* (Oxford, Oxford University Press, 2017).

Born, Gary B, *International Commercial Arbitration* Vol I–III, 2nd edn (The Netherlands, Wolters Kluwer, 2014).

Born, Gary B, *International Arbitration: Cases and Materials* (The Netherlands, Wolters Kluwer, 2011).

Brekoulakis, Stavros and Devaney, Margaret, 'Public–Private Arbitration and the Public Interest Under English Law' (2017) 80 *Modern Law Review* 22.

Brekoulakis, Stavros, 'On Arbitrability: Persisting Misconceptions and New Areas of Concern' *Queen Mary University of London School of Law Legal Studies Research Paper* No 20/2009. Available at: https://ssrn.com/abstract=1410285.

Brekoulakis, Stavros, 'The Relevance of the Interests of Third Parties in Arbitration: Taking a Closer Look at the Elephant in the Room' (2009) 113 *Penn State Law Review* 1165.

de Búrca, Gráinne, 'The European Court of Justice and the International Legal Order after Kadi' (2010) 51 *Harvard International Law Journal* 1.

Buxbaum, Hannah, 'Territory, Territoriality, and the Resolution of Jurisdictional Conflict' (2009) 57 *American Journal of Comparative Law* 631.

Calliess, Gralf-Peter, 'Lex Mercatoria' in Basedow, Jürgen et al (eds), *Encyclopedia of Private International Law* (Cheltenham, Edward Elgar, 2017) 1119.

Cappelletti, Mauro, Seccombe, Monica, Weiler, Joseph HH (eds), *Integration through Law: Europe and the American Federal Experience* Vols 1–3 (New York, de Gruyter, 1986–1987).

Cartwright, John, 'Interpretation of English Law in Light of the Common Frame of Reference' in Snijders, Henk J and Vogenauer, Stefan (eds), *Content and Meaning of National Law in the Context of Transnational Law* (Munich, Sellier, 2009) 197.

Caruso, Daniela, 'The Missing View of the Cathedral: The Private Law Paradigm of European Legal Integration' (1997) 3 *European Law Journal* 3.

Chalmers, Damian, Jachtenfuchs, Markus and Joerges, Christian, *The End of the Eurocrats' Dream: Adjusting to European Diversity* (Cambridge, Cambridge University Press, 2016).

Chong, Adeline, 'The Public Policy and Mandatory Rules of Third Countries in International Contracts' (2006) 2 *Journal of Private International Law* 27.

Collins, Hugh, 'The Hybrid Quality of European Private Law' in Brownsword, Robert, Micklitz, Hans-Wolfgang, Niglia, Leone and Weatherill, Stephen (eds), *The Foundations of European Private Law* (Oxford, Hart Publishing, 2011) 453.

Collins, Hugh, *Regulating Contracts* (Oxford, Oxford University Press, 1999).

Contartese, Cristina and Adenas, Mads, 'EU Autonomy and Investor-state Dispute Settlement under *inter se* Agreements between EU Member States: *Achmea*' (2019) 56 *Common Market Law Review* 157.

Contartese, Cristina, 'The Autonomy of the EU Legal Order in the ECJ's External Relations Case Law: From the "Essential" to "Specific Characteristics" of the Union and Back Again' (2017) 54 *Common Market Law Review* 1627.

Court of Justice of the European Union, Research and Documentation Directorate, 'Fact sheet: Urgent Preliminary Ruling Procedure and Expedited Procedure' (April 2019). Available at: https://curia.europa.eu/jcms/upload/docs/application/pdf/2019-10/tra-doc-en-div-c-0000-2019-201906086-05_00.pdf.

Court of Justice of the European Union, 'The Future of the Judicial System of the European Union (Proposals and Reflections)', Court of Justice and Court of First Instance (Joint Report, May 1999). Available at: www.alanuzelac.from.hr/Pdf/eu-postdip/Buducnost%20suda%20Europskih%20zajednica%20-%20ave.pdf.

Cremona, Marise, 'Introduction' in Cremona, Marise (ed), *Structural Principles in EU External Relations Law* (Oxford, Hart Publishing, 2018).

Croquet, Nicolas AJ, 'The Import of International Customary Law into the EU Legal Order: The Adequacy of a Direct Effects Analysis' (2013) 15 *Cambridge Yearbook of European Legal Studies* 47.

Cross, Ciaran and Kube, Vivian, 'Is the Arbitration Clause of the Energy Charter Treaty Compatible with EU law in its Application between EU Member States?' Analysis commissioned by the Munich Environmental Institute (February 2018). Available at: www.bilaterals.org/IMG/pdf/180226_gutachten_english_b.pdf.

Dalhuisen, Jan H, *The Transnationalisation of Commercial and Financial Law, and of Commercial, Financial, and Investment Dispute Resolution: The New Lex Mercatoria and its Sources*, 7th edn (Oxford, Hart Publishing, 2019).

Dammann, Jens and Hansmann, Henry, 'Globalizing Commercial Litigation' (2008) 94 *Cornell Law Review* 1.

Davies, Gareth, 'Constitutional Disagreement in Europe and the Search for Pluralism' in Avbelj, Matej and Komárek, Jan (eds), *Constitutional Pluralism in the European Union and Beyond* (Oxford, Hart Publishing, 2012) 269.

Dehousse, Franklin R, 'The Reform of the EU Courts (II): Abandoning the Management Approach by Doubling the General Court' *Egmont Paper* 83, The Royal Institute of International Relations (March 2016).

Dezalay, Yves and Garth, Bryant G, *Dealing in Virtue: International Commercial Arbitration and the Construction of Transnational Legal Order* (Chicago, University of Chicago Press, 1996).

Diez-Hochleitner, Javier, 'The European Union Facing Investment Arbitration' in Eeckhout, Piet and López-Escudero, Manuel (eds), *The European Union's External Action in Times of Crisis* (Oxford, Hart Publishing, 2016) 453.

Dimopoulos, Angelos, 'The Principle of Autonomy and its Implications for Intra and Extra EU BITs' *EJIL: Talk!* (27 March 2018). Available at: www.ejiltalk.org/achmea-the-principle-of-autonomy-and-its-implications-for-intra-and-extra-eu-bits/.

Dowes, Neil and Tang, Zeng Sophia, 'Arbitration in EU Jurisdiction Regime: Brussels I Recast and a New Proposal' (2015) 3 *Groningen Journal of International Law* 125.

Dryzek, John S, *Deliberative Global Politics: Discourse and Democracy in a Divided World* (Cambridge, Polity Press, 2006).

Dupont, Cedric G, Schultz, Thomas and Yackee, Jason W, 'Investment Arbitration and Political Systems Theory' in Schultz, Thomas and Ortino, Federico (eds), *Oxford Handbook of International Arbitration* (Oxford, Oxford University Press, 2019). Available at: https://ssrn.com/abstract=3351343.

Eeckhout, Piet, 'Integration of Public International Law in EU Law: Analytical and Normative Dimensions' in Eeckhout, Piet and López-Escudero, Manuel (eds), *The European Union's External Action in Times of Crisis* (Oxford, Hart Publishing, 2016) 189.

Eeckhout, Piet, 'Opinion 2/13 on EU Accession to the ECHR and Judicial Dialogue – Autonomy or Autarky?' *Jean Monnet Working Paper* 01/15. Available at: http://jeanmonnetprogram.org/paper/opinion-213-on-eu-accession-to-the-echr-and-judicial-dialogue-autonomy-or-autarky/.

Enchelmaier, Stefan, 'The Development of the Free Movement Principles over Time' in Garben, Sacha and Govaere, Inge (eds), *Internal Market 2.0*, Modern Studies in European Law, 102 (Oxford, Hart Publishing, 2020).

EU Commission, 'Report to the European Parliament, the Council and the European Economic and Social Committee on the application of Council Regulation (EC) No 44/2001 on Jurisdiction and the Recognition and Enforcement of Judgments in Civil and Commercial Matters', COM(2009) 174 final (21 April 2009).

EU Commission (Staff Working Document), Report 'Online public consultation on investment protection and investor-to-state dispute settlement (ISDS) in the Trade and Investment Partnership Agreement', SWD(2015) 3 final (31 January 2015).

EU Commission Staff Working Paper, Impact Assessment, Accompanying document to the Proposal for a Regulation of the European Parliament and of the Council on jurisdiction and the recognition and enforcement of judgments in civil and commercial matters (Recast), SEC(2010) 1547 final.

European Commission, Communication from the Commission to the Council, the European Parliament, the European Economic and Social Committee and the Committee of the Regions 'Towards a Comprehensive European International Investment Policy', COM(2010) 343 final (7 July 2010).

Fassbender, Bardo, 'Sources of Human Rights Obligations Binding the UN Security Council' in Becker, Pieter HF, Dolzer, Rudolf and Waibel, Michael (eds), *Making Transnational Law Work in a Global Economy: Essays in Honour of Detlev Vagts* (Cambridge, Cambridge University Press, 2010) 71.

Fischer-Lescano, Andreas and Teubner, Gunther, 'Regime Collisions: The Vain Search for Legal Unity in the Fragmentation of Global Law' (2004) 25 *Michigan Journal of International Law* 999.

Franck, Susan D, 'The Nature and Enforcement of Investor Rights Under Investment Treaties: Do Investment Treaties Have a Bright Future?' (2005) 12 *UC Davis Journal of International Law and Policy* 47.

Franck, Susan D, 'The Legitimacy Crisis in Investment Treaty Arbitration: Privatizing Public International Law Through Inconsistent Decisions' (2005) 73 *Fordham Law Review* 1521.

Fry, James D and Stampalija, Juan I, 'Forged Independence and Impartiality: Conflicts of Interest of International Arbitrators in Investment Disputes' (2014) 30 *Arbitration International* 189.

Friedland, Mark R and Adams-Prassl, Jeremias, *Viking, Laval and Beyond* (Oxford, Hart Publishing, 2016).

Fukuyama, Francis, *Identity: The Demand for Dignity and the Politics of Resentment* (London, Profile Books, 2018).

Gaillard, Emmanuel, Darrigade, Coralie and Reich, Daniel, 'Shearman & Sterling Secures Victory for EDF in Dispute Over German Power Company Sale'. Available at: www.shearman.com/en/newsinsights/news/2016/05/secures-victory-for-edf-in-dispute-over-german (13 May 2016).

Gaillard, Emmanuel, *Legal Theory of International Arbitration* (The Netherlands, Brill Nijhoff, 2010).

Garben, Sacha, 'The Constitutional (Im)balance between "the Market" and "the Social" in the European Union' (2017) 13 *European Constitutional Law Review* 23.

Gazzinni, Tarcisio, 'General Principles of Law in the Field of Foreign Investment' (2009) 10 *Journal of World Investment and Trade* 103.

Geradin, Damien and Villano, Emilio, 'Arbitrability of EU Competition Law-Based Claims: Where Do We Stand After the CDC Hydrogen Peroxide Case?' *TILEC Discussion Paper* 2016. Available at: http://ssrn.com/abstract=2851112.

van Gestel, Rob, Micklitz, Hans-Wolfgang and Maduro, Miguel P, 'Methodology in a New Legal World' EUI Working Papers Law 2012/13. Available at: http://ssrn.com/abstract=2069872.

Goode, Roy, Kronke, Herbert and McKendrick, Ewan, *Transnational Commercial Law: Texts, Cases and Materials*, 2nd edn (Oxford, Oxford University Press, 2015).

Granger, Marie-Pierre and Guinchard, Emmanuel, 'Introduction' in Granger, MP and Guinchard, E (eds), *The New EU Judiciary: An Analysis of Current Judicial Reforms*, European Monographs Series Set 102 (The Netherlands, Wolters Kluwer, 2018) 1.

Grierson, Jacob, 'Comment on West Tankers Inc v RAS Riunione Adriatica di Sicurta SpA (The Front Comor)' (2009) 26 *Journal of International Arbitration* 891.

Griffiths, John 'What is Legal Pluralism' (1986) 24 *Journal of Legal Pluralism and Unofficial Law* 1.

Hachez, Nicolas and Wouters, Jan, 'International Investment Dispute Settlement in the Twenty-first Century: Does the Preservation of the Public Interest Require an Alternative to the Arbitral Model?' in Freya Baetens (ed), *Investment Law within International Law: Integrationist Perspectives* (Cambridge, Cambridge University Press, 2015) 417.

Haggard, Stephan and Simmons, Beth A, 'Theories of International Regimes' (1987) 41 *International Organization* 491.

Halberstam, Daniel, 'It's the Autonomy Stupid! A Modest Defense of Opinion 2/13 on EU Accession to the ECHR, and the Way Forward' *Michigan Public Law and Legal Theory Research Paper Series* No 432 (February 2015). Available at: http://ssrn.com/abstract=2567591.

Halliday, Terence C and Shaffer, Gregory, 'Transnational Legal Orders' in Halliday, Terence C and Shaffer, Gregory (eds), *Transnational Legal Orders* (Cambridge, Cambridge University Press, 2014).

van Harten, Gus, 'A Case for an International Investment Court', *Society of International Law* (SIEL) *Inaugural Conference 2008 Paper.* Available at: https://ssrn.com/abstract=1153424.

van Harten, Gus, 'Investment Treaty Arbitration as a Species of Global Administrative Law' (2006) 17 *European Journal of International Law* 121.

Hartkamp, Arthur S, *EU Law and National Private Law: Effect of EU Law and European Human Rights Law on Legal Relationships between Individuals*, 2nd edn (Cambridge, Intersentia, 2016).

Henckels, Caroline, 'Balancing Investment Protection and the Public Interest: The Role of the Standard of Review and the Importance of Deference in Investor–State Arbitration' (2013) 4 *Journal of International Dispute Settlement* 197.

Hepburn, Jarrod, 'In Accordance with which Host State Law: Restoring the "Defence" of Investor Illegality in Investment Arbitration' (2014) 5(3) *Journal of International Dispute Settlement* 531–59. Available at: https://ssrn.com/abstract=2428859.

Hess, Burkhard, 'The Fate of Investment Dispute Resolution after the Achmea Decision of the European Court of Justice' (2018) *Max Planck Institute Luxemburg Working Paper Series* 3. Available at: www.mpi.lu/research/working-paper-series/2018/wp-2018-3/.

Hess, Burkhard, Pfeiffer, Thomas and Schlosser, Peter, 'Report on the Application of Regulation Brussels I in the Member States', *Heidelberg University* Study JLS/C4/2005/03. Available at: http://courtesa.eu/wp-content/uploads/2019/03/study_application_brussels_1_en.pdf (September 2007).

Hilpold, Peter, 'EU Law and UN Law in Conflict: the Kadi Case' (2009) 13 *Max Planck Yearbook of United Nations Law* 141.

Hinarejos, Alicia, 'Social Legitimacy and the Court of Justice of the EU: Some Reflections on the Role of the Advocate General' (2012) 14 *Cambridge Yearbook of European Legal Studies* 615.

Hindelang, Steffen, 'Conceptualisation and Application of the Principle of Autonomy of EU Law: The CJEU's Judgment in *Achmea* Put in Perspective' (2019) 44 *European Law Review* 383.

Hindelang, Steffen, 'Study on Investor-State Dispute Settlement (ISDS) and Alternatives of Dispute Resolution in International Investment Law' in European Parliament, Directorate-General for External Policies of the Union (Directorate B, Policy Department), *Study: Investor-State Dispute Settlement (ISDS) Provisions in the EU's International Investment Agreements Vol 2 – Studies*, EXPO/B/INTA/2014/08-09-10, Part II (September 2014).

Horwitz, Morton J, 'Republicanism and Liberalism in American Constitutional Thought' (1987–1988) 29 *William & Mary Law Review* 57.

Howse, Rob, Langille, Joanna and Sykes, Katie, 'Sealing the Deal: The WTO Appellate Body's Report in EC-Seal Products' (2014) 18 *American Society of International Law*. Available at: www.asil.org/insights/volume/18/issue/12/sealing-deal-wto%E2%80%99s-appellate-body-report-ec-%E2%80%93-seal-products.

Innerarity, Daniel, 'Does Europe Need a Demos to be Truly Democratic?' (2014) *LSE 'Europe in Question' Discussion Paper Series* 77. Available at: www.lse.ac.uk/european-institute/Assets/Documents/LEQS-Discussion-Papers/LEQSPaper77.pdf.

Ip, Eric C, 'Reconceptualizing the International Legal Regime: Law, Politics and Institutions' (2009) 2 *Northwestern Interdisciplinary Law Review* 57.

Jensen, Thomas, 'The Democratic Deficit of the European Union' (2009) *Living Reviews in Democracy*. Available at: https://pdfs.semanticscholar.org/f45d/b3bdd50dd40d06df9ad974d8acf8df168a4b.pdf.

Kennedy, David, 'The Political Economy of Centers and Peripheries' (2013) 26 *Leiden Journal of International Law* 7. Available at: http://blogs.sciences-po.fr/pilagg/files/2012/05/David-Kennedy-Paper-PILAGG-FM.pdf.

Keukelaire, Stephan and Justaert, Arnout, 'Policy Networks and the Analysis of EU Foreign Policy' GARNET Conference: The European Union in International Affairs (Brussels 24–26 April 2008). Available at: www.ies.be/files/repo/conference2008/EUinIA_VIII_4_KeukeleireJustaert.pdf.

Klabbers, Jan, *Treaty Conflict and the European Union* (Cambridge, Cambridge University Press, 2009).

Klamert, Marcus, 'The Autonomy of the EU (and of EU Law): Through the Kaleidoscope' (2017) 42 *European Law Review* 815.

Klein, Nicolas, *Das Investitionsschutzrecht als völkerrechtliches Individualschutzrecht im Mehrebenensystem*, Studies in International Investment Law 27 (Baden-Baden, Nomos, 2018).

Kingsbury, Benedict et al, Foreword: Global Governance as Administration – National and Transnational Approaches to Global Administrative Law (2005) 68 *Law and Contemporary Problems* 1 (2005). Available at: https://scholarship.law.duke.edu/lcp/vol68/iss3/1.

Kochenov, Dimitri, 'EU Law without the Rule of Law: Is the Veneration of Autonomy Worth It?' (2015) 34 *Yearbook of European Law* 1.

Komninos, Assimakis P, 'Arbitration and EU Competition Law'. Available at: http://ssrn.com/abstract=1520105 (19 April 2009).

Koskenniemi, Martti, 'It's Not the Cases, It's the System' (2017) 18 *Journal of World Investment and Trade* 343.

Koskenniemi, Martti, Chairman of the Study Group of the International Law Commission (ILC), 'Fragmentation of International Law: Difficulties Arising From the Diversification and Expansion of International Law', ILC 56th Session (1 May–9 June and 3 July–11 August 2006) A/CN.4/L.682.

Korzun, Vera, 'The Right to Regulate in Investor-State Arbitration: Slicing and Dicing Regulatory Carve-Outs' (2017) 50 *Vanderbilt Journal of Transnational Law* 355.

Koutrakos, Panos, (Editorial) 'More on Autonomy – Opinion 1/17 (CETA)' (2019) *European Law Review* 293.

Kramer, Xandra E, 'Judicial Cooperation in Civil Matters' in Kuijper, Pieter J et al (eds), *The Law of the European Union* (The Netherlands, Kluwer, 2018) 721.

Kramer, Xandra E, 'EU Overriding Mandatory Law and the Applicable Law on the Substance in International Commercial Arbitration' in Ferrari, Franco (ed), *The Impact of EU Law on International Commercial Arbitration* (New York, Juris, 2017) 285.

Kramer, Xandra E, 'The Interaction between Rome I and Mandatory EU Private Rules – EPIL and EPL: Communicating Vessels?' in Stone, Peter and Farah, Youseph (eds), *Research Handbook on EU Private International Law* (Cheltenham, Edward Elgar, 2015) 248.

Kramer Xandra E, Ontanu, Alina and de Rooij, Michiel (eds), 'The Application of Brussels I (Recast) in the Legal Practice of EU Member States: Synthesis Report', Erasmus University/TMC Asser Institute 2016–2018. Available at: www.asser.nl/media/5018/m-5797-ec-justice-the-application-of-brussels-1-09-outputs-synthesis-report.pdf.

Krasner, Stephen D, *International Regimes* (Ithaca, Cornell University Press, 1983).

Kulaga, Lukasz, 'A Brave, New International Investment Court in Context: Towards a Paradigm Shift of the ISDS' (2012) 38 *Polish Yearbook of International Law* 115. Available at: https://ssrn.com/abstract=3448233.

Landa, Isabella Bellera, 'State Parties in Contract-Based Arbitration: A Report from the 16th Annual ITA-ASIL Conference'. Available at: http://arbitrationblog.kluwerarbitration.com/2019/06/17/state-parties-in-contract-based-arbitration-a-report-from-the-16th-annual-ita-asil-conference (17 June 2019).

Lavranos, Nikos, 'Comment: When 23 Member States Terminate Their Intra EU BITS' (6 May 2020). Available at: https://borderlex.eu/2020/05/06/comment-when-23-eu-member-states-terminate-their-intra-eu-bits/.

Leibfried, Stephan, 'Social Policy Left to the Judges and the Market?' in Wallace, Helen, Pollack, Mark A and Young Alasdair R (eds), *Policy-Making in the European Union*, 7th edn (Oxford, Oxford University Press, 2014) 263.

Lew, Julian MD, 'Achieving the Dream: Autonomous Arbitration' (2006) 22 *Arbitration International* 179.

Lew, Julian, 'The Law Applicable to the Form and Substance of the Arbitration Clause' in Albert Jan van den Berg (ed), 'Improving the Efficiency of Arbitration Agreements and Awards: 40 Years of Application of the New York Convention', *ICCA Congress Series* 9 (The Netherlands, Kluwer Law International, 1999) 114.

Lianos, Iannis, 'In Memoriam Keck (…)', *CLES Research Paper Series* 5/2014 10, 20 et seq. Available at: www.ucl.ac.uk/cles/research-paper-series.

Lock, Tobias, *The European Court of Justice and International Courts* (Oxford, Oxford University Press, 2015).

Lourenco, Ana, 'Autopoietic Social Systems Theory: Co-Evolution of Law and the Economy' *Centre for Business Research, University of Cambridge Research Paper* No 409 (2010). Available at: www.austlii.edu.au/au/journals/AUJlLegPhil/2010/4.pdf.

Luhmann, Niklas, *Introduction to Systems Theory* (Cambridge, Polity Press, 2013).

Luhmann, Niklas, Das Recht der Gesellschaft, *Suhrkamp Taschenbuch Wissenschaft, 1183*, 1st edn (Frankfurt, Suhrkamp, 1995).

Luhmann, Niklas, Gibt es in unserer Gesellschaft noch unverzichtbare Normen? *Heidelberger Universitätsreden*, 4 (Heidelberg, CF Müller, 1993).

Luhmann, Niklas, Legitimation durch Verfahren, *Soziologische Texte*, 66, 3rd edn (Darmstadt, Luchterhand, 1978).

Luhmann, Niklas, *Vertrauen: Ein Mechanismus der Reduktion sozialer Komplexität*, 2nd edn (Stuttgart, F Enke Verlag, 1973).

Maduro, Miguel P, *We The Court: The European Court of Justice and the European Economic Constitution* (Oxford, Hart Publishing, 1998).

Mahiou, Ahmed, 'Du droit économique au nouvel ordre économique international: quelques réflexions' (2013) 27 *Revue international de droit économique* 523.

Majone, Giandomenico, 'The Regulatory State And Its Legitimacy Problems', *Reihe Politikwissenschaft/ Institut für Höhere Studien, Politikwissenschaft* 56 (Wien, July 1998). Available at: https://nbn-resolving.org/urn:nbn:de:0168-ssoar-246700.

Menkel-Meadow, Carrie, 'Why and How to Study "Transnational Law"' (2011) 1 *University of California (Irvine) Law Review* 97. Electronic copy available at: http://ssrn.com/abstract=1851634.

Menz, Georg and Crespy, Amandine (eds), *Social Policy and the Eurocrisis: Quo Vadis Social Europe?* (London, Palgrave Macmillan, 2015).

Mertens, Hans-Joachim, 'Lex Mercatoria: A Self-applying System Beyond National Law?' in Gunther Teubner (ed), *Global Law without a State* (Dartmouth, Aldershot, 1997) 31.

Micklitz, Hans-Wolfgang, 'Rethinking the Public/Private Divide' in Maduro, Miguel P, Tuori, Kaarlo, Sankari, Suvi (eds), *Transnational Law: Rethinking European Law and Legal Thinking* (Cambridge, Cambridge University Press, 2014) 271.

Monti, Giorgio, 'The Global Reach of EU Competition Law' in Marise Cremona and Joanne Scott (eds), *EU Law Beyond EU Borders: The Extraterritorial Reach of EU Law* (Oxford, Oxford University Press, 2019) 174.

Moravcsik, Andrew, 'Reassessing Legitimacy in the European Union' (2002) 40 *Journal of Common Market Studies* 603.

Mulder, Jotte, *Social Legitimacy in the Internal Market: A Dialogue of Mutual Responsiveness*, Modern Studies in European Law (Oxford, Hart Publishing, 2018).

Muir Watt, Horatia, 'Integration and Diversity: The Conflict of Laws as a Regulatory Tool' in Cafaggi, Fabrizio (ed), *The Institutional Framework of European Private Law* (Oxford, Oxford University Press, 2006) 107.

Nazzini, Renato, 'Global Solution Arbitrability of Cartel Damages Claims in the European Union: CDC, KEMIRA, and Microsoft Mobile' *King's College London Dickson Poon School of Law Legal Studies Research Paper Series* Paper No 2019-12. Available at: https://ssrn.com/abstract=3249051.

Nobles, Richard and Schiff, David, *Observing Law Through Systems Theory* (Oxford, Hart Publishing, 2013).

Nyombi, Chrispas, Mortimer, Tom and Lewis, Rhidian, 'Italian Torpedoes in the Shadow of the Recast Brussels Regulation 2012' (2015) 36 *European Competition Law Review* 263.

Odermatt, Jed, 'The Principle of Autonomy: An Adolescent Disease?' in Cremona, Marise (ed), *Structural Principles in EU External Relations Law* (Oxford, Hart Publishing, 2018) 291.

Ortolani, Pietro, 'Anti-Suit Injunctions in Support of Arbitration under the Recast Brussels I Regulation' (2015) *Max Planck Institute Luxemburg Working Paper Series* 1. Available at: www.mpi.lu/research/working-paper-series/2015/wp-2015-1/.

Otis, James, *The Rights of the British Colonies* (Boston/London Repr., J Almon, 1764).

Panighetti, Thomas, 'Has London Outmaneuvered the Italian Torpedo?' (2013) 5 *Arbitration Law Review* 276.

von Papp, Konstanze '"Benefit Tourism" Post Brexit: Tackling the Ghost by More EU Social Engagement' (2018) 69 *Northern Ireland Legal Quarterly* 271.

von Papp, Konstanze, 'The Role and Powers of the Court of Justice' in Emmanuel Guinchard and Marie-Pierre Granger (eds), *The New EU Judiciary: An Analysis of Current Judicial Reforms*, European Monographs 102 (The Netherlands, Wolters Kluwer, 2018) 101.

von Papp, Konstanze, 'Biting the Bullet or Redefining Consent in Investor–State Arbitration? Pre-Arbitration Requirements after BG Group v Argentina' (2015) 16 *Journal of World Investment and Trade* 695.

von Papp, Konstanze, 'Solving Conflicts with International Investment Treaty Law from an EU Law Perspective: Article 351 TFEU Revisited' (2015) 42 *Legal Issues of Economic Integration* 325.

von Papp, Konstanze, 'Clash of "Autonomous Legal Orders": Can EU Member State Courts Bridge the Jurisdictional Divide between Investment Tribunals and the ECJ? A Plea for Direct Referral from Investment Tribunals to the ECJ' (2013) 50 *Common Market Law Review* 1039.

Park, William W, 'Private Adjudicators and the Public Interest: The Expanding Scope of International Arbitration' (1986) 12 *Brooklyn Journal of International Law* 62.

Parra, Antonio R, *The History of ICSID*, 2nd edn (Oxford, Oxford University Press, 2017).
Pellet, Alain, 'Contre la tyrannie de la ligne droite; aspects de la formation des normes en droit international de l'économie et du dévelopment' (1992) 19 *Thesaurus Acroasium* 291.
Pernice, Ingolf, 'Study on International Investment Protection Agreements and EU Law' in European Parliament, Directorate-General for External Policies of the Union (Directorate B, Policy Department), *Study: Investor–State Dispute Settlement (ISDS) Provisions in the EU's International Investment Agreements Vol 2 – Studies*, EXPO/B/INTA/2014/08-09-10, Part III (September 2014).
Peters, Anne, *Beyond Human Rights: The Legal Status of the Individual in International Law* (Cambridge, Cambridge University Press, 2016).
Petrochilos, Georgios, *Procedural Law in International Arbitration* (Oxford, Oxford University Press, 2004).
Podgorecki, Adam, Whelan, Christopher J and Khosla, Dinesh (eds), *Legal Systems and Social Systems* (London, Croom Helm, 1985).
Puig, Sergio, 'Network Analysis and the Sociology of International Law' (2018) *Arizona Legal Studies Discussion Paper* No 18-06. Available at: https://ssrn.com/abstract=3130256.
Raeschke-Kessler, Hilmar, 'Germany' in Carter, James H (ed), *The International Arbitration Review*, 5th edn (London, Law Business Research, 2014) 250.
Reinisch, August, 'Jurisdiction and Admissibility in International Investment Law' in Gattini, Andrea, Tanzi, Attila and Fontanelli, Filippo (eds) *General Principles of Law and International Investment Arbitration* (The Netherlands, Brill Nijhoff, 2018) 130.
Reinisch, August, 'The European Union and Investor–State Dispute Settlement: From Investor-State Arbitration to a Permanent Investment Court' (2016) *Centre for International Governance Innovation* (CIGI) *Inestor-State Arbitration Series* 2. Available at: www.cigionline.org/sites/default/files/isa_paper_series_no.2.pdf.
Rensmann, Thilo (ed), *Mega-Regional Trade Agreements* (Cham, Springer, 2017).
Ritwik, Ankita, 'Tobacco Packaging and the State's Ability to Legislate' (2013) 54 *Harvard International Law Journal* 523.
Roberts, Anthea and Trahanas, Christina, 'Judicial Review of Investment Treaty Awards: BG Group v Argentina' (2014) 108 *American Journal of International Law*. Available at: https://ssrn.com/abstract=2767889.
Roberts, Anthea, 'The Next Battleground: Standards of Review in Investment Treaty Arbitration' (2011) 16 *International Council for Commercial Arbitration Congress Series* 170. Available at: https://ssrn.com/abstract=2186208.
Rodrik, Dani, *Straight Talk on Trade: Ideas for a Sane World Economy* (Princeton, Princeton University Press, 2018).
Rosenfeld, Friedrich, 'Arbitral Praeliminaria: Reflections on the Distinction between Admissibility and Jurisdiction after BG v Argentina' (2016) 29 *Leiden Journal of International Law* 137.
van Rossem, Willem, 'The Autonomy of EU Law: More is Less?' in Wessel, Ramses A and Blockmans, Steven (eds), *Between Autonomy and Dependence: The EU Legal Order under the Influence of International Organisations* (The Hague, TMC Asser Press, 2013).
Roth, Wulf-Henning, *Case C-381/98, Ingmar GB Ltd v Eaton Leonard Technologies Inc.* (2002) 39 *Common Market Law Review*369 (note).
Rutgers, Jakobien W, 'European Competence and a European Civil Code: A Common Frame of Reference or an Optional Instrument' in Hartkamp, Arthur S et al (eds), *Towards a European Civil Code*, 4th edn (The Netherlands, Wolters Kluwer, 2011).
Sauvant, Karl P (ed), *Appeals Mechanism in International Investment Disputes* (Oxford, Oxford University Press, 2008).
Shaffer, Gregory, 'How Do We Get Along? International Economic Law and the Nation State' (2019) 117 *Michigan Law Review* 1229. Available at: www.ssrn.com/abstract=3249249.
Scharpf, Fritz W, *Governing in Europe: Effective and Democratic*? (Oxford, Oxford University Press, 1999).
Schiek, Dagmar, 'Towards More Resilience for a Social EU – The Constitutionally Conditioned Internal Market' (2017) 13 *European Constitutional Law Review* 611.

Schill, Stephan, 'The Mauritius Convention on Transparency: A Model for Investment Law Reform?' *EJIL:Talk!* (8 April 2015). Available at: www.ejiltalk.org/the-mauritius-convention-on-transparency-a-model-for-investment-law-reform/.

Schill, Stephan, 'W(h)ither Fragmentation: On the Literature and Sociology of International Investment Law' (2011) 22 *European Journal of International Law* 875.

Schill, Stephan, 'The Multilateralization of International Investment Law: The Emergence of a Multilateral System of Investment Protection on the Basis of Bilateral Treaties' (2008) *Society of International Economic Law Online Proceedings Working Paper* 18/08. Available at: https://ssrn.com/abstract=1151817.

Schill, Stephan, 'International Investment Law and Comparative Public Law – an Introduction' in Schill, Stephan (ed), *International Investment Law and Comparative Public Law* (Oxford, Oxford University Press, 2010).

Schmidt, Vivien A, 'The Eurozone's Crisis of Democratic Legitimacy: Can the EU Rebuild Public Trust and Support for European Economic Integration?' *European Commission Directorate-General for Economic and Financial Affairs Discussion Paper* 015 (2015). Available at: http://publications.europa.eu/resource/cellar/b4f269c4-8907-11e5-b8b7-01aa75ed71a1.0001.02/DOC_2.

Schneiderman, David, 'Against Constitutional Excess: Toquevillian Reflections on International Investment Law' (2018) 85 *University of Chicago Law Review* 585.

Schultz, Thomas, *Transnational Legality: Stateless Law and International Arbitration* (Oxford, Oxford University Press, 2014).

Schütze, Robert, 'Models of Demoicracy: Some Preliminary Thoughts' (2020) *EUI Department of Law Research Paper* No 2020/08. Available at: https://ssrn.com/abstract=3658493.

Shackleton, Michael, 'Transforming Representative Democracy in the EU? The Role of the European Parliament' (2017) 39 *West European Politics* 191.

Shany, Yuval, *The Competing Jurisdictions of International Courts and Tribunals* (Oxford, Oxford University Press, 2004).

Shany, Yuval, 'Jurisdiction and Admissibility' in Romano, Cesare PR, Alter, Karen J and Shany, Yuval (eds), *The Oxford Handbook of International Adjudication*, 781 (Oxford, Oxford University Press, 2014).

Sigler, Jay A, 'A Cybernetic Model of the Judicial System' (1968) 41 *Temple Law Quarterly* 398.

Simma, Bruno, 'Self-contained Regimes' (1985) *Netherlands Yearbook of International Law* 111.

Snyder, Francis and Yi, Lu, 'Transnational Law and the EU: Reflections from WISH in China' (2013) *European Law Journal* 705.

Somek, Alexander, *The Cosmopolitan Constitution*, Paperback edn (Oxford, Oxford University Press, 2016).

Sornarajah, Muthucumaraswamy, *The International Law on Foreign Investment*, 4th edn (Cambridge, Cambridge University Press, 2017).

Stegmann, Philipp, 'The Application of the Financial Responsibility Regulation in the Context of the Energy Charter Treaty: Case for Convergence or "Square Peg Round Hole"?' (2017) *Beiträge zum Transnationalen Wirtschaftsrecht* 145. Available at: http://telc.jura.uni-halle.de/de/forschungen-und-publikationen/beitr%C3%A4ge-transnationalen-wirtschaftsrecht.

Steinbach, Armin, *EU Liability and International Economic Law*, Modern Studies of European Law (Oxford, Hart Publishing, 2017).

Stephan, Paul, 'Nothing to Say for the FAA: Why Arbitration Does Not Offer Unparalleled and Mutual Benefits' *University of Memphis Law Review (forthcoming)*. Available at: https://ssrn.com/abstract=3580227.

Stolleis, Michael, *Öffentliches Recht in Deutschland: Eine Einführung in seine Geschichte (16.–21. Jahrhundert)* (Munich, CH Beck, 2014).

Stone Sweet, Alec and Grisel, Florian, *The Evolution of International Arbitration: Judicialization, Governance, Legitimacy* (Oxford, Oxford University Press, 2017).

Tams, Christian J, 'An Appealing Option: The Debate About an ICSID Appellate Structure' *Beiträge zum Transnationalen Wirtschaftsrecht*, 57 (June 2006). Available at: http://telc.jura.uni-halle.de/sites/default/files/altbestand/Heft57.pdf.

Teubner, Gunther, 'Quod Omnes Tangit: Transnational Constitutions Without Democracy?' (2018) 45 *Journal of Law and Society* S5–S29. Available at: https://ssrn.com/abstract=3177062.

Teubner, Gunther, *Constitutional Fragments: Societal Constitutionalism and Globalization* (Oxford, Oxford University Press, 2012).

Teubner, Gunther, 'Breaking Frames: Economic Globalisation and the Emergence of *lex mercatoria*' (2002) 5 *European Journal of Social Theory* 199.

Teubner, Gunther and Korth, Peter, 'Two Kinds of Legal Pluralism: Collision of Laws in the Double Fragmentation of World Society' in Young, Margaret A (ed) *Regime Interaction in International Law: Theoretical and Practical Challenges* (Cambridge, Cambridge University Press, 2012) 23.

Tietje, Christian, 'The Applicability of the Energy Charter Treaty in ICSID Arbitration of EU Nationals vs EU Member States' *Beiträge zum Transnationalen Wirtschaftsrecht*, 78 (2008). Available at: http://telc.jura.uni-halle.de/sites/default/files/altbestand/Heft78.pdf.

Tietje, Christian and Baetens, Freya, 'The Impact of Investor–State Dispute Settlement (ISDS) in the Transatlantic Trade and Investment Partnership' *Study Prepared for the Minister for Foreign Trade and Development Cooperation, Ministry of Foreign Affairs, The Netherlands* (24 June 2014). Available at: www.rijksoverheid.nl (singling out challenges to national *legislation*).

Titi, Catherine, 'Most-Favoured Nation Treatment, Survival Clauses and Reform of International Investment Law' (2016) 33 *Journal of International Arbitration* 425.

Titi, Catherine, 'International Investment Law and the European Union: Towards a New Generation of International Investment Agreements' (2015) 26 *European Journal of International Law* 639.

Touscoz, Jean, *Transferts de technologie: sociétés transnationales et nouvel ordre international* (Paris, PUF, 1978).

UNCTAD International Investment Agreements (IIA) Issues Note (June 2019). Available at: https://unctad.org/en/PublicationsLibrary/diaepcbinf2019d5_en.pdf.

Vandenbroucke, Frank (ed), *A European Social Union After the Crisis* (Cambridge, Cambridge University Press, 2017).

Virally, Michel, 'Vers un droit international du développement' (1965) 11 *Annuaire Français de Droit International* 3.

Wagner, Markus, 'Regulatory Space in International Trade and International Investment Law' (2014–2015) 36(1) *University of Pennsylvania Journal of International Law* 1–87. Available at: https://ssrn.com/abstract=2403959.

Wagner-von Papp, Florian, 'Competition Law in EU Free Trade and Cooperation Agreements (and What the UK Can Expect After Brexit)' 2017 *European Yearbook of International Economic Law* 301.

Weatherill, Stephen, *Contract Law of the Internal Market* (Cambridge, Intersentia, 2016).

Weiler, Joseph HH, 'The Transformation of Europe' (1991) 100 *Yale Law Journal* 2403.

Weiler, Joseph HH, 'After Maastricht: Community Legitimacy in Post-1992 Europe' in Adams, William J (ed), *Singular Europe: Economy and Polity of the European Community After 1992* (Ann Arbor, University of Michigan Press, 1992) 11.

Weiler, Joseph HH, Haltern, Ulrich R and Mayer, Franz C, 'European Democracy and its Critique' (1995) 18 *West European Politics* 4.

Wendehorst, Christiane, 'Internationales Privatrecht' in Katja Langenbucher (ed), *Europarechtliche Bezüge des Privatrechts*, 2nd edn (Baden-Baden, Nomos, 2008) 376.

de Wet, Erika, 'Jus Cogens and Obligations Erga Omnes' in Shelton, Dinah (ed), *The Oxford Handbook on Human Rights* (Oxford, Oxford University Press, 2013) 555.

Wilhelmsen, Louise Hauberg, 'The Recast Brussels I Regulation and Arbitration: Revisited or Revised?' (2014) 30 *Arbitration International* 169.

Wischmeyer, Thomas, 'Generating Trust Through Law? Judicial Cooperation in the European Union and the Principle of "Mutual Trust"' (2016) 17 *German Law Journal* 339.

Wisner, Robert and Campbell, Neil, 'Bringing the Home State Back In: The Case for Home State Control in Investor-State Dispute Settlement' (2018) 19 *Business Law International* 5.

de Witte, Bruno, 'The Continuous Significance of Van Gend en Loos' in Maduro, Miguel P and Azoulai, Loïc (eds), *The Past and Future of EU Law: The Classics of EU Law Revisited on the 50th Anniversary of the Rome Treaty* (Oxford, Hart Publishing, 2010) 9.

de Witte, Bruno, 'Direct Effect, Primacy, and the Nature of the Legal Order' in Craig, Paul, and de Búrca, Gráinne, *The Evolution of EU Law*, 2nd edn (Oxford, Oxford University Press, 2011) 324.

Wong, Jarod, 'BG Group v Argentina: A Supreme Misunderstanding' (2016) 43 *Pepperdine Law Review* 541.

Wurmnest, Wolfgang, 'International Jurisdiction in Competition Damages Cases under the Brussels I Regulation: CDC Hydrogen Peroxide' (2016) 53 *Common Market Law Review* 225.

Zamir, Noam and Segal, Peretz, 'Appeal in International Arbitration: An Efficient and Affordable Arbitral Appeal Mechanism' (2019) 35 *Arbitration International* 79.

Ziegler, Katja, 'The Relationship between EU Law and International Law' (2015) *University of Leicester School of Law Research Paper* No 15-04. Available at: https://ssrn.com/abstract=2554069.

Zumbansen, Peer, 'Where the Wild Things Are: Journeys to Transnational Legal Orders, and Back', *King's College London Dickson Poon School of Law Legal Studies Research Paper Series*, Paper No 2016-11. Available at: http://ssrn.com/abstract=2723990.

Zumbansen, Peer, 'Defining the Space of Transnational Law: Legal Theory, Global Governance & Legal Pluralism' (26 September 2011) *Osgoode CLPE Research Paper* No 21/2011. Available at: www.ssrn.com/abstract=1934044.

INDEX

www.ingramcontent.com/pod-product-compliance
Ingram Content Group UK Ltd.
Pitfield, Milton Keynes, MK11 3LW, UK
UKHW021031041026
15470UKWH00013B/1291

9 781509 931170